Movements of Thought
in Modern Education

Movements of Thought in Modern Education

George F. Kneller
University of California, Los Angeles

John Wiley & Sons

New York   Chichester   Brisbane   Toronto   Singapore

Cover photo: The New York Public Library.

Copyright © 1984, by John Wiley & Sons, Inc.

All rights reserved. Published simultaneously in Canada.

Reproduction or translation of any part of
this work beyond that permitted by Sections
107 and 108 of the 1976 United States Copyright
Act without the permission of the copyright
owner is unlawful. Requests for permission
or further information should be addressed to
the Permissions Department, John Wiley & Sons.

Library of Congress Cataloging in Publication Data:

Kneller, George F. (George Frederick), 1908–
  Movements of thought in modern education.

  Sequel to: Introduction to philosophy of education.
  Bibliography: p.
  Includes index.
  1. Education—Philosophy—History—20th century.
I. Title.
LA133.K57 1984   370′.1   83-14696
ISBN 0-471-88328-X (hard)
ISBN 0-471-88635-1 (pbk.)

Printed in the United States of America
10 9 8 7 6 5 4 3 2 1

Preface

This work is a sequel to my *Introduction to Philosophy of Education* (Wiley, 1971). It is written primarily for students of education, and especially for those studying the philosophy of education. It is intended to be a critical summary of educational ideas in today's leading philosophic movements, brief enough to be mastered in a single term.

Philosophy, as I see it, attempts to clarify and answer the deepest and most difficult questions that people raise. Philosophy of education deals with the most fundamental questions raised by educators. As such, philosophy is not limited to treatises but may take many forms, such as personal testaments (Kohl, Kozol), reflective essays (Illich), and works on psychology (Piaget), sociology (Apple), and economics (Friedman). In this book, then, I consider not only formal philosophies (analysis, phenomenology, hermeneutics, positivism) but also movements of thought with strong philosophic cores (structuralism, Marxism, romanticism, conservatism). Many thinkers whom I discuss draw on their experience as educators. Now, as in the past, the educational process is a powerful stimulus to philosophic thought.

Some of my classifications may provoke disagreement. Freire, it may be said, is a Marxist as well as a phenomenologist; Habermas, a hermeneuticist as well as a Marxist; and Chomsky and Piaget more than structuralists. I agree. But my aim is to present movements of thought first, individuals second, and I believe that my assignments capture what is philosophically most important in these thinkers as well as most relevant to educational thought and practice.

I hope that this book helps teachers to present their material more effectively and students to grapple with ideas as I myself have tried to do in my Critiques and Appraisals. With basic philosophic positions explained and assessed, both students and teachers will have more time to pursue ideas and problems that appeal to them personally.

For the help they gave me in preparing this book I am especially grateful to Steven Hackbarth, Ph.D., and John Harrison, M.A. (Oxon.).

George F. Kneller
University of California, Los Angeles

Contents

1 Analysis   **1**

2 Phenomenology   **27**

3 Hermeneutics   **65**

4 Structuralism   **99**

5 Positivism   **137**

6 Marxism   **167**

7 Romanticism   **197**

8 Conservatism   **219**

For Further Reading   **257**

Index   **261**

Analysis

1

Words and Concepts

What is the purpose of philosophy? Is it to explain what the world is like? To advise people how to live? To lay the foundations of other branches of knowledge? How philosophers answer such questions gives us the key to their thoughts. In this chapter we consider the views of those thinkers for whom the true business of philosophy is *analysis*. During the past 35 years their approach has dominated philosophy in the English-speaking world. What is meant, then, by "analysis"?

To analyze something is to take it apart, to reveal its components and tell how they are related. A chemist, for instance, analyzes a substance by identifying its constituents and their molecular structure. A historian anatomizes a battle by breaking it down into moves and counter-moves and showing how these led to victory or defeat. What does the philosopher analyze? Primarily *concepts*.

What is a concept? It is a notion or idea that signifies what is common to a number of specific things or states of affairs. The concept of a school, for example, stands for what is present in a certain range of institutions—nursery schools, day schools, kindergartens, private schools, public schools, and the like— and makes them all schools rather than laboratories or colleges. The concept of intelligence denotes what it is about a variety of acts and achievements that makes them intelligent as opposed to idle, inept, or ill-conceived.

Since we think with the aid of words, we use them to label our concepts. The word "intelligence," for example, labels our concept of what is common to all intelligent acts and attainments, just as the word "school" names our concept of the common properties of kindergartens, *lycées*, high schools, and so on.[1] Nevertheless, words and concepts are not identical, since the same word may be used for different concepts on different occasions. Thus, depending on context, the word "school" names the concept of a group of philosophers, a collection of fish, or a class of institutions. Still, words and concepts are closely related and, as we will see, it is important when analyzing concepts to examine the words that express them.

But why analyze concepts at all? Concepts are crucial because they filter our experience of the world. This world does not come to us already labeled with all its parts in order. On the contrary, we have to categorize our experience of it, so that the world makes sense to us. As philosophers, we wish to decide whether the particular concepts we apply to the world are adequate and, if so, where they apply and why. It is naive to suppose that we simply can reflect on things as they are in themselves; we also must consider the concepts through which we interpret them.[2]

How, then, are concepts analyzed? We begin as a rule by examining the words in which they are expressed. To analyze a concept like teaching, we first consider how the word "teaching" is used in different contexts, such as teaching children,

---

[1]It is conventional to put quotation marks around words when they are referred to as words but not around the corresponding concepts.

[2]On the relation between words and concepts, see P.H. Hirst and R.S. Peters, *The Logic of Education* (London: Routledge & Kegan Paul, 1970), pp. 3–8; John Barrow, *The Philosophy of Schooling* (New York: Wiley, 1981), pp. 7–14; John Wilson, *Fantasy and Common Sense in Education* (Oxford: Robertson, 1979), ch. 2, and "Concepts, Contestability and the Philosophy of Education," *Journal of Philosophy of Education*, 15:1 (1981), 3–16.

teaching badly, teaching French, and teaching ourselves. Yet we do not stop there. For what we want to know is not just the meaning of the word, but what precisely this meaning includes and excludes, what it implies and presupposes, and under what conditions its use is appropriate. For example, if we reflect on the four contexts just mentioned, we find that they tell us one important truth about teaching: that we always teach something to someone; that is, teaching is a transfer of information between persons.

Still, this analysis may not satisfy us. What is involved, we may ask, in the transfer of information? How do we *know* that we have taught someone? Suppose we "teach" but the student learns nothing? Have we really taught him? Probably not. Here we have hit on another truth about teaching—that it involves learning. We cannot teach someone something unless he learns from us.[3] This is called a "conceptual" truth—a truth gained by considering what is involved in our concepts. It should be distinguished from an "empirical" truth, which is based on observation of the world. Most analytic philosophy is a search for conceptual truths.

What is the difference, then, between an analysis of a concept and a dictionary definition of the corresponding word? Whereas a dictionary states the meaning of the word, an analysis provides the rationale for that meaning. It tells us why the things or states of affairs to which the word is applied are all instances of the same concept. This distinction is sometimes simply put by saying that a successful analysis identifies the "necessary and sufficient conditions" for a concept's application. For example, it is a *necessary* condition of teaching that I present some information and intend that it be learned. If I simply mention something to a student without intending that she learn it, I am not teaching. On the other hand, submitting information with this intention does not in itself guarantee teaching. A further, *sufficient* condition also must be satisfied—the information must actually be learned.

Concepts are especially important in the construction of *ar-*

---

[3]Some analysts, however, distinguish between "ordinary" teaching and "successful" teaching. The first is teaching that may be competent but does not lead to learning (because the student is too prejudiced, say, or simply determined not to learn); the second is teaching that does produce learning.

guments. Suppose I am interested in the concept of indoctrination and wish to consider whether indoctrination is legitimate in schools. I first must analyze the concept and find out what it covers. I then am ready to construct an argument—that is, to present a reason or set of reasons in support of or against a claim. Philosophers not only construct but also appraise arguments. They determine whether the reasons given are good ones, whether they lead logically to the conclusion, and whether each step in the argument is valid. Thus, whether it makes sense to say that indoctrination is justified turns in the first instance on what indoctrination is taken to be, and, in the second, on whether the argument is sound.

Most concepts are more complex than we might think. Consider how much is covered by the concept of education. First, education is a *process* through which knowledge, values, and skills are transmitted and acquired. Next, it is the *product* of this process, or the knowledge and experience gained from it. Then, it is a *profession* requiring special training and certification. Yet again, it is an *academic discipline*—the organized study of process, product, and profession by means of history, philosophy, and the human sciences. Each of these subconcepts of education, in turn, can be unpacked further.

Analytic philosophers maintain that many concepts and arguments, especially in philosophy, are expressed misleadingly. Some analysts say that our ordinary language simply is not clear enough to make the precise distinctions required by philosophy. Others say that ordinary language is clear but that philosophers have misused it. Analysts of the first kind employ symbolic logic[4] (logic that uses quasi-algebraic symbols) with the intention of representing concepts and arguments more exactly. So far, however, they have had little influence on educational thought, largely because education is a practical endeavor difficult to codify in abstract, symbolic schemes.[5]

Analysts of the second kind contend that in order to expli-

---

[4]Logic is the study of valid reasoning, of the types of argument that it is rational to employ.

[5]For some recent attempts to do so, see David Harrah, "What Should We Teach About Questions?"; Jaako Hintikka, "A Dialogical Model of Teaching"; and James E. McClellan, "The Concept of Learning: Once More with (Logical) Expression," *Synthese*, **51**:1 (April 1982), 21–38, 39–60, and 87–116, respectively.

cate concepts, we must examine the ordinary uses of words and sentences. When we know what words and sentences ordinarily are used to say, we are able to see what the corresponding concepts cover and what validly can be argued by means of them. We may ask, for example, whether people usually say such things as "I am teaching Mary long division," or "I taught Jim but he didn't learn," or "Teaching is an art." The answers to these and similar questions will tell us what sensibly can be said about teaching and what cannot. The rationale for this view is that ordinary usage must make sense or it would not have survived; hence the concepts it expresses can be relied on. This mode of analysis usually is known as "linguistic analysis" or "ordinary language philosophy." It is the mode most congenial to educational philosophers and hence our main concern in this chapter.

Language Games and Speech Acts

A key notion in ordinary language philosophy is that of a "language game." According to Ludwig Wittgenstein (1889-1951), one of the founders of this philosophy, a language game is the way in which words are used in some communal activity. Think, he said, of some workers building a house. Master masons tell their apprentices what they want by pointing out pieces of stone and lumber and calling out "block," "pillar," "slab," "beam," and so forth. These utterances belong to the language game involved in construction work. Similarly, such words as "teach," "learn," "memorize," and "study," have their principal uses in the language games involved in educating.

A language, then, is like a collection of games, each with its own rules. An act of speech or writing is an act within a language game. To understand the act, you must know the game being played and what its rules are. A word's meaning is what that word is used for in a language game. A word that appears in several language games normally has several meanings. Take the word "strike," for example, which can mean "delete," or "stop work," or "hit," or many other things. When you know how the word "strike" is *used*, you know what it means. Or, as

Wittgenstein put it, "Don't ask for the meaning, ask for the use."

Many ordinary language philosophers have described the uses of words in particular language games, such as those of religious worship, art appreciation, and education itself. Others have been more ambitious. John Austin, for example, sought to explicate a concept that underlies all language games, that of a "speech act."[6] Speaking, he said, actually combines a number of acts. First, there is the act of saying words—the "locutionary" act. In performing this act I do several things at once: I make certain sounds, combine them grammatically, and utter meaningful words. But I do more; I say something with a certain force. I assert something, ask something, promise something, warn someone, thank someone. Thus, I also perform what Austin calls an "illocutionary" act, an act done in (or while) uttering words. Finally, I may speak in order to affect my hearer—to persuade, frighten, amuse, or annoy. Austin named these "perlocutionary" acts. A complete speech act, then, consists of a locutionary act with its subacts and also an illocutionary and/or a perlocutionary act.

Speech Acts and Teacher Authority

Speech act theory illuminates a host of educational topics, such as that of teacher authority. In the traditional view of this topic—as expressed, for instance, by analyst Richard Peters—authority and power are logically independent concepts.[7] To be in authority is to be entitled to decide what is the case and what should be done. To have power is to be able to ensure, by force if necessary, that such decisions are accepted. Now it so happens, says Peters, that people in authority usually have power. But it is not logically necessary that they should.[8] We do not contra-

---

[6] J. L. Austin, *How to Do Things with Words* (Cambridge, Mass.: Harvard University Press, 1962). For an introduction to speech acts, see John Searle, "Philosophy of Language," in *Men of Ideas*, ed. Bryan Magee (New York: Harper & Row, 1979), pp. 180–200.

[7] Richard S. Peters, *Ethics and Education* (London: Allen & Unwin, 1966), pp. 238–240.

[8] Ibid., p. 239: "Authority . . . may be and usually is supported by various forms of power. . . . But this is no reason for blurring the distinction between the two concepts."

dict ourselves if we suppose that someone in authority has no power, whereas we do contradict ourselves if we suppose that a person in authority has no right to make decisions. For example, even if a mob has sealed off a police station, a judge still is entitled to order people off the streets. Although the judge may be powerless to enforce the order, he or she has a right to issue it. We can conceive of this state of affairs (authority without power) perfectly well, because our concepts of authority and power are logically separate. If they were logically interdependent, we could not conceive of it, for the very idea of authority without power then would be self-contradictory, like the idea of a circle without shape or a curriculum without content.

Peters also distinguishes between being "in" authority and being "an" authority. To be *in* authority, he says, is to be entitled to say what the rules are in some social sphere (e.g., the school) and how they should be obeyed. This may be called "social/political" authority. To be *an* authority is to have a special right to speak on a sphere of knowledge in which one is trained or competent. This may be called "epistemic" authority, or authority in matters of knowledge or skill. Epistemic authority generally does not include the right to decide what is the case in a sphere of knowledge or what should be done in it. A teacher, for example, is (or should be) *an* authority on one or more academic subjects (or skills). A teacher has the right to teach accepted knowledge in these subjects but not, states Peters, to decide whether it is genuine knowledge or not. A physics teacher, for example, must present the laws of physics as known facts rather than as propositions on which he or she is entitled to pass judgment. Now the teacher also is *in* authority with power of decision, but only, says Peters, in the sphere of school and classroom control. The teacher is entitled to decide, for instance, what noise level is acceptable and when an assignment should be completed, but not whether noise can be measured in decibels or whether the rules of grammar may be suspended when writing essays.

Is Peters right? Not entirely. To begin, the concepts of authority and power, in my view, *are* logically connected. To be in authority involves more than the right to decide what is and what should be the case in some sphere. It also involves the right to ensure, if necessary by force, that others accept these decisions. Authority without power no longer is authority. Suppose, for example, an umpire declares someone out. If the player refuses to leave and the other players ignore the umpire's decision, the umpire definitely has lost his authority. Authority relations, then, are best seen as power relations that are regarded as legitimate. This is not to equate the concepts of authority and power. Instead, it is to say that all authority includes power, but that not all power is included in authority. Although a student in effect may run the class from the back row, he or she does not have the authority to do so.

Next, let us consider whether being *an*, and being *in*, authority are as distinct as Peters maintains. Although the two forms can be distinguished conceptually, is this distinction generally observed in practice? We can answer this question by examining certain speech acts in which authority is expressed.[9] Austin contrasts "verdictive" speech acts (such as grading, ranking, and assessing) with "exercitive" speech acts (such as ordering, choosing, and demoting).[10] A *verdictive*, he says, is a judgment, "the delivering of a finding upon the evidence or reasons as to value or fact." An *exercitive* is "the giving of a decision in favor of or against a course of action . . . a decision that something is to be so, as distinct from a judgment that it *is* so." Verdictives usually are issued by people with epistemic authority. A teacher, for instance, may tell a student that she has used a relative pronoun incorrectly or that she has forgotten to bracket one of the expressions in a mathematical equation. Exercitives are characteristic of people with social/political authority. A playground supervisor, for instance, may tell a student that he is to put his shirt on or keep out of a certain area.

People with social/political authority also issue verdictives that are, and are intended to be, exercitives—that is, judgments that are simultaneously decisions. Suppose a baseball umpire and a spectator both say that a runner is out. The spectator may know as much about the game as the umpire, and he may have had a better view of the ball. But it is only when the umpire says so that the runner is out. The umpire's speech act not only is a judgment that something is so (a verdictive) but also a decision

[9]See also Peter Goldstone and Donald Tunnell, "A Critique of the Command Theory of Authority," *Educational Theory*, 25:2 (Spring 1975), 131–38.

[10]Op. cit., pp. 152–154.

that makes it so (an exercitive). In performing such speech acts people with social/political authority *make* things the case. They define situations and the actions appropriate to them, and only their definitions are legitimate.

Now some people with epistemic authority also combine both forms of speech act and both forms of authority. Teachers, for instance, make many judgments about knowledge that have consequences their students must accept.[11] Take such acts as evaluating a student's performance, appraising the relevance of a remark, and deciding on the suitability of a topic for discussion. Here a teacher's verdictives often function as exercitives. If a teacher constantly finds a student's comments irrelevant, she may pass over him during a discussion in favor of someone else. In doing so, the teacher forms a judgment of the student's potential, and in due course she may advise him to take a different set of courses or, if possible, to choose a teacher whose methods are more congenial to him. Thus, a teacher's judgment that something *is* so often is a decision that it is *to be* so. In stating that an essay deserves an "A" or a "D," the teacher *makes* it an "A" or a "D." In calling a remark irrelevant, the teacher *makes* it irrelevant. And we can only hope that the decisions will have a healthy effect on the students concerned.

Thus although being *in*, and being *an*, authority can be distinguished in the abstract, the two cannot always be separated in practice. In certain contexts, such as schools, the distinction often breaks down. Teachers do not simply apply the standards of their disciplines; they often apply them in such a way as to make something the case with direct consequences for the student. In the sphere of knowledge they act not only with epistemic authority but also with an authority appropriate to the social/political sphere.

---

[11]For a similar view, see Helen Freeman, "Authority, Power, and Knowledge: Politics and Epistemology in the 'New' Sociology of Education," in *Philosophy of Education 1980: Proceedings of the Thirty-Sixth Annual Meeting of the Philosophy of Education Society*, ed. C.J.B. Macmillan (Normal, Ill.: Philosophy of Education Society, 1981), pp. 80–93.

Analysis in Action:
The Concept of Discipline

As the above example shows, ordinary language analysis is well suited to the study of education. It eschews symbolic logic, which is too inflexible to represent the meaning and structure of most talk about education and, instead, examines the language games of education in their own terms. Again, in attending to the ordinary rather than the technical uses of words, this form of analysis tends to support the common sense beliefs reflected in these uses. As Austin once noted,[12] ordinary words and the concepts they express have met people's everyday needs for centuries. Hence they are likely to be more serviceable in all ordinary and practical affairs than any technical terminology. Now education epitomizes the "ordinary" and the "practical." It is formative for all persons, and the activities it involves, such as teaching and learning, are found in less refined form in nearly all human endeavors. Education, therefore, lends itself to exploration by a philosophy that values the language and concepts of ordinary life.

How, then, does analysis work?[13] Here is one approach. Take the concept of discipline. Your ultimate goal is to state the necessary and sufficient conditions for the correct use of this concept. Ask yourself what things you ordinarily would call "discipline" and what not. Think, for example, of disciplining a student, an army, a workforce, the mind, even disciplining yourself. Make a list of words related to "discipline," such as "punish," "browbeat," "reprimand," "train," "guide," "control," and "teach." Ask yourself where you would use one of these words rather than the word "discipline", and vice versa. What sort of thing would you call disciplining rather than, say, browbeating or punishing, and the reverse? Your answers to such questions will begin to reveal what the concept of discipline embraces.

---

[12]J. L. Austin, "A Plea for Excuses," *Philosophical Papers,* 3rd ed., ed. G. J. Warnock and J. O. Urmson (Oxford: Clarendon Press, 1979), p. 182.

[13]For an excellent account of the analytic method in education, see Jonas F. Soltis, *An Introduction to the Analysis of Educational Concepts,* 2nd ed. (Reading, Mass.: Addison-Wesley, 1978). For two other highly relevant approaches, see Keith Graham, *J. L. Austin: A Critique of Ordinary Language Philosophy* (Atlantic Highlands, N.J.: Humanties, 1977), ch. II; and William Lyons, *Gilbert Ryle: An Introduction to His Philosophy* (Atlantic Highlands, N.J.: Humanities, 1980), ch. 2.

Suppose, for example, a student is persistently late and a teacher decides to put a stop to it. When would you say the teacher "punishes" the student? Most probably when the teacher causes the student physical discomfort with the intention of deterring him or her from being late in future. The teacher may choose to keep the student after school, perhaps, for twice as long as he or she was late or may assign an essay on the subject of punctuality. Now when would you say the teacher is "browbeating"? Most probably when he or she seeks to deter the student through humiliation. The teacher speaks harshly, perhaps, dismisses the student's explanations, and uses the prestige of office to put the student down.

When would you say the teacher "disciplines" a student? Most probably when he or she explains why punctuality matters and how the student can achieve it. The teacher gives reasons for valuing punctuality and describes steps that the student can take to arrive on time. If the student explains why he or she was late, the teacher listens with respect, decides whether the explanation is reasonable, states the reasons for this decision, and motivates the student to follow the rules for getting anywhere on time.

Next you might ask whether the concept of discipline refers to a single kind of thing (such as an activity, an achievement, a disposition, or an undergoing) or whether it covers a range of things. Since we already have noted the *activity* of discipline, let us consider discipline as a combination of an achievement and a disposition—as an *achieved disposition*. Think of disciplined learning, disciplined thinking, disciplined writing. What do these cases have in common? All involve a readiness, attained through persistent practice, to follow the rules of an activity. Since the rules have been internalized, the activity is almost automatic. Disciplined learning, for instance, is the acquired readiness to open your books at a moment's notice, focus your mind, and study uninterruptedly for a long period of time. Or consider the *undergoing* of discipline. Think of being disciplined by a teacher, by an athletic coach, by a sergeant, by life, or by yourself, for the sake of mastering the rules themselves or, sometimes, of attaining some further end such as better health or an academic degree.

Now distinguish between central and marginal cases of the concept. For example, it seems more meaningful to say that a person is disciplined than to say that an animal or a machine is.

This is because a person cooperates consciously in the process of discipline (and indeed may direct it), whereas an animal cooperates unconsciously and a machine has no choice at all. A person who does not cooperate is said to be coerced rather than disciplined. A poet might speak of "the cool discipline of machinery" to contrast the reliability of a machine (which follows automatically the rules built into it) with the volatility of its operators.

Ask, next, whether the concept is employed descriptively or to express approval or disapproval. "Discipline" is used to commend as well as describe. We admire disciplined troops but not undisciplined people. Yet we also have reservations about discipline. For example, we tend to respect a sympathetic teacher more than a disciplinarian. This is because we value personal freedom as an end in itself and discipline mainly as a means to this end. Self-discipline, too, seems desirable largely for the personal freedom it makes possible.

Now consider how you would teach students to understand the concept of discipline. What examples would be persuasive? You might describe how a trained nurse escorts frightened patients from a blazing sanitorium, or how a karate expert floors a mugger. Both nurse and Black Belt follow the rules they have learned and thus keep their emotions from overwhelming them. Or you might choose examples of self-discipline. You could mention someone who gives up partying in favor of learning to play the piano, or someone who spends his evenings studying accounting. Although the first examples are more dramatic, the last are preferable. If you want to teach a class about discipline, it may be best to emphasize self-discipline. For the more that students learn to discipline themselves, the less discipline they will need from you or the school.

Finally, try to specify enough conditions to distinguish between discipline and related concepts such as upbraid and browbeat. Upbraiding, for instance, may not lead to the desired action. When I upbraid someone, I seek to shame the person for falling short of the standards expected. But if the student does not accept those standards, I may have little favorable effect. Again, when I browbeat a student, I intimidate rather than discipline. If I tell a student to, he or she will clean the blackboards or empty the wastebaskets but will probably not internalize the rules of these activities. Obviously, you may not be able to state the necessary and sufficient conditions for the use of a concept; it may be too vague or too complex to define exactly. If so, you should state what conditions you can. My purpose here is to start you on the road of analysis rather than to cover a concept exhaustively.[14]

Do the distinctions we have drawn really matter? Emphatically. They correspond to different ways in which teachers act toward students, and they mark differences in teaching practice. If we are aware of relevant concepts, we can adapt our practices. Granted, good teachers will distinguish intuitively among the practices of upbraiding, browbeating, and disciplining. For example, they will tend to discipline unpunctual students rather than browbeat them. Yet their intuitions can be blocked by bias and emotion. When this happens, a knowledge of relevant concepts and a habit of controlled reflection can correct a teacher's judgment and change his or her response.

True, analysis may not produce agreement. An inquiry into such concepts as authority and discipline may trigger years of debate, and even the terms of that debate may be swept aside by the next wave of Young Turks. Nevertheless, this ongoing discussion can deepen our understanding of important concepts and reflect changes in cultural values. Like other philosophies, analysis promotes growth in understanding even when it reaches no permanent solution.

Analysis and Educational Research

Analysis helps clarify the concepts employed in educational research.[15] Whereas the mature sciences (physics, chemistry,

---

[14]For an analysis of the concept of an academic discipline such as history or mathematics, see Tasos Kazepides, "Discipline in Education," in *Philosophy of Education 1977: Proceedings of the Thirty-Third Annual Meeting of the Philosophy of Education Society,* ed. Ira S. Steinberg (Urbana, Ill.: Philosophy of Education Society, 1977), pp. 54–63.

[15]Analysts also have proposed models (i.e., mini-theories) for research to test. See Donna H. Kerr and Jonas F. Soltis, "Locating Teacher Competency: An Action Description of Teaching," *Educational Theory,* **24**:1 (Winter 1974), 5–16; and Nel Noddings, "Teacher Competency: An Extension of the Kerr-Soltis Model," *Educational Theory,* **24**:3 (Summer 1974), 284–90.

biology) use precise, technical concepts (such as electron, valence, and gene), the human sciences take most of their basic concepts from ordinary life. Think of motive, role, learning, development, and action. Ordinarily, for example, we explain an action by citing the intention with which it was done. But what do we mean by an action? Some analysts maintain that the standard case of an action is something done *with an intention* as opposed to something produced by a cause.[16] If a student nudges his neighbor to spoil her painting, he does so intentionally and performs an action. But if he nudges her because he has been shoved, the nudge is unintentional. It is a reflex, the effect of a cause.

Other analysts argue that an intention is a *kind* of cause, since it is the agent's intention that causes him or her to act.[17] If the student had not intended to annoy his neighbor, he would not have nudged her intentionally. It was his intention that led him to do so. Nevertheless, these analysts insist that a distinction still must be drawn between two types of explanation: explanations of actions by reference to their intentions, and explanations of other phenomena by reference to contingent causes—or causes as *scientists* understand them.

What in fact is the scientific concept of a cause? For a scientist, a cause is connected only extrinsically with its effects. An event (the cause) happens, and certain other events (the effects) are *observed* to follow. But they do not *logically have to* follow. For example, when the temperature falls below 32 degrees Fahrenheit, liquids are observed to congeal and metals to contract. Yet these effects are not *logically* required. We do not contradict ourselves if we imagine that the causes occur without their customary effects. We say that the effects will follow be-

---

[16]For example, R. S. Peters, *The Concept of Motivation* (London: Routledge & Kegan Paul, 1960); and A. I. Melden, *Free Action* (London: Routledge & Kegan Paul, 1961). I may also act *unintentionally* (e.g., because I am absentminded) or I may *fail* to do what I intend (e.g., because I am tired or timid). However, unintentional actions and failures to act are deviations from the standard form of action (which we consider here) and are to be considered in the light of it rather than the reverse.

[17]For example, Donald Davidson, "Actions, Reasons and Causes," in *Essays on Action and Events* (Oxford: Clarendon Press, 1980), pp. 3–19.

cause so far as we know they always have. But we do not—indeed we cannot—insist that they *must* follow, because there is no logically necessary connection between causes and effects of this type.

An intention, on the other hand, *is* logically connected with the action it informs. The intention makes it an act of that kind. Change the intention, and the action itself also changes. Suppose I ask a student to stay after class. If I intend to punish him, my behavior is an act of detention; if I intend to tutor him, it is an act of invitation. What distinguishes these acts is my intention. Act and intention thus are necessarily connected. Hence it would be self-contradictory to say that I "detain" the student in order to tutor him, or that I "invite" him to stay in order to punish him. I may also, it is true, fail to carry out my intention. For example, I may intend to punish a student but be unable to go through with it. When the moment comes for me to say, "Stay after school tonight," I may find myself saying instead, "Don't do that again or you'll have to stay after school." In this case my intention ceases to govern my action. The *logical* connection between intention and act, therefore, is not an empirical compulsion. I do not *have* to do what I intend. Rather, it is a *conceptual* connection between the act and the intention (if any) that actually informs it, such that I *conceive* what I do in terms of the intention with which I do it. If I do what I intend (e.g., invite the student or detain him), then my action must be described in terms of that intention—that is, as an act of invitation or detention. If I fail to do what I intend, then, clearly, the act is not governed by the intention and cannot be described in terms of it—except insofar as one might say, "He tried, and failed, to invite (or detain) the student."

What do these distinctions contribute to educational research? Among other things they show that behaviorist research programs in education generally are misconceived. Behaviorists seek to explain all human behavior, including purposive action, as the direct or indirect effect of stimuli. But since purposive actions must be explained by reference to intentions, most behaviorist research programs are both logically incoherent and empirically false. They are logically incoherent, because if actions are defined by reference to their intentions, they cannot also be treated as effects in the scientific sense of that term. They are empirically false because people do in fact act to realize their intentions.[18]

What concepts need analysis most? Generally those that belong to a range of fields: the concept of knowledge, for instance, which is central to a grasp of educational aims, curriculum, and instruction; and the concept of justice, which is crucial to the understanding of rights, equality, and due process. In analyzing such concepts we examine various assumptions in which they figure—the assumption, for instance, that knowledge is something to be *placed in* the mind (rather than *formed by* the mind in the course of experience), or that justice is a creation of laws (rather than an ideal to which laws should conform). Such assumptions often are charged with emotion and they can grip us strongly. Thus, analysis enables us to confront some of our more powerful beliefs. In the next section we consider how one analyst, Paul Hirst, has handled the key concept of liberal education.

Concept of Liberal Education

Writing during the mature phase of the ordinary language movement,[19] Hirst has followed a broader, less linguistically focused mode of analysis than such early masters as Wittgenstein, Ryle, and Austin. Although he appeals to the concept of a

---

[18]Behaviorist Burrhus F. Skinner, for example, states that to learn is to be conditioned. The learner is led (i.e., caused) by a teacher or learning program to respond in certain ways to certain stimuli—for example, to conjugate various French verbs when asked to do so. The analytic philosopher points out that this explanation applies only to rote learning. More complex and demanding types of learning—such as learning to write a paragraph or learning to dissect a frog—are forms of action governed by the learner's intentions.

[19]Paul H. Hirst, "Liberal Education and the Nature of Knowledge," in *Philosophical Analysis and Education,* ed. Reginald D. Archambault (London: Routledge & Kegan Paul, 1965), pp. 113–38; P. H. Hirst and R. S. Peters, *The Logic of Education* (London: Routledge & Kegan Paul, 1970), ch. 4; and Paul H. Hirst, "The Forms of Knowledge Re-Visited," *Knowledge and the Curriculum: A Collection of Philosophical Papers* (London: Routledge & Kegan Paul, 1974), ch. 6. "Liberal Education and the Nature of Knowledge" also is reprinted in *Knowledge and the Curriculum.* For Hirst's most recent summary of his position, see his contribution to "Symposium" (*Philosophy and Education: Eightieth Yearbook of the National Society for the Study of Education,* ed. Jonas F. Soltis), *Harvard Educational Review,* 51:3 (August 1981), 418.

language game,[20] he is interested less in ordinary language usage than in the logical features of typical statements in various branches of knowledge. This emphasis on concepts and arguments rather than on fine points of language is characteristic of much analytic philosophy today.

The problem Hirst addresses is a classic: What knowledge or experiences should the curriculum include? Clearly, students can handle only a small part of the knowledge and experiences available to them. How is this part to be chosen? Are some forms of knowledge and experience basic to others, or are all forms of equal worth? These questions have been considered by philosophers as diverse as Plato, Locke, Kant, Rousseau, and Dewey. How does Hirst deal with them?

Hirst maintains that the basic (though not the only) purpose of education is to develop the mind. Education that fulfills this purpose he calls "liberal." The mind develops, he says, by acquiring knowledge. In fact, mental growth *is* the acquisition of knowledge: "The achievement of knowledge is necessarily the development of mind—that is, the self-conscious rational mind of man—in its most fundamental aspect."[21] This is because the concepts of mind and knowledge are "logically related," so that a statement about the mind "in its most fundamental aspect" entails a corresponding statement about knowledge, and vice versa.

For Hirst the forms of knowledge are "the complex ways of understanding experience which man has achieved, which are publicly specifiable and which are gained through learning."[22] Hence he also calls them "modes" of knowledge and experience.[23] Each mode or form develops the mind "in ways that are peculiar to [the form] itself as a way of understanding experience." Each mode, moreover, can be seen in two ways: as a collection of true propositions and as a set of symbols (usually words) expressing concepts. These concepts, and the propositions in which they appear, enable us to "structure" not only

---

[20]"Language and Thought," *Knowledge and the Curriculum*, pp. 80–83.

[21]"Liberal Education and the Nature of Knowledge," *Knowledge and the Curriculum*, p. 39.

[22]Ibid, p. 38.

[23]*Logic of Education*, p. 62.

knowledge but "all other forms of consciousness, including, for example, emotional experiences, or mental attitudes and beliefs." Hence the forms of knowledge are "the basic articulations whereby the whole of experience has become intelligible to man; they are the fundamental achievement of mind." To acquire knowledge, then, is to learn "to see, to experience the world in a way otherwise unknown, and thereby come to have a mind in a fuller sense."[24]

What are the forms of knowledge and how can they be distinguished? Hirst identifies seven forms: mathematics, empirical science, history, religion, moral and interpersonal knowledge, literature and the fine arts, and philosophy.[25] Each form can be distinguished by three criteria. First, each has unique, central concepts, such as space, time, and causality in empirical science, and God, sin, and predestination in religion. Next, each has its own "logical structure" or "network of possible relationships" among its concepts. That is, the concepts and statements of history, say, can be "meaningfully related" only in certain ways and used meaningfully only to say certain things. Ways of talking that make sense in history need not do so in mathematics or religion. Finally, each has a unique way of testing the truth of its propositions—logical deduction from axioms in the case of mathematics, for instance, and observation and experimentation in the case of empirical science.[26]

What does this analysis tell educators? It tells them, says Hirst, that a liberal education must supply an understanding of all seven forms of knowledge and that a total education must include more than this—for example, special studies, physical education, and character education. Thus, Hirst's analysis both

---

[24]"Liberal Education and the Nature of Knowledge," pp. 38, 40.

[25]*Logic of Education*, pp. 63–64; "Forms of Knowledge Re-Visited," pp. 86–87. Hirst allots those propositions in history and the human sciences, which are testable by observation, to the form of empirical science, and those which are "explanations of human behavior in terms of intentions, will, hopes, beliefs, etc." to the form he calls "interpersonal knowledge."

[26]Hirst originally proposed a fourth criterion—"the method used to establish [or discover] true propositions"—but he now regards it as logically "secondary," though "most important in education and research." "Forms of Knowledge Re-Visited," pp. 85–86; "Liberal Education and the Nature of Knowledge," p. 44.

demarcates a "distinctive" concept and reveals the need for another "much wider" concept.[27] What makes the concept of a liberal education most important, however, is that it draws together "those elements in a total education that are logically basic."[28] That is, the forms of knowledge not only are "the logically basic objectives" of any worthwhile curriculum, they also "categorize" all other curricular objectives, for they provide "not only the kinds of true statement there are . . . but also the kinds of experience, feeling, attitudes, skills, etc."[29]

How are the other objectives to be "categorized"? Hirst does not answer this question directly. Relating the forms to the curriculum, he says, is "a matter of practical planning" that involves psychological, administrative, and other considerations in addition to the "purely philosophical." A total curriculum pattern can be composed "in an infinite variety of ways," provided that "the logical priority of intellectual objectives be recognized" and their "logical structure" not denied.[30] It seems that the content of the forms may be conjoined with any other content (as in "a practical project of design and building") and sequenced in any way,[31] provided that this arrangement is designed "to develop understanding of all the various forms . . . , and explicit steps [are] taken to see that this end is achieved." However, Hirst does point out that this arrangement in the end must lead to a study of the forms in their own right, for otherwise they will remain implicit in the curriculum instead of being the logically basic objectives at which the curriculum is aimed.[32]

---

[27]"Symposium," p. 418.

[28]"Forms of Knowledge Re-Visited," p. 96.

[29]"Realms of Meaning and Forms of Knowledge," *Knowledge and the Curriculum*, p. 67.

[30]"Liberal Education and the Nature of Knowledge," p. 43; "Realms of Meaning and Forms of Knowledge," pp. 67–68; "Forms of Knowledge Re-Visited," p. 99.

[31]"The logic of a subject is relevant to being taught, for its patterns must be accepted as essential to the form of knowledge. But how these patterns are best discerned [by the student] is a matter for empirical investigation." "Liberal Education and the Nature of Knowledge," p. 50.

[32]Ibid., p. 51.

Critique   Hirst's account of liberal education is a signal achievement in at least two respects. First, he insists that the intellectual core of any worthwhile curriculum must be based on a philosophic analysis of the nature of knowledge and the mind. Technical details aside, the heart of the curriculum must be well thought out and justified philosophically. Second, he maintains that this intellectual core should furnish the student with a number of ways of experiencing, viewing, and judging the world. Reality and the mind are manysided, and every student should be able to understand, rather than merely encounter, a range of experiences—moral, religious, and aesthetic as well as purely cognitive.

A major analysis invites analysis in turn. Let us therefore ask: To what extent does Hirst's achievement succeed *on its own terms?* Do his criteria indeed pick out distinct forms of knowledge? Take the first criterion—the possession of unique, central concepts. One might argue that it is the goal of mathematics at least, and possibly of empirical science, to explain its findings by means of a single theory and hence a single set of concepts. This goal, however, has yet to be realized; at present, not even physics qualifies as a distinct Hirstian form.[33] Moreover, it is open to question whether concepts such as life, heredity, and natural selection, still less culture, society, and the economy,[34] ever will be defined in terms of the concepts of space, time, and cause that (according to Hirst) are unique to the empirical sciences.[35] Again, what central concepts are unique to history but not to interpersonal knowledge? And what unique concepts unify literature and the fine arts?[36] Hirst does not say.

The second criterion—possession of a unique logical structure—fails to apply for the same reason as the first. Without a

---

[33]Physics currently is divided between quantum theory and general relativity; mathematics consists of algebra, analysis, and topology; and Gödel's theorem proves that mathematics cannot be unified.

[34]See pp. 86–87.

[35]*Logic of Education*, p. 64.

[36]For other criticisms of Hirst's first criterion, see D. C. Phillips, "The Distinguishing Features of Forms of Knowledge," *Educational Philosophy and Theory*, 3:2 (October 1971), 27–35; and D. C. Phillips, "Perspectives on Structure of Knowledge and the Curriculum," in *Contemporary Studies in the Curriculum*, ed. P. W. Musgrave (Sidney: Angus and Robertson, 1974), pp. 15–29.

unifying theory there can be no unifying structure. It may be said that a form of knowledge possesses structure so long as its concepts are logically related in some way. For example, in the form of interpersonal knowledge, many statements including the concepts of action, purpose, and decision presuppose statements including the concept of intention. Nevertheless, there is no hierarchy here but only a single level of entailment. An array of logically parallel concepts, all dependent on a more basic concept (in this case that of intent), constitutes a collection of concepts rather than a structure.

Under the third criterion—possession of a unique way of testing truth claims—Hirst's forms hardly fare better. Mathematics might seem to use a unique method—the logical deduction of theorems from axioms. Yet empirical science, which employs observation, also relies on deduction to derive test statements from generalizations and on deduction from axioms to derive test statements from theoretical principles. As for the remaining forms, some seem to employ the above methods (e.g., philosophy uses logic), while at least one of them—literature and the fine arts—does not consist of propositions and does not make truth claims that can be tested methodically.

Consider Hirst's view on this last form. A work of art, he says, comprises a number of elements that are combined like the words of a sentence to express a meaning that may be judged true or false. The scenes of a play or the movements of a symphony correspond to words or phrases, and like a sentence, the play or symphony expresses a proposition. Thus, he writes, Picasso's *Guernica*, George Eliot's *Middlemarch*, Mozart's *Fidelio*, and a Haydn symphony, each can be taken as "a statement expressing a truth we can properly be said to know."[37]

Yet if we ask *what* truth a work of art expresses, the answer almost invariable trivializes the effect the work has on us. Is *Macbeth*, for instance, primarily a statement that crime does not pay? No, it seems better described as a portrait of a murderer who becomes appalled by his crimes. Macbeth, to be sure, comes to realize the particular truth that his crimes have corrupted him. Yet the play itself is not a statement of the proposi-

---

[37]"Literature and the Fine Arts as a Form of Knowledge," *Knowledge and the Curriculum*, pp. 152, 160.

tion contained in this insight, but rather the representation of a man coming to have this insight and much else beside. In short, it is what Aristotle in his *Poetics* called the "representation of an action." Again, is *Guernica* simply a statement that war is hell or fascism inhumane? Hardly. It seems first and foremost to be the depiction of a city under the fury of aerial bombardment. True, Picasso's painting makes us aware that war is hell. It does so, however, not because it is a statement of the proposition, but because it is a representation of a catastrophe that leads us to draw this conclusion.

Works of art, then, are not primarily statements but representations of reality, including psychical reality, that move our emotions. The writer or artist expresses an attitude toward this reality and, if he or she is mature, the work will convey a kind of truth. But this truth does not take the form of a proposition. The meaning or significance of a novel or painting is not like the meaning of a statement. On the contrary, it is a combination of thought, emotion, and sensation that is more like the impression made on us by a person we have met or a sunset we have seen. Indeed, a work of art seems not so much to contain knowledge as to depict what the world looks like to someone who believes (say), as did the novelist Joseph Conrad, that human beings deep down are mysterious and irrational or, like the Impressionists, that what we see are not things in themselves but sense data.

Hirst also may be faulted for relying on "planners" to relate his liberal curriculum to the curriculum as a whole. All he stipulates is that his own curriculum be included in the latter, on the grounds that the forms of knowledge are "logically basic" (since they structure the range of intelligible experience). Yet it does not follow that a knowledge of the forms is the most important goal of education. As Hirst himself says, education has other goals than the purely intellectual, especially in the narrow sense in which he uses this term (e.g., so that it excludes acquiring the skills of a second language).[38] In the nature of things, however, education as a whole must have some more general goal than liberal education in Hirst's sense—to develop the personal and social self, for example, or to lead to

---

[38]"Forms of Knowledge Re-Visited," p. 96.

the good life. This general goal not only will subordinate other goals, such as moral growth, intellectual development, and the good of society, it will also, depending on how it is interpreted, cause them to be ranked differently. If so, moral growth or community service, say, may be ranked higher than intellectual development. Indeed, these goals may be ranked so much higher that they exclude part of the liberal curriculum Hirst recommends. If, therefore, Hirst believes that his liberal education is the most important part of education as a whole, he first should relate the goal of his liberal education to any conceivable overall goal of the curriculum. He then should *prove* that his goal *is* the overall goal's most important part.

Let me conclude by saying that I have discussed Hirst's analysis, not because I think it seriously flawed, but because I wish to show how analysis is done. It is only one of many examples I could have chosen. In fact, I agree with much that Hirst says. I believe, for instance, that intellectual development is the chief goal of the curriculum. I also believe that Hirst's forms are fundamental, though I do not think he has defined them satisfactorily. I would use them to structure the (American) high school curriculum and the first two years of college. I would, for example, treat sex education within the form of empirical science, especially biology, and career education within the form of interpersonal knowledge. Above all, I honor Hirst for providing an analysis that has challenged us to think more deeply about the curriculum and take steps to improve it.

APPRAISAL

Analysis has brought rigor and clarity to educational thought. It has drawn sharp distinctions, exposed hidden assumptions, and detected flaws in reasoning. Analysis has identified the conceptual muddles of behaviorism and has improved curriculum design by distinguishing among the forms of knowledge. It tentatively has "mapped the logical geography" of many key concepts, such as education, schooling, teaching, learning, knowledge, intelligence, and equality. It has shown some of the things that sensibly can be thought and said with the aid of these concepts. It has demonstrated, for instance, that schooling necessarily involves teaching (for you cannot school people without teaching them) yet learning does not (for you can learn without being taught). A clearer understanding of concepts in turn can lead to wiser decisions, for some of the heat in the educational debate arises from confusion about the different concepts and principles at stake, especially when the concepts are at once related and opposed, like rights and responsibilities, freedom and authority, and teaching and indoctrination.

Analysis has made the philosophy of education more professional—more of a craft. In preanalytic times students would read any or all of the following: the educational ideas of leading philosophers, the implications for education of traditional philosophic schools (such as realism and idealism), and general theories of education (such as perennialism and progressivism). For the most part, they studied the results of other people's thinking. With analysis, however, students are forced to consider specific educational problems. They no longer only read philosophy, says the analyst, they also *do* it.

Analysis is a philosophy to which many people can contribute. It focuses as a rule on single concepts or groups of concepts and examines them in detail. It aims at continuous dialogue, in the belief that every distinction drawn, every obscurity uncovered, enlightens us further. Anyone who studies analysis seriously can choose some conceptual puzzle and work toward its solution.

The analyst has a special message for teachers. "You are responsible for what you think and say," he declares. "Unless you think and speak clearly, you will pass on your confusion and prejudice to your students." Among other things, teachers must disclose their intentions, know the nature of their authority, and distinguish among actions such as disciplining, punishing, browbeating, and upbraiding.

Yet a price has been paid for these achievements. The interest in language too often has become an obsession. Sensitivity to usage has degenerated into wordplay and a drawing of distinctions for their own sake. When analysis is bad, it can be frivolous, pedantic, and even obscure. It is ironic that the search for clarity should lead to so much misunderstanding among analysts themselves.

Many analysts have failed to stress the implications of their work for educational practice. They have talked to one another rather than to the policymaker, the administrator, or the teacher. Complained one critic, "I am come from the trenches of teaching to the Pentagon of philosophy, and am dismayed to find the generals playing chess."[39] Now analysis *does* contribute to practice. It provides a clearer understanding of concepts and principles operative in the professional and private lives of educators. But too many analysts have stated this truth rather than illustrated it in detail.

Again, analysis is apt to be cautious. True, no less a philosopher than John Austin declared that analysis only begins with ordinary language and need not end with it. Yet most analyses *have* ended with it. Ordinary language frequently has had both the first word and the last. Analysts on the whole seem to assume that the central truths about human life have been attained and that philosophy's task is to vindicate them. Although analysts may sympathize with piecemeal reforms, they generally resist radical critique.

Analysts are inclined to be skeptical of large-scale theories. They tend to overlook the fact that problems usually arise against a background of theory, and that experience becomes problematic just when it contradicts some theory of what experience should be like.[40] In education, few analyses have been both deep and comprehensive and thus genuine theories. (Hirst's analysis of liberal education is as good a theory as the movement has produced.) If analysis is to attract younger philosophers, it must produce more theories that can be tested by examining their practical consequences. This means that analysts must do more than expose obscurity and confusion in a theory. They also must consider whether the theory throws new light, however crude, on some aspect of what it purports to explain.

During the last decade, however, analysts have become less obsessed with ordinary language and readier to engage in moral

---

[39]Cited by Abraham Edel, "Analytic Philosophy of Education at the Cross-Roads," *Educational Theory*, **22**:1 (Spring 1972), 132.

[40]R. J. Haack, "Philosophies of Education," *Philosophy*, **51**:196 (April 1976), 164ff., 174.

and social criticism.[41] Some have begun to evaluate educational institutions and recommend reforms. They are tackling such controversial issues as the right to equal education, the rights of children, affirmative action, and reverse discrimination. They are speaking out on such practical problems as desegregation, moral education, curriculum choice, and teaching as a profession.[42]

One stimulus to this practical turn has been the challenge of other philosophies. During the postwar years three major philosophies have made the crossing from Europe: phenomenology, hermeneutics, and structuralism. Together with other philosophies considered in this book, they now influence a wide range of educational thinking. Let us see what they can tell us about life in general and education in particular. I begin with phenomenology, which in its existentialist form caught the attention of educators at the same time as analysis.

---

[41]See Richard Rorty, "Philosophy in America Today," *American Scholar,* **51**:2 (Spring 1982), 183–200; and Arthur C. Danto, "Analytical Philosophy," *Social Research,* **47**:4 (Winter 1980), 612–34. On analysis in education today, see Richard Pratte, "Analytic Philosophy of Education: A Historical Perspective," *Teachers College Record,* **81**:2 (Winter 1979), 145–65; R. F. Dearden, "Philosophy of Education, 1952–82," *British Journal of Educational Studies,* **30**:1 (February 1982), 57–71; and John Wilson, "Philosophy and Education: Retrospect and Prospect," *Oxford Review of Education,* **6**:1 (1980), 41–52.

[42]See, for example, *Ethics and Educational Policy,* ed. Kenneth Strike and Kieran Egan (London: Routledge & Kegan Paul, 1978). For educational philosophy that is both vigorous and morally committed, read two books by Mary Warnock: *Schools of Thought* (London: Faber & Faber, 1977) and *Education: A Way Ahead* (Oxford: Blackwell, 1979).

Phenomenology 2

Husserl: Early Phenomenology

Like analysis, phenomenology seeks to describe our basic concepts, but uses another method and other data. Whereas analysis turns to language considered as the repository of concepts, phenomenology goes to the stream of individual experience—to the process of perceiving, thinking, feeling, deciding, remembering, and other mental acts.[1] This stream is our access to all that exists. To understand the world and ourselves, says the phenomenologist, we must look clearly and directly—without presuppositions—at these basic data of our experience, at what actually is there in our minds.

Why the name "phenomenology"? Edmund Husserl (1859–1938), founder of this philosophy, called the contents of the conscious mind "phenomena" after the Greek word for "appearances." Any mental content, he said, is an appearance of something, whether real or imaginary, present or absent, object

---

[1]On phenomenology and analysis, see *Linguistic Analysis and Phenomenology,* ed. Wolfe Mays and S. C. Brown (London: Macmillan, 1972).

or idea. It is the form that something takes in the mind rather than the thing itself. Phenomenology is the systematic study (*logos*) of these appearances.

What are the phenomena like? Are they a chaos of streaks, blurs, and flashes? No, as a rule they are relatively integrated. They come as objects, ideas, memories, and coherent images. I see a football field, think of the next lesson, remember my best friend, imagine a vandalized school. Why are the phenomena organized like this? According to Husserl, the mind structures its contents by means of concepts. If things are to appear to us at all, their appearances—the phenomena—must conform to our concepts. What cannot be conceptualized, cannot be experienced.

Concepts range from the general (e.g., space, time, and education) to the specific (e.g., teacher, student, and text). Particular individuals may apply these concepts differently, but they still apply the same concepts. For example, the first grader, the dropout, the chemistry whiz, and the principal all regard the science laboratory differently; yet they all regard it as a laboratory. Phenomenology seeks to describe the nature and scope of the concepts underlying all branches of knowledge, including education, and thus to place these branches on foundations that are "absolutely certain."

The Phenomenological Method

How do you discover and describe these fundamental concepts? First, you set aside all presuppositions that might distort the nature of what appears to you. To use Husserl's term, you "bracket" them, as a mathematician brackets an expression or an equation, so that it does not interfere with the immediate mathematical operation. Above all, you bracket the common-sense presupposition that you live in a world of objects that are independent of you and give rise to your experiences. For what you actually encounter are not objects but experiences of objects, experiences that you yourself structure through your concepts.

Suppose you wish to isolate the concept through which you structure the experience of teaching. You bracket all your ideas of teaching, all pedagogical, psychological, sociological theories, all notions of authority and responsibility. You even bracket your belief that the classroom you now enter or imagine exists independently of you. You seek to become what the novelist Henry James called a "perfect reflector,"[2] an unprejudiced eye.

Next, you compare this experience of teaching with other actual or possible experiences of teaching. How do you do this? In your mind's eye you alter one feature of the experience and then another and another. In each case you ask yourself whether the altered experience basically is the same as the original experience (or as a variant of it that you now consider more representative). You ask yourself whether it has the same essence or structure and so reflects the same organizing concept. By considering a wide range of experiences, you isolate the essential features of the concept you are examining. If you follow this procedure rigorously, says Husserl, and compare your results with those of other investigators, together you will describe the basic concepts that are common to members of your society.

So think of a teacher you admired. How did she present her subject, capture your interest, answer questions, discipline you, grade you, and the like? Let her teaching be your initial experience. Next, recall other teachers who differed from her in some way—in attitude, in the subjects they taught, in age, sex, or temperament, in teaching method, knowledge, and so forth. Try to identify the common features of their teaching and hers. Now cast your mind further. Imagine parents, politicians, salespeople, preachers, shop stewards. Think of computers, TV commercials, newspapers. Do these ever teach? If so, when and how? Imagine listening to a sales pitch, a sermon, a storm warning, a piece of advice, a political harangue. Are you still being taught? If so, in what sense? If not, why not? When you meet some feature that you realize does not belong to teaching, you have reached the boundaries of the concept. Unlike a teacher, for example, a salesperson aims chiefly at your pocketbook and a preacher at your soul. But be aware that the core

---

[2]In his later novels (e.g., *The Ambassadors, The Golden Bowl*) Henry James sought to present the main action and characters through the eyes of a subordinate character who would observe and infer without bias or favoritism.

features of teaching rarely are grasped at once. You move slowly and deliberately from vagueness toward clarity. When you think that you have established these core features, you can compare your findings with those of other inquirers.

The Lifeworld

According to Husserl, we derive most of our basic concepts from the "lifeworld" (*Lebenswelt*).[3] This is the everyday human world of homes, jobs, and hobbies, the world in which we work, socialize, eat, and sleep. We think of this world as objective and independent, yet it is we who sustain it and give it meaning. Social institutions and practices—money, markets, recreations, and schools—mean what they do because we have learned to think and talk about them in common ways. (Each of us, being unique, also gives these common concepts his or her own shades of meaning.) To understand the lifeworld properly, we must describe—phenomenologically—the concepts through which we give it meaning.

Husserl contrasted the lifeworld with the world as described by science. Modern science, he said, was born in Galileo's decision to idealize and mathematicize nature—that is, to postulate ideal constructs (e.g., infinitesimal particles and frictionless motion), to state the relations between them in mathematical equations, and to treat these constructs and relations as the ultimate reality to which the observable world approximates. Reality is reduced to what can be measured and expressed mathematically, and it is treated as independent of man. Everything else is ignored. Yet, declared Husserl, the abstractions of science presuppose the world of lived experience. Science itself is built on our immediate experience of the world.

Science, said Husserl, not only has replaced nature with abstractions, it also has sought to explain human beings as though we too were natural phenomena, objects without inner lives. Psychology and sociology especially have focused on observable behavior, ignoring the thoughts and intentions that give meaning to that behavior. They have given us a picture of ourselves that we hardly recognize. If we wish to explain

---

[3] Edmund Husserl, *The Crisis of the European Sciences and Transcendental Phenomenology*, trans. with an introd. by David Carr (Evanston, Ill.: Northwestern University Press, 1970).

human beings, we must relate the activities and findings of the human sciences to the basic concepts with which we understand and organize our everyday experience.[4]

For example, we can use the phenomenological method to describe in detail the actual phenomena of the educational process. Many of these phenomena are human actions and responses. To describe them accurately, we need to state what they mean to the persons involved. We need to look at education through the eyes of those who are engaged in it. Thus, we can ask different teachers how they feel and what they do when they size up a new group of students, get a question they cannot answer, spot a potential troublemaker, watch a class break up, wade through a pile of exams, and so forth. The ultimate purpose of our investigations is to describe the major concepts through which people structure their experiences of education. Since persons with different roles in the educational system (e.g., students, teachers, administrators, and janitors) structure their experiences of the educational process differently, we must identify the basic features of each group's concepts of (say) teaching, learning, punishment, disobedience, and play. We then may find that each group (and perhaps subgroup) has its own versions of these concepts.

Another important task is to describe how concepts are acquired. As the phenomenologist points out, children form many commonsense concepts (e.g., of ordinary physical objects) without schooling at all. They interact with people, animals, plants, sports, artworks, and (through TV) with aspects of history, politics, commerce, and culture. One prime role of the school is to help children build their informal concepts into the more complex and differentiated concepts they will need in later life. Formal concepts and the knowledge that goes with them are established by the academic disciplines—history, science, mathematics, and so on. The school must match the concepts and findings of the disciplines to the concepts and knowledge of the child. If this is to be done effectively, educators

[4]On Husserl and phenomenology, see David Stewart and Algis Mickunas, *Exploring Phenomenology: A Guide to the Field and Its Literature* (Chicago: American Library Association, 1974), ch. 2; Don Ihde, *Experimental Phenomenology: An Introduction* (New York: Putnam, 1977); *Philosophy and Phenomenological Understanding*, ed. Edo Pivčević (Cambridge: Cambridge University Press, 1975); Edo Pivčević, *Husserl and Phenomenology* (London: Hutchison, 1970).

need to know not only how trained investigators conceptualize objects in the different disciplines but, more importantly, how children themselves come to perceive these objects.

The choice of materials for the curriculum should be guided, then, by phenomenological research. Phenomenologists should ascertain how practitioners in each discipline studied in school come to understand the facts and theories they use—how biologists, for example, come to grasp photosynthesis and evolution, and how historians come to comprehend the Fall of the Bastille and the French Revolution. Here the best course is for phenomenologists versed in these disciplines to ask how they formed their own understanding, what features were crucial to them in learning, and so forth.

Even more important, phenomenologists should find out from teachers and students how youngsters can see in their mind's eye the facts and theories they study, how they can experience them vicariously, and how they can connect them with the kinds of people, processes, and things they already know. Suppose, for example, students are to learn how Father Junipero Sera and his band explored California and founded the first missions. The names and dates will be almost meaningless unless the students can picture the band on their travels, visualize the mountains and valleys they crossed, imagine their plans and ambitions, and relate their joys and setbacks to experiences the students themselves have had. In addition, students should use their own grasp of politics, geography, and social life to discern the influence of those early Spanish settlements on the culture of California today. A phenomenologically based curriculum will enable youngsters to build a bridge from their own concepts to those of the disciplines and, at the same time, to preserve their earlier concepts.[5]

Heidegger: From Anxiety to Authenticity

Husserl issued the challenge. What was the response?[6] In the 1920s, one of Husserl's most gifted students, Martin Heidegger

---

[5]See Donald Vandenberg, "Charlatans, Knowledge, Curriculum and Phenomenological Research," in *Working Papers in Distance Education*, No. 5 (St. Lucia, Queensland, Australia: University of Queensland Press, 1982).

[6]For selections from existential phenomenologists, see *Existentialism from Dos-*

(1889–1976), broke with his former teacher. For most of his career Husserl had focused on the operations of the conscious mind. How the world exists outside the mind, and whether it affects the mind, mattered little to him. To Heidegger, however, it was obvious that we inescapably are involved in the world. We are born in it, educated in it, work in it, die in it. Heidegger therefore applied Husserl's method[7] not to the mind alone but to human existence as a whole. What basic characteristics do we find, he asked, if we look without presuppositions at ordinary human life? Other philosophers, indebted to Husserl and Heidegger, have asked the same question. They are known as existential phenomenologists. Their answers form a tradition that has real meaning for education.

In his *Being and Time* (1927) Heidegger asked what it means to be human. Basically, he said, to be human is to interact with the world. For Heidegger, unlike Husserl, I do not merely contemplate this world, I use it and am affected by it. I am surrounded by things that play a part in my life, by charts, classrooms, playgrounds, cars. I live among people who matter to me—among family, friends, students, colleagues. I meet this world in different moods—buoyantly, studiously, angrily, suspiciously. For Heidegger, the most important of these moods is *anxiety*.

Anxiety arises when my everyday life seems pointless and I find myself isolated with nothing and no one to sustain or guide me. Now I realize that I alone am to blame for my life and that nothing in the world matters so much to me. Anxiety shows me the three basic traits of the human condition—*my* condition. First, I am free. Unlike the papers and pencils on my desk, I can

---

toevsky to Sartre, ed. with an introd. by Walter Kaufmann, rev. ed. (New York: New American Library, 1979); *Phenomenology and Existentialism,* ed. Richard M. Zaner and Don Ihde (New York: Putnam, 1973); *Existentialism,* ed. and introd. by Robert C. Solomon (New York: Modern Library, 1974). A good history of the movement is Mary Warnock's *Existentialism* (London: Oxford University Press, 1970). Two collections of essays on phenomenology in education are: *Phenomenology and Education: Self-Consciousness and Its Development,* ed. Bernard Curtis and Wolfe Mays (London: Methuen, 1978); and *Existentialism and Phenomenology in Education: Collected Essays,* ed. David E. Denton (New York: Teachers College Press, 1974).

[7]Strictly speaking, a weaker version of this method. See Herbert Spiegelberg, *The Phenomenological Movement: An Introduction,* vol. 1, rev. ed., (The Hague: Nijhoff, 1976), pp. 247–252.

do and be what I choose. Hence I am responsible for what I become. Next, I am "thrown" into the world. I did not pick my parents, my genes, my teachers, my epoch. I am simply here. And I must die alone, with no one to stand in for me. The thought of death drives home to me that my life is my own to make and my only one. Finally, I live most of the time like everyone else. I teach the same lessons, watch the same shows, keep the same schedules, take the same vacations. Nothing distinguishes me. Yet I might have been different.

Anxiety makes me choose. I can flee from it and pick up my life as before, reassured that at least I am like everyone else. Or I can face it and do what I alone am capable of. My life up to now has been standardized and impersonal. I have done as "one" does and not what "one doesn't."[8] Thus, I am inauthentic much of the time. But I do not have to be. I can start to live authentically. Instead of following convention, I can choose my own goals and standards and pursue my own vision. What does this tell me as a teacher?

It tells me that I must teach authentically. But how do I do this? First, I teach for a purpose of my own: to cherish and protect the young, for instance, or to pass on a tradition (such as the study of literature), or to improve society through its next generation, or to spread a certain virtue such as tolerance or courtesy. Next, I teach in my own way. I create a style of my own, or I mold one I have learned and apply it to my own ends. Then I take responsibility for what I do. I am not content to say, "I'm supposed to do it" or "The principal wants it." Even if these things are so, they are not *my* reasons for acting. If I take my class to the local museum, I do so because I admire the museum or value the project, not because everyone goes there or because I don't know what else to do.

In pursuing these aims I also seek a more general goal—to arouse the student's own desire for authenticity. Each student has the right and responsibility to choose who he or she will be. I therefore treat students as ends in themselves. I don't identify with them, I don't court them, I don't steer them toward a major

---

[8]Martin Heidegger, *Being and Time*, trans. John McQuarrie and Edward Robinson (New York: Harper & Row, 1962), p. 165.

or career. I simply am an example to them. By setting my own standards, by following my own path, by teaching wholeheartedly, I show my students what the authentic life can be. I tell them that they are responsible for their successes and failures, as I am for mine, and I give them the opportunity to achieve what they can.

The greatest obstacles to authenticity are fear and conformity. Following Heidegger, I encourage my students to stand by their beliefs in situations that require moral courage. If a girl likes to play with tractors rather than dolls, I tell her to be proud of this and experiment with all the machines she can find. If a boy prefers collecting shells to playing basketball, I advise him to collect them because sooner or later the world will be interested in them too. If a student is bullied or sidelined, I am there for him to turn to. If he is true to what is best in himself, I must defend him against all comers.

Authentic teaching reflects the uniqueness of the individual teacher. It is a form of self-expression, but directed toward the self-realization of others. The authentic teacher spurns the cult of efficiency, the worship of numbers. The authentic teacher also rejects the attempt to hold teachers and students "accountable" to distant administrators through standardized tests. Such tests state how someone has scored in relation to others; they are not an indication of who the teacher is. Teachers are not first and foremost accountable to the authorities but, instead, are *responsible*—to themselves and to the students, colleagues, parents, and others with whom they deal face to face.

Authenticity arises out of anxiety. How does the teacher handle this mood? To answer this question, we must distinguish betwen existential and neurotic anxiety.[9] *Existential* anxiety is a highly painful form of illumination that dissolves my beliefs, values, and defenses and reveals me as I am—solitary, finite, free. It is the most powerful experience I can have; it is the source of creativity, the prerequisite of growth. It can arise at any time. If there is any advice a teacher can give, it is "Allow

---

[9]See Peter Koestenbaum, *The New Image of the Person: The Theory and Practice of Clinical Philosophy* (Westport, Conn.: Greenwood Press, 1978), pp. 231–233; and Bernard J. Boelen, *Personal Maturity: The Existential Dimension* (New York: Seabury, 1978), chs. 4, 5.

yourself to be anxious!" The more anxiety I can tolerate, and the more I can bear the truth of the human condition, the more authentic I am. *Neurotic* anxiety results from suppressing existential anxiety. It is the pain and dissatisfaction I feel when I limit myself and deny my real possibilities.

Existential anxiety emerges mostly during adolescence. The 12-year-old seeks security and identity in the gang. He hangs out with them, dresses like them, talks like them, thinks like them. Within a few years, however, he is bored and disgusted with everything. Like J. D. Salinger's Holden Caulfield, he thinks, "The whole damn world is phoney." In reality he is withdrawing from everything inauthentic. And within himself he finds—nothing. He is free to be whatever he chooses. But what should he choose? This is existential anxiety. Teachers should let the experience take its course. They should be ready with advice and compassion when the student seeks it. But the student must come to them.

In the high noon of adolescence, beneath habits learned from parents and school, the student finds a self of his own. Now he knows who he is. Whatever he does—write, educate, reform, heal the sick—will enhance his life. To find himself, however, he may have to reject the culture in which he has been raised. This takes courage. Most adults are impatient with the ideals he takes so seriously. They want him to behave "normally," that is, like everyone else. As a teacher, however, I must encourage self-exploration. I must urge my students to hold fast to their visions in adult life. What matters, I must say, is not to fit into the world or even to dazzle it, but to use what the world offers—money, contacts, career—to realize the best in oneself.

The second great onset of existential anxiety is in middle age. At the peak of my career I may find that teaching holds no more surprises for me. I ask, Is this what I promised myself? I have taught all these youngsters, but what have I learned myself? I now must look at the person I have become. I may have chosen to teach originally in response to my inner voice. But now that voice may be saying something different. Now I must choose again. I must be honest with myself and fair to my students. Either I find a new purpose in teaching or I quit (start a restaurant, write that novel, become a realtor). I, who will die sooner than I think, must realize once more the unique potential I always have borne.

Critique   Authenticity involves personal responsibility. The authentic teacher must do what she or he believes in rather than follow convention. But authenticity also has limitations. For example, Heidegger overvalues anxiety. Why should this mood alone show me what I really am? Intimacy, meditation, therapy, communion with nature, handling professional responsibility, and the experience of taking a moral stand surely reveal as much of me and do so less bleakly. If I wish to grow, I should seek a wider range of experiences than Heidegger proposes.

Again, Heidegger's concept of authenticity is incomplete. It prescribes little and forbids less. For any act whatever—no matter how ruthless or antisocial—can be authentic, provided it is chosen sincerely. Heidegger also takes individualism to extremes. Although he grants that I can live authentically in the crowd, he dwells on solitary reflection. Yet surely we may be no less honest, and enter no less deeply into ourselves, when we are intimate with others. Integrity notwithstanding, the authentic teacher must be careful not to seem too distant and self-enclosed to students.

Finally, in his attack on conformism Heidegger underestimates the decency and vitality of ordinary social life. Casual contacts tend to be stylized, but they also may cheer us and sometimes lead to deeper relations. The camaraderie of the classroom and the playground enable us to relax between more serious endeavors. Heidegger's social views leave much to be desired. On the one hand, he seems uninterested in reforming society. On the other hand, he announced his support for national socialism, whose conformist society he regarded as ideal for the German people. True, he later withdrew that support, but not without revealing the fundamental poverty of his social thought.[10]

Sartre: Freedom and Choice

Where Heidegger is concerned with authenticity, Jean-Paul Sartre (1905–1980) is preoccupied with freedom. Where Heidegger emphasizes choosing your own standards and following them over time, Sartre stresses choosing *afresh in each situation*. Each of us, Sartre says, is completely free. To be free is to choose, and I can choose whatever I like—to criticize the princi-

---

[10]Recent works on Heidegger include: Roger Waterhouse, *A Heidegger Critique* (Brighton: Harvester, 1980); and George Steiner, *Martin Heidegger* (New York: Viking, 1979).

pal, teach my class the way I want, advocate suicide, lose my temper. True, I may be restrained from doing these things (by other people, for example, or physical weakness), but I cannot be stopped from choosing them. If one of my choices is blocked, I can try another. If the principal retaliates, for example, I can ignore him. The fact remains: I am still free. Whether I like it or not, whether I know it or not, I am "condemned" to freedom.

Freedom, says Sartre, can be agonizing. I have no right to say, "I can't help doing this, it's not my fault." I *can* help doing it and it *is* my fault. I am absolutely responsible for my life. This thought torments me, so I tend to suppress it by lapsing into what Sartre calls "bad faith," the pretence that I am not really free. The most common form of bad faith is surrender to a role. I become "the good teacher," say, and nothing more, a person who does certain things and not others, who cedes her initiative to her function. I get up at 6, for instance, to be at school by 8, saying that I *have* to be there. But I *need* not. I can choose to sleep in and risk being fired. Again, I read through the text before class, telling myself that I must be prepared. But I need not. I can toss the text in my drawer and improvise. If I do not do so, it is not because I cannot or must not. It is because I do not *choose* to.

I am burdened not only by my own freedom but also by that of my students and fellow teachers. They behave unexpectedly, pursue purposes at odds with mine, and at times actively frustrate me. In self-defense I try to control or manipulate them. I think of them as things, as though they were not really free. I see a girl studying, and I think "She is methodical," and henceforth I expect her to be so. I catch a student cheating and I say "He is a cheat," and thereafter I watch him like a hawk. But that is not the end of it. For Sartre, all human relations are a battle with three possible outcomes: sadism, masochism, and indifference. Everyone's freedom threatens mine, and mine threatens everyone else's. Either I dominate my students, or they dominate me, or we remain indifferent. "Hell," says a Sartrean character, "is other people."[11]

Where does this last view leave the school? On a *pessimistic* reading of the early Sartre, a genuinely humane education is

---

[11]Jean-Paul Sartre, *No Exit* (New York: Vintage, 1946), p. 47.

impossible. As a teacher, I must be in control. I must get my students to learn what I think they need to learn. If I can do so gently, well and good. If not, either my students or I go to "the Wall." From this perspective much formal education is, for the students, forced labor. They are compelled to attend school, subjected to discipline, and made to read, write, and memorize. In response, they either hit back or knuckle under.

However, if we take certain Sartrean themes and do not ask for overall consistency, we find a more congenial view. As a Sartrean teacher, I reject all formulas, all techniques. I even hesitate to learn from experience, if that means stereotyping or classifying students and situations. Each problem, each lesson, each student is a new challenge. I question, explain, discuss, advise, and grade as though for the first time. I present myself not as a functionary but as a unique person seeking to learn and grow as much as my students. I make my choices on the spot, doing what seems right to me in that moment. In short, I teach by personal example rather than by precept. By my spontaneity, independence, and love of life, I inspire my students to seek and live the free life themselves.

I make a point, too, of encouraging *conscious* choice. I show students that they have far more room for choice than they probably realize. Again and again students choose without knowing it, either because the choice is a habit or because they think they have no choice (as when they blindly obey school rules and parental commands). They therefore should choose with awareness.

I also describe the temptations of bad faith, especially the lure of glamorous roles (the Stud, the Letterman, the Campus Queen, the Brain) that falsify the self. A boy may suppress his tenderness in order to appear cool; a girl may deny her intellect to appear attractive. Unfortunately, too many students succumb to bad faith. Writes Sartre: "The attentive pupil who wishes to *be* attentive, his eyes riveted on the teacher, his ears wide open, so exhausts himself in playing the attentive role that he ends up by no longer hearing anything.[12] The best antidote to youthful bad faith is the example of teachers who refuse to play a part,

---

[12]Jean-Paul Sartre, *Being and Nothingness*, trans. with an introd. by Hazel E. Barnes (New York: Philosophical Library, 1956), p. 60.

who do things for their own reasons, not those of the administration or the curriculum supervisor.

Finally, I expect the unexpected. I do not assume that a particular student will be the person he was yesterday. It is his intrinsic right to be unpredictable. I do not seek security in a stable classroom, or resent it when a student stridently asserts himself. I ask him, however, to deal with the consequences of his actions, however unforeseen, for if I protect him from these, I make him dependent.

Critique   What are we to say of Sartre? On the one hand, we must admire his strenuous commitment to individual freedom, coupled with his insistence on choice and self-responsibility. For Sartre, freedom means not less effort but more, not laxity but decisiveness. Again, he says that life must be lived in risk and uncertainty and in the permanent possibility of despair. This is a salutary corrective to the view, so prevalent today, that life is manageable, that all problems are soluble, and that one is *entitled* to be happy. Finally, there is a healthy truth in Sartre's somber view of the place of conflict in human affairs. In their eagerness to cooperate and compromise, Sartre implies, parents, teachers, and administrators are all too quick to resolve their differences rather than stand up courageously for their views.

On the other hand, we are not, in my view, as free as Sartre maintains. Each of us bears the deep marks of his childhood, the constraints of language and culture, and the impress of race, religion, and class. Until high school the student has been formed largely by others. Moreover, contrary to Sartre, society is the source of many of our strengths. Without it I could not learn to think or talk or make any worthwhile choices. Again, Sartre exaggerates the interpersonal struggle. Think how many friendships are formed in school. Think how much affection there is for teachers who like their students, and how much respect there is for a teacher who is conscientious and fair. As a teacher, then, I may well choose to combine a Sartrean admiration for individual freedom with an equal and un-Sartrean commitment to cooperation. I also must walk a fine line between encouraging individual choice and teaching my students what they need to know. Sartre would insist, however, and rightly, that I draw that line for myself.

Again, Sartre says that each of us must exercise his or her freedom to the utmost. But is this code compatible with the school's responsibility to prepare the young for life in society? Some critics argue that, if there are no supraindividual values and if there is no harmony between persons, social morality is impossible.[13] Others reply[14] that Sartre's big existentialist work, *Being and Nothingness*, implies a social ethic that is spelled out later in the popular essay, "Existentialism Is a Humanism."[15] In the essay Sartre declares that if you seek to realize your own freedom, you should commit yourself equally to the freedom of others.[16] In my view, even enthusiastic Sartreans should put Sartre's insights to their own use, not follow the philosopher slavishly. I therefore believe that teachers should incorporate into their code a twin commitment to their own and to their students' freedom, while at the same time doing all they can to create or preserve a society that encourages individual freedom and responsibility.

Merleau-Ponty: Bodily Perception

Maurice Merleau-Ponty (1908–1961) agrees with Husserl that phenomenology must go to the world of lived experience. He maintains, however, that I am not basically a thinker who creates mental pictures of the world, but an actor directly linked to the world through my body. My body is unique in nature; unlike anything nonhuman, it is both subjective and objective. My body is a subject because I perceive with it and act through it,

---

[13]For example, Mary Warnock, *Existentialist Ethics* (London: Macmillan, 1967), p. 3.

[14]For example, Hazel Barnes, *An Existentialist Ethics* (New York: Knopf, 1967), ch. III; and Thomas C. Anderson, *The Foundations and Structure of Sartrean Ethics* (Lawrence, Kansas: Regents Press of Kansas, 1979).

[15]In Kaufmann, ed., *Existentialism from Dostoevsky to Sartre*, pp. 345– 369.

[16]Two fine introductions to Sartre are Iris Murdoch, *Sartre: Romantic Rationalist* (New Haven: Yale University Press, 1953); and Mary Warnock, *The Philosophy of Sartre* (London: Hutchinson, 1965). The best recent introduction is by Peter Caws, *Sartre* (London and Boston: Routledge & Kegan Paul, 1979).

and am nothing without it. My body is an object because I can stand back and look at it. I can feel and touch it and know it is mine. If I fall and hurt my ankle, I touch it to see if it is broken. In the same movement I act with my body and upon it. Nothing else in the world is both subject and object at the same time.

Because I am "embodied"—that is, live in my body—I relate to the world primarily through my senses. Both thought and knowledge are based on perception. Perception, in turn, is rooted in childhood. For Merleau-Ponty, the crucial lifeworld is that of infancy; the adult's world is only an "elaboration" of the world of the child. Young children, he says, do not differentiate themselves sharply from their mothers or their playpens. They do not construct the world. They are immersed in it. The child's mind, too, works differently from an adult's. Children perceive globally rather than in detail. They will draw the outline of a bicycle, for instance, without relating the pedals to the rear wheels. Their perceptions also are more strongly felt. If a girl draws a cube as four or five juxtaposed squares on the same plane, it is not because she believes the cube has this form, but because she is describing the impression that the sides of the cube make on her.[17]

According to Merleau-Ponty, perception involves action. I perceive an object because I do something with my body. I glance at my watch to check the time, cross the schoolyard to speak to a colleague, climb the stairs to teach my class. In Merleau-Ponty's own words,[18]

All movement proceeds from a perceptual foundation, and all sensation implies a motor exploration or an attitude of the body. Vision would be reduced to little if it were not oriented by the orientation to see.

I know the world because I explore it bodily.

Again, much perception is "prereflective." I often move bodily among things and persons without thinking what I am

[17]Maurice Merleau-Ponty, "The Child's Relation with Others," in *The Primacy of Perception,* trans. J. M. Edie (Evanston, Ill.: Northwestern University Press, 1964), p. 188.

[18]Ibid., p. 175.

doing. Only from time to time do I focus on myself and ask, "What's going on here?" Thus, much perception is not a conscious act but the background against which acts stand out. This prereflective mode of being is not superseded as I grow but is the source of all my later achievements.[19] I think, act, and feel as I do because of the omnipresent, prereflective stratum of my experience. Since culture is created and recreated by individuals, this stratum also is the source of all cultural achievements—of art, science, politics, and social life.

How does the work of Merleau-Ponty help me as a teacher? It tells me, first, that especially at the elementary level, concrete experience should precede abstract thought. Children should learn by moving their bodies, manipulating objects, and generalizing from what they discover. They also should draw on the prereflective concepts that they formed in their earliest years and that they have elaborated ever since. These concepts, says Merleau-Ponty, are dispositions to think, act, and perceive; they are "sedimented" into the child's lived body (*corps vécu*), enabling him to orient himself to new situations.[20]

Suppose, then, I wish to teach a child what a perimeter is.[21] I ask him to walk along each wall of the classroom, counting his paces. In this way he learns that the side, S, of a figure is like something you can walk on, and that the perimeter, P, of a figure equals $S + S + S + S$ and is like something you can walk right around. The concept of a perimeter thus is sedimented into his lived body, and he is disposed to respond to perimeter problems both mentally and physically. As he matures, his response becomes increasingly mental.

In this episode I also enable the child to draw on his pre-

[19]See Neil Bolton, "Piaget and Pre-Reflective Experience," and Wolfe Mays, "Piaget Formal and Non-Formal Elements in the Child's Conception of Causality," in Curtis and Mays, ed., *Phenomenology and Education*, pp. 28–41, 42–79. Both essays contrast Piaget with Merleau-Ponty.

[20]These sedimentations give the individual ". . . power to respond with a certain type of solution to situations of a certain general form." Merleau-Ponty, *The Phenomenology of Perception*, trans. Colin Smith (New York: Humanities Press, 1962), p. 130.

[21]See James Palermo, "'Direct Experience' in the Open Clasroom: A Phenomenological Description," in *Philosophy of Education 1974: Proceedings of the Thirtieth Annual Meeting of the Philosophy of Education Society*, ed. Michael J. Parsons (Edwardsville, Ill.: Philosophy of Education Society, 1974), pp. 241–254.

reflective experience of the school. As he runs in the playground and sits in class, the child becomes familiar with the different sized spaces of the school. He has bounded along corridors, leaped over chairs, opened windows and doors. He now uses the sedimented traces of these experiences to form mathematical concepts.

Merleau-Ponty also tells me that teaching is a conversation, not a Sartrean struggle between unequals. Because I am linked physically to my world, I am linked physically to people. My students and fellow teachers are not an external threat but an inevitable part of my life. They do not invade my space, but are already present in it, as I am in theirs. Even speech has its origin in the body. Before children can speak, they gesticulate, and even the most sophisticated conversation relies on intonation, gesture, and expression.

Moreover, says Merleau-Ponty, none of us is totally free. If we were, we could not distinguish, as we do, between certain of our acts that are free and others that are determined by our situations. We are partly free and partly conditioned by our past and by our present situation. For all of us, the classroom is both a constraint and an opportunity. As a teacher, how can I use it most fruitfully?

For Merleau-Ponty, teaching is an intensely personal process. As a teacher, I must be in touch with my own past, especially with my early perceptions and concepts, which are the source of my strongest emotions. This is the only way I can respond fully and spontaneously to my students and help them deepen the curiosity, élan, and sense of identity inherited from early childhood. The life of reason develops against a background of prereflective experience. If I divorce myself from this background, I become arid and unable to convey the intellectual excitement I would like to feel.

Again, I must face the fact that I have formed a definite picture of the world. Like most people, I took my basic concepts from parents, peers, and school. But how many of these concepts did I accept passively? If I have not questioned my concepts and beliefs before, I must question them now and see how they were formed. Unless I do, I will not stimulate my students to seek their own meaning in life.

How can I help my students interpret the world for themselves? First, they can learn to look at the world and their own experiences through the perspectives of the different disciplines—history, civics, biology, Spanish. Why so? Because the disciplines supplement, question, and sometimes refute the commonsense notions held by parents and peers. They offer general concepts and principles by which to reflect on the world. By their variety they refute the idea that there is a single truth and a single morality. Used in this way, they foster an independent mind.

Second, my students should study literature and the arts. In reading a novel, observing a painting, or listening to a symphony, the student enters a different realm, one which interprets, intensifies, or departs altogether from the everyday world. Thus, the work of art offers students a new content and a new experience by which to appreciate and criticize the life around them. Again, by taking them out of their everyday selves and stirring their emotions, art enables them to recover a lost spontaneity and the unprejudiced eye of early childhood.[22]

Critique   Of the leading phenomenologists, Merleau-Ponty is perhaps the closest in spirit to most English-speaking educators. Although wedded neither to common sense nor to pragmatism (the testing of ideas by their practical consequences), he nevertheless is always moderate, always the philosopher of the middle way. From his perspective, teaching is a personal art, but not one that requires the extremes of Heideggerian authenticity or Sartrean freedom. In his view, too, the young child should learn abstract concepts by combining thought with bodily movement and sensory experience. He also respects the human sciences more than his predecessors. For example, his major work, *The Phenomenology of Perception*, examines both behaviorist and Gestaltist findings in some detail.

On the other hand, we cannot help noticing certain shortcomings. Although he maintains that science, like other cultural endeavors, is based on prereflective perception, he does not illustrate this or prove it by argument. Again, his work lacks the sweeping, if onesided, insights of more speculative thinkers

---

[22]See Maxine Greene, *Landscapes of Learning* (New York: Teachers College Press, 1978), *passim*.

like Heidegger and Sartre. Moreover, outside his political writings, he has little to say about discipline, morality, and the harsher side of life. Most of all, his educational message is uncritically individualist. As a consequence, his English-speaking interpreters have treated the disciplines as avenues to personal growth rather than to public knowledge, and nothing in his philosophy leads me to think he would have disagreed with them. Let us remember, however, that he died fairly young, before he could systematize his ideas. Had he been granted the "golden years" of most philosophers, he might well have done so.

Like other thinkers we have examined in this chapter so far, Merleau-Ponty is a philosopher whose work throws important light on education. However, the phenomenological tradition also includes some more explictly educational thinkers, to whom we now turn.

Buber: Education as Dialogue

Martin Buber (1878–1965), the first of these thinkers, believes in individual freedom and self-responsibility. But, unlike Heidegger and Sartre, and more strongly than Merleau-Ponty, he maintains that the self grows only through communion with others. Without "the other," he says, the "I" cannot develop. Buber also is deeply religious. For him, the ultimate purpose of communion and growth is to imitate God, Who created us in His image.

According to Buber, I may interact with people and things in two ways, the "I-You" and the "I-It." The paradigm of an I-You relation is when two people meet in genuine appreciation. Each welcomes the other for the other's sake; neither uses the other for his or her own purposes. Buber calls this relation "dialogue" or "communion." I also can relate in this way to nature (e.g., to animals and trees) and to art. But this relation is highly demanding, for at the same time that I participate intensely in the life of the other, I recognize the other's separateness from me.

This polarity necessarily shortens the encounter. Thus Buber writes:[23]

In the darkened opera-house there can be established between two of the audience, who do not know one another, and who are listening with the same intensity to the music of Mozart, a relation which is scarcely perceptible and yet is one of elemental dialogue, and which has long vanished when the lights blaze up again.

The I-You relation, then, falls again and again into the ordinary mode of relating, the I-It.

The I-It relation tends to be self-interested and practical. I use the other person (or thing) for some purpose outside himself (itself). I ask a student to mail a letter for me, or I mark a tree that I intend to fell. I-It relations are necessary, however, and need not be inauthentic or dehumanizing. They become so only when I use them to escape from genuine dialogue or when I persistently exploit another for my own ends. Nevertheless, even at their best, these relations are only a threshold to full communion. In Buber's words, "The *It* is the eternal chrysalis, the *Thou* the eternal butterfly."[24]

Dialogue involves "inclusion," the simultaneous perception of both sides of a shared experience. I imagine what it is like for the other to experience an event, and at the same time allow the other to imagine what it is like for me to do so. Each of us lives through the event both from his own point of view and from the other's. Each of us welcomes the other, but neither surrenders himself. Buber points to three elements in inclusion.[25]

. . . first, a relation, no matter what kind, between two persons, second, an event experienced by them in common, in which at least one of them actively participates, and, third, the fact that this one person, without forfeiting anything of the felt reality of this activity,

---

[23]Martin Buber, "What is Man?" in *Between Man and Man,* trans. Ronald Gregor Smith with an introd. by Maurice Friedman (New York: Macmillan, 1965), p. 204.

[24]Martin Buber, *I and Thou,* 2nd ed., trans. Ronald Gregor Smith (New York: Scribner, 1958), p. 17.

[25]"Education," in *Between Man and Man,* p. 97.

at the same time lives through the common event from the standpoint of the other.

Each of us, then, is a full self for the other. Each of us consciously "confirms" the other and knows that the other confirms him. Without such mutual confirmation we cannot grow as persons.

According to Buber, the aim of education is to enable the young to grow by expressing their instincts—chiefly for creation and communion. At first, however, these instincts are potentials without objects, since children know little of the world. Thus, teachers provide children with knowledge and know-how—with a selection from the world to work on—so that the children may express themselves. Creativity alone, however, does not produce genuine growth. So teachers not only present knowledge, they also enter into a dialogue about it with the students, and thus elicit the instinct for communion.

Buber contrasts communion with freedom. Freedom, he says, is not the goal of education but something that makes education and communion possible. In his own words,[26]

Freedom in education is the possibility of communion; it cannot be dispensed with and it cannot be made use of in itself; without it nothing succeeds, but neither does anything succeed by means of it; it is the run before the jump, the tuning of the violin, the confirmation of that primal and mighty potentiality which it cannot even begin to actualize.

What the child needs is not freedom without direction but communion in an educative context. As Buber puts it, "the decisive influence is to be ascribed not to the release of an instinct but to the forces which meet the released instinct, namely, the educative forces."[27] The most important of these forces is the teacher.

As a teacher, I recognize that each of my students is a unique being whom the world will never see again. Each deserves to express this uniqueness in her own, chosen way of life. It is my task to help each student do this. If I form a youngster myself,

---

[26]"Education," p. 90.

[27]Ibid., p. 86.

by transmitting knowledge and inculcating values, I may deny her uniqueness. Yet if I let her learn as she pleases, she will develop little character and acquire few skills. How do I find a mean? According to Buber, I maintain a dialogue with the student in which, with all my soul, I take both her point of view and my own, and at the same time fully respect her independence. How I do this?

First, I put myself in the student's place. I "listen" to her and discover what she needs now and what she will need later, and thus what knowledge I can usefully offer and what I must withhold. I also allow the student to explore a subject first for herself. By these two steps I encourage her to trust me and to be curious. I try not to prod the student or interfere with her; instead, I radiate goodwill and respect, so that she knows I am on her side. As Buber says,[28]

For educating characters you do not need a moral genius, but you do need a man who is wholly alive and able to communicate himself directly to his fellow beings. His aliveness streams out to them and affects them most strongly and purely when he has no thought of affecting them.

Thus I wait for the student to approach me, and my attitude gives her every encouragement to do so.

Now I respond to the first hint of an overture. I offer the student the knowledge I have been keeping for her, and we discuss it. By making this knowledge part of my life, by presenting it as something I have weighed and felt, not as an item from a book, I make it appealing to the student. But what if she is not convinced? What if we disagree strongly? If the student is sincere, I must "love her still," for I must allow her to be true to herself. It is my responsibility to help her, not hers to help me (though she in fact may do so). In Buber's words,

A conflict with a pupil is a supreme test for the educator. He must use his insight wholeheartedly . . . but he must at the same time have in readiness the healing ointment for the heart pierced by it. . . . and if he cannot conquer the self-willed soul that faces him (for victories

---

[28]"The Education of Character," *Between Man and Man*, p. 105.

over souls are not so easily won), then he has to find the word of love which alone can help to overcome so difficult a situation.[29]

This incident points to an important difference between dialogue in education and dialogue elsewhere. My dialogue with the student is onesided. I can enter his mind, but as a rule he lacks the knowledge and experience to enter mine. If he does so, the teaching relation is over and we become either friends or antagonists or indifferent to each other. By maintaining this dialogue I enable the student to be free within a framework of order, and I provide knowledge without imposing it on him.

How do I offer the student values to live by? How do I help him build character? Buber believed that there are absolute values (such as the Ten Commandments) but that the individual must discover them for himself and decide when to apply them. As a teacher I must exemplify these values rather than impose them. I also may present moral dilemmas for discussion, such as whether to be candid and lose one's friends and whether to meet terrorism with terror. Above all, I must encourage my students to reflect on their own lives, suggesting that it is both admirable and personally satisfying to be a well-rounded person, and that by living up to a range of moral values (e.g., being patient, as well as courageous) they can achieve this.

Critique   In many ways Buber is on the side of the angels. He is an optimist. He believes that people are naturally cooperative, that they seek to grow, and that they do so through experiences of mutual affection and respect. He also is an individualist. He advocates personal relations for the sake more of individual fulfilment than of social harmony (in which, however, he also believed). Furthermore, Buber loves teaching. For him, teachers take the initiative, personalize knowledge, and radiate enthusiasm. If students oppose their teachers, the teachers must find it in their hearts to love them. Finally, Buber proposes a way to combine student freedom with teacher authority. By being patient, intuitive, and benevolent, teachers can encourage students to turn to them for knowledge and can offer it when students do so.

---

[29]"The Education of Character," pp. 107–108.

On the other hand, Buber provides a number of insights into education rather than a complete program. He presents most of these insights in aphorisms instead of arguing for them. If we accept his ideas, it generally is because they either "feel right" or "confirm" our experience, not because we are rationally persuaded. Again, although he regards I-You relations as the heart of education, he also believes that they usually are fleeting and infrequent, and that they depend on "grace" and hence cannot be sought or anticipated. It is hard to see how teachers can maintain either authority or enthusiasm if they are waiting for moments of mutual affection that may not occur.

Buber seems to be thinking mainly of small classes, in which I-You relations are easier to achieve. Indeed, he recommends life in small, close-knit communities.[30] He focuses on teacher-student relations rather than the students' relations with one another and does not consider the possibility of persistent peer group opposition. Although he does not explicitly introduce God into education, his principles seem applicable almost exclusively to parochial schools. In a large, urban, racially mixed school, a teacher facing widespread hostility and even violence cannot await the student's spark of interest or keep discipline with "the raising of a finger, perhaps, or a questioning glance."[31] The teacher's best course, then, is either to find general inspiration in Buber's writings or to develop particular techniques that reflect some of his very noble spirit.[32]

Freire: Consciousness-Raising

For the Brazilian educator Paolo Freire (b. 1921) phenomenology becomes a philosophy of social change. Like Buber, though unlike most existential phenomenologists, Freire believes that people should work together to see their world differently, to reform it, and to improve the lot of humankind everywhere. For Freire, as for the phenomenologists, we are by nature active and

---

[30]For example, "The Education of Character," p. 116.

[31]*Between Man and Man*, p. 89.

[32]On Buber, see Maurice Friedman, *Martin Buber: The Life of Dialogue*, 3rd rev. ed. (Chicago: University of Chicago Press, 1981); *The Philosophy of Martin Buber*, ed. Paul Arthur Schilpp and Maurice Friedman (LaSalle, Ill.: Open Court, 1967); and Adir Cohen, "Martin Buber and Changes in Modern Education," *Oxford Review of Education*, 5:1 (1979), 81–103.

exploratory. We stand on our own feet and construct our own picture of the world around us. Yet, especially in the Third World, but even in advanced societies, people have been "dehumanized" by oppressive governments and elites that, through education, propaganda, and the media, have led them to internalize the oppressor's view of them. The true purpose of education, says Freire, is to enable people to see themselves and their lifeworld afresh and to transform both, so that they can lead more fulfilling lives.[33]

To do this, says Freire, the poor and the powerless must throw off the stereotypes imposed on them by the ruling class. In the eyes of the latter, the poor are lazy, dishonest, shifty, and unproductive—in short, "marginal." The proper role of education, say the elite, is to "cure" the poor of their harmful ways, make them literate, law-abiding, and willing to work. Freire rejects this notion of marginality. The poor, he says, voluntarily or involuntarily, knowingly or unknowingly, have been led by the rich and powerful to define themselves as naturally ignorant and inferior. Their minds have been invaded. They "see reality with the outlook of the invaders rather than their own . . . and the more they mimic the invaders, the more stable the dominant position of the latter becomes."[34] As long as the poor perceive themselves to be powerless, they will remain so.

To expel the internalized oppressor and recover their own capacity for perception, the poor need an entirely new education. According to Freire, education never is neutral. It is either an "instrument of domination," reinforcing the oppressor's ideas and bringing about conformity, or else the "practice of freedom," which enables the masses to reflect on their condition and change it.

As an instrument of domination, says Freire bitterly, education is a form of "banking." It is

an act of depositing in which the students are the depositories and the teacher is the depositor. Instead of communicating, the teacher issues

[33]Paolo Freire, "Cultural Action and Conscientization," *Harvard Educational Review,* **40**:3 (July 1970), 205.

[34]Paolo Freire, *Pedagogy of the Oppressed,* trans. Myra Bergman Ramos (New York: Herder and Herder, 1970), p. 151.

communiques and "makes deposits" which the students patiently receive, memorize, and repeat. This is the "banking" concept of education, in which the scope of action allowed to the student extends only as far as receiving, filing, and storing the deposits . . . where knowledge is a gift bestowed by those who consider themselves knowledgeable upon those they consider to know nothing. [35]

In Freire's view, the school divides knowledge into separate subjects and presents them as something unalterable and "out there." The teacher inducts students into a world that seems quite independent of the students' perceptions. Students neither initiate nor experiment. They are "spectators," not "recreators." [36] The more they submit to this role, says Freire, the more they adapt to the oppressor's world.

How, then, is education to become the "practice of freedom"? How can education help students think with their own rather than the oppressor's concepts? First, says Freire, education must become a dialogue of equals. Students cannot rethink and remake their world if, as their teacher, I tell them, "This is what you must do." Instead, each of us must become both teacher and student. The students must help me see what their world is like, and I must present back to them clearly and explicitly what they show me obscurely. In this way we become "jointly responsible for a process in which all grow." [37] Next, we must focus on the people's actual experiences, abandoning the oppressor's ideas, and striving to see these experiences as they really are. We must "take our own culture as always problematic and . . . question it without accepting the myths that ossify it and ossify us." [38] Consequently, we must not simply reapply lessons learned in other situations. "Experiments cannot be transplanted; they must be reinvented." [39] Finally, together we

---

[35]*Pedagogy of the Oppressed*, p. 4.

[36]Paolo Freire, "Adult Literacy as Cultural Education for Freedom," *Harvard Educational Review*, **40**:2 (April 1970), 62.

[37]*Pedagogy of the Oppressed*, p. 67.

[38]Paolo Freire, "A Few Notions about the Word 'Conscientization'," trans. Manuel Vaquerizo, in *Hard Cheese* (Liverpool: Free Press, 1971).

[39]Paolo Freire, *Pedagogy in Process: The Letters to Guinea-Bissau*, trans. Carman St. John Hunter (New York: Seabury Press, 1978), pp. 9–10.

must "problematize" the people's situation. We must approach it, not as an external given, but as something open and unresolved, something to be understood and acted on. Freire calls this entire process "conscientization"—consciousness-raising.

Our experience is shaped by language, since words fix and color our concepts. If the oppressed people are to take charge of their experience, they must discard the language of the oppressor. They must find words that fit their own perceptions. They must name things as they see them. Learning to read and write, then, "is no inconsequential matter of memorizing an alienated word but a difficult apprenticeship in naming the world."[40] Literacy training, says Freire, is a weapon for the oppressed in their self-defense against exploitation and in their struggle for self-determination and self-government. Literacy, then, must be wedded to action. One must learn to "read one's own reality" and "write one's own future." Freire writes of some villagers in Guinea-Bissau, West Africa, who were trying his program. The villagers financed the literacy project themselves by first growing their own banana crop. These people, says Freire, rewrote their material world in order to learn to read and write a language, and learning a language will help them rewrite their world still more.

Freire proposes a special method of literacy training. The learners choose one or more important themes from their common life, such as the reality of the slum. Next, they examine a "codification," a photo or filmstrip of a slum scene, and discuss what it means for them. In this way they break down the oppressor's code and replace it with one that is more realistic. Only after several hours of discussion do they begin to read and write.

To do so, they use generative words—those whose syllables can be recombined by the learner to create new words. In Latin America no more than seventeen such words supposedly are needed to teach adults to read and write Spanish and Portugese.[41] Each word is trisyllabic and known to the students (e.g., *favela*—"slum" in Portugese). Members of the group con-

---

[40]"Cultural Action and Conscientization," 211.

[41]Paolo Freire, *Cultural Action for Freedom* (Cambridge: *Harvard Educational Review* and Center for the Study of Development and Social Change, 1970), p. 19n.

sider a word that names something in the scene. They break the word into syllables (e.g., *fa-ve-la*) and the syllables into letters, and see what new words they can construct from the letters. In this way, group members explore their culture through both words and visual representations.

Critique   Freire's work is admirable in many ways. Freire has great faith in the power of education to liberate people. He insists that education can do this only if people educate themselves. He also believes that people actually can transform the way they perceive and use the world. He points out that all education is political in the sense that it is for or against freedom (as he sees it) and for or against the status quo. He offers a striking criticism of the "banking" concept of education. Finally, he is not dogmatic. He says that he seeks to stimulate his readers to think, not to tell them how to act. In his own words,[42]

> . . . *one of the best methods of reading my letters would be . . . to try to extract from them possible lines of work that I may not have perceived but which may be found hidden in one or another affirmation within the body of the letter. In essence, to read a letter deeply is to rewrite it.*

Will his program work? In my view, it will have difficulty succeeding on a large scale. Freire expects a great deal from education. Any radical, populist movement is bound to meet strong resistance, not only from regimes and groups that perceive it as a threat, but from individuals who are content with their lives and do not wish to overturn the society that keeps them comfortable enough. Freire proposes no way to deal with this resistance.

Next, his idea of "oppression" is highly abstract. This term is expected to cover aspects of the status quo anywhere in the world, from Latin America to Eastern Europe to the United States. Yet in too many of these cases the most we can fairly say is that this is not the best of all possible worlds. Nor does Freire

---

[42]*Pedagogy in Process*, pp. 128–129.

meet the very reasonable objection that the lot of the oppressed often is as much their own fault as that of their oppressors.

Finally, Freire's work not only is utopian but also, ironically, potentially elitist. Literacy campaigns led by dissidents, intellectuals, and radical students may create a new class of "conscientizing" leaders. Granted, the oppressed plan their education with their "teachers," yet the latter are the main moving forces for change. Being more sophisticated, are they not likely to press for what they perceive as "best" for the people? Indeed, the oppressed may even find themselves oppressed by their own leaders. Moreover, consciousness-raising may well prove most suited not so much to the Third World as to groups in the affluent West who do not need to draw on outsiders to stimulate the process of examining and changing their lives.[43]

The "New Sociology" of Education[44]

The "New Sociology" of Education began in England and the United States in the 1970s as a phenomenologist riposte to the dominant positivist tradition.[45] The New Sociologists agree with the Husserlians that research begins with description. It is pointless, they say, to explain why things happen as they do in education unless you first describe precisely what does happen. You must bracket (set aside) the concepts devised by researchers, such as "intelligence," "social class," and "organization," and observe at firsthand what actually goes on in the educational lifeworld—in classrooms, in playgrounds, at home, and on the streets. Like Merleau-Ponty, for example, the New Sociologists believe that the child experiences the world quite differently than the adult and that conventional education mistakenly subordinates the child's "prereflective sedimentations"

---

[43] A good collection of essays on Freire is *Literacy and Revolution: The Pedagogy of Paolo Freire*, ed. Robert Mackie (London: Pluto Press, 1980). For further criticism, see Manfred Stanley, *The Technological Conscience: Survival and Dignity in the Age of Expertise* (New York: Free Press, 1978), ch. 8.

[44] In this section I stress the philosophical rather than the sociological aspects of the movement.

[45] For a comprehensive manifesto of the movement, see *Knowledge and Control*, ed. Michael F. D. Young (London: Collier Macmillan, 1971).

to theoretical subject matter. And, with Freire, the New Sociologists dislike the "banking" mode of education.

Society, say the New Sociologists, seems to be a given, because it preexists me and because it is formed by groups and whole populations sharing concepts and conventions. However, since we carry these concepts and conventions in our minds, we can change them and so, eventually, the practices and institutions that depend on them. Similarly with knowledge. All knowledge is based on experience and especially on perception. A particular group, such as teachers or psychiatrists, tries to legitimate a way of seeing and understanding the world as *the* way. Yet it is only *their* interpretation. Because each of us perceives and experiences the world, each of us constructs knowledge. Instead of constructing it in line with the "received view," we can interpret it personally in the light of our own experience.

The New Sociologists criticize most educators for believing that knowledge is fixed rather than relative and that some types of knowledge are intrinsically superior to others. This view, they say, depreciates the child's perspective. It imposes on students an external curriculum that alienates them from their lived experience and hinders their attempt to make their lives meaningful. The received view of the world also is imposed on most teachers who have not absorbed it in their youth, since teachers generally have little choice over the broad outlines of what is taught. To discover what the transmission of the received view really is doing to teachers and students, we must ask them how they as individuals experience the process of education. We must take not the scientist's but the actor's standpoint.

The New Sociologists are especially interested in how and why teachers and students misunderstand one another, because these misunderstandings reveal basic assumptions on both sides. One researcher, for example,[46] videotaped a number of lessons in which teachers asked students to perform apparently simple tasks and then judged whether the students "understood" what they had done. Students were asked, for instance,

---

[46]Hugh Mehan, "Accomplishing Classroom Lessons," in Aaron Cicourel et al., *Language Use and School Performance* (New York: Academic Press, 1974), pp. 76–142.

to draw a line across their papers, and a triangle beneath the line: Then they were asked, "Where is the triangle?" The correct answer was "The triangle is under the line." This answer allegedly showed "understanding." Answers such as "near the line," "on the paper," or even "under the line" were judged incorrect, since they indicated (so teachers thought) that the students either did not understand the right preposition to use or did not understand that the answer had to be a complete sentence.

According to this research, teachers give instructions that they assume are "obvious," yet often students do not know what is expected of them. Teachers treat responses as evidence of either understanding or misunderstanding, yet the meaning of even the simplest response often calls for much interpretation. Because they themselves seek to discard assumptions and take the participant's view, the New Sociologists have been particularly good at probing the assumptions of teachers and students in face-to-face interactions.

The New Sociologists maintain that people create "social structures" simply by interacting with one another. They seek to observe how "objective social facts"—such as students' academic achievements and school career paths, and "routine patterns of behavior," as seen in the ebb and flow of action and speech during a lesson—are formed in the interplay between teachers and students, principals and teachers, and so on.[47] As phenomenologists, the New Sociologists seek to show that, far from being creatures of their social environments, people *make* those environments.

In their classroom studies the New Sociologists have singled out two processes in particular: "labeling" and "negotiation." Labeling is the process by which a weak or deviant group is categorized to its disadvantage. Now, all of us must classify to make sense of our worlds, and it seems reasonable to classify according to one's needs and principles. But when teachers label students as "bright" and "stupid," "interesting" and "boring," they are apt to harm them. They also use their own rather than the students' classifications. Labels, then, are apt to guide

---

[47]Hugh Mehan, *Learning Lessons: Social Organization in the Classroom* (Cambridge, Mass.: Harvard University, 1979), and "Structuring School Structure," *Harvard Educational Review,* 48:1 (February 1978), 32–64.

the teacher's expectations of students and, worse still, students' expectations of themselves. Labels also tend to bring about the success or failure they imply.[48] Thus, teachers both expect and elicit different performances from upper and lower stream students. A searching question put by a lower stream student, for instance, often is interpreted as an attempt to embarrass the teacher or raise a laugh. The student internalizes the teacher's view of him and thinks that he must be either stupid or "agin' the system." Thus, streaming may manufacture rather than reflect the differences that are said to justify it.

Negotiation is the process by which teachers and students influence one another's responses. According to the New Sociologists, students generally learn not because teachers impose their will on them but because the two sides reach an accommodation. True, the sides are unequal. By and large, teachers deliver established, theoretical knowledge and bypass the commonsense knowledge absorbed at home and on the streets. Nevertheless, teachers must concede something to the students' point of view; and provided teachers explain themselves, students generally will accept their teacher's view of a situation. It is when teachers are autocratic, or grade unfairly, or make personal remarks—in short, break the *students'* rules— that students recoil and sometimes rebel.

Critique The New Sociology sets out to demystify the processes of education. In the phenomenological spirit, it challenges our assumptions, especially about the objectivity of educational research and the judgments of educators. Instead of correlating abstractions (such as race, class, and achievement), the New Sociology examines, from the participant's point of view, the day-to-day, face-to-face interplay of students, teachers, and others. It shows how teachers and students, albeit from positions of unequal strength, negotiate with one another, and it exposes the harm done by labeling. In spite of these achievements, however, the New Sociology faces two serious problems.

First, phenomenological sociologists are inclined to write as though material things and mental processes are real and inde-

---

[48]See, for example, Nell Keddie, "Classroom Knowledge," in *Knowledge and Control,* pp. 133–160.

pendent, whereas the social world is not. For them, social phenomena exist in the form in which we conceive and perceive
them. This belief breeds undue optimism about the possibilities
of social change. Teachers, they think, have only to understand
their situation in order to alter it. Such optimism underestimates the force of precedent. Teachers and students do not negotiate in a historical vacuum. At every point, custom itself, the
fact that things "always have been done this way," constrains
them. So does the law. (If teachers do not follow prescribed
programs and procedures, they are in trouble.) Finally, education is shaped by the forces of material production and those
who control them. If we wish to change education fundamentally, we must change more than the minds of teachers. We also
must modify the social, political, and economic power relations
that shape the very life of education. And that would be a co-
lossal undertaking.

The second problem is that of relativism. The New Sociologist maintains that we must look at things from the point of
view of the people we are studying. By what right, then, does
the New Sociologist criticize the authoritarian teacher and the
positivist researcher? If all views are equal, what is the point of
his criticism? Worse still, if all views are equal, relativism itself
no longer is a privileged position.

Thus, the New Sociology seems to contradict itself. For if
relativism is correct, and *all* views *are* equal, relativism has no
right to assert itself—that is, to say that absolutism (the view
that only one or some views are correct) is mistaken. On the
other hand, if relativism *is* entitled to assert itself and make a
statement about all views, it cannot be correct, for it says that all
views, including the *opposite* of itself, are correct. [49]

In response to these problems many of the New Sociologists
have turned to Marxism (see Chapter 6). Nevertheless, the
problems themselves do not hinder phenomenologists from
doing empirical research and from reflecting on it. Although
less widespread than it was in the early 1970s, the phenomenological movement in sociology is innovative still. [50]

---

[49]Admittedly this is an old argument against relativism, but it may be new for
some readers.

[50]For a sympathetic presentation and critique of the phenomenological strain in

Appraisal[51]

The phenomenological movement is as rich and varied as any philosophy in the English-speaking world.[52] In both its Husserlian and existential forms phenomenology is a philosophy of freedom. Existential phenomenology emphasizes freedom of action. Both teachers and students must make their own choices for their own reasons. Students must assert themselves as unique persons by choosing, as far as possible, what they will learn and how. Teachers encourage students by being free themselves as well as noninterfering. Buber moderates this intense individualism by saying that both teacher and student must be involved in the student's learning. By her interest in the subject matter, by her unique approach to it, and by the fact that she finds it a challenge, the teacher awakens a similar response in the student.

Husserlian phenomenology stresses an almost boundless freedom of thought. With discipline and effort, it says, we can question *all* our assumptions, even those of common sense, and

---

the New Sociology, see Madan Sarup, *Marxism and Education* (London and Boston: Routledge & Kegan Paul, 1978), Part One. Two other critiques are Michael J. Apple, "The New Sociology of Education: Analyzing Cultural and Economic Reproduction" [review], *Harvard Educational Review*, **48**:4 (November 1978), 495–503; and Richard J. Bates, "New Developments in the New Sociology of Education," *British Journal of Sociology*, 1:1 (1980), 67–79.

[51]In this Appraisal I do not repeat many observations made in my Critiques.

[52]On contemporary phenomenology, see Hugh J. Silverman, "Phenomenology," *Social Research*, **47**:4 (Winter 1980), 704–720. Some appraisals of phenomenology in education include Donald Vandenberg, "Existential and Phenomenological Influences in Educational Philosophy," in *Philosophy of Education since Mid-Century*, ed. Jonas F. Soltis (New York: Teachers College Press, 1981), pp. 38–63; David Neil Silk, "The Poverty of a Phenomenology of Education," and Philip G. Smith, "Response to Silk," in *Philosophy of Education 1977: Proceedings of the Thirty-Third Annual Meeting of the Philosophy of Education Society*, ed. Ira S. Steinberg (Urbana, Ill.: Philosophy of Education Society, 1977), pp. 222–234; and Leroy F. Troutner, "The Promise of Phenomenology: A Response to Silk's 'The Poverty of . . .'," Maxine Greene, "Response to Troutner," and David N. Silk, "Rejoining the Argument," in *Philosophy of Education 1980: Proceedings of the Thirty-Sixth Annual Meeting of the Philosophy of Education Society*, ed. C. J. B. Macmillan (Normal, Ill.: Philosophy of Education Society, 1981), pp. 62–79.

uncover the basic concepts with which we structure our experience, concepts such as knowledge, education, and teaching. A phenomenological description of these concepts, as distinct from a linguistic analysis of them, will (it is claimed) reveal what is essential in the human condition and what is not. The description will tell us what knowledge must be, what education means, what teaching must include. It will enable us to conceive an education that is commensurate with our needs as holders of these concepts.

The phenomenologist points out that all our experience of the world is interpreted experience. Yet, he says, we forget our own contribution to the world. We come to think of roles and institutions—teaching and schools—as quasi-physical realities, independent of us and unalterable. We see schools, teachers, students, curriculums, tests, and grades as parts of a world "out there" to which we must adapt. We ignore the mental and physical activities by which we help to make this world what it is.

The phenomenologist tells us that to learn a subject matter satisfactorily, students must use it to illuminate what they have experienced themselves. It is not enough for students to grasp that a theorem is deduced correctly from the relevant axioms. They also must see that it agrees with or adds to their experience of space in the park or on the street. Similarly, it does not suffice to memorize the grammar of another language. Students also must appreciate that the French subjunctive, say, conveys something about the nature of human thought or action, or about natural processes that they themselves have observed or now can recognize. By learning this way, students incorporate formal knowledge into their life experience and thus make that experience compatible with yet further knowledge.

Teachers, too, will teach satisfactorily only what they have absorbed into their own experience. When preparing a topic, they should associate at least the central point with an aspect of their experience that corresponds to something the student can either find in his own experience or add to it. When the point is presented, the student then is more likely to reach into his experience to match it. Suppose, for example, the topic is the fall of the Bastille. To help the student feel how a crowd can occupy a capital and topple a regime, a teacher can draw on his or her memory of crowd emotions or on scenes of crowds that the student may have seen on the news.

On the other hand, to some readers, much phenomenological writing at first is alien and unattractive. It appears obscure, riddled with strange terms ("thrownness," "body-subject," "sedimentation"), and dependent on assertion rather than argument. It seems irrational, a philosophy of extremes.

Take existential phenomenology. The Heideggerians and Sartreans seem unwarrantedly pessimistic, finding the essence of the human situation in such relatively uncommon experiences as existential anxiety and the thought of one's death. They prefer to regard freedom as agonizing and inescapable rather than as conducive to happiness and success. They believe that society diminishes rather than fosters the individual. Yet most people's experience belies this. Most of us find our colleagues congenial, our students cooperative, and the schools we teach in at least tolerable. We believe that public morality is as important as private. A student, we say, must be true to himself, but only if he seeks, or at least respects, the welfare of others.

Other existential phenomenologists appear overoptimistic. Buber and Freire both propose striking and original models for education. Yet Buber does not consider the possibility of determined opposition. He believes that school discipline is unnecessary and that a good teacher never need be punitive. Freire believes that his model can make the oppressed masters of themselves. He does not show how his model could meet the need of an industrially advanced society for knowledgeable, skilled workers and professionals. Hence his model is less suited to such societies.

Finally, phenomenologists of a Husserlian cast, such as the New Sociologists, have failed to explain convincingly how history develops and why social reality is constituted as it is. They seek to show how I as an individual tend to form the social-cultural world around me by seeing that world in a certain way. What they neglect to stress is that society and culture themselves enable me to do this and yet constrain how I do it. For I am born, raised, and educated within a society, a language, and a system of ideas that precede me. I may create words, ideas, and practices, but only within a tradition that supports me. My students and I construct knowledge and social forms through the concepts we apply. But how did these concepts arise, and why these and not others?

Phenomenology has immense promise as an account of how the individual, whether student or teacher, can experience the educational process. But we also need a philosophy of history and culture to explain why education exists at all and what it can mean to different eras and peoples. Let us turn, therefore, to the philosophy of hermeneutics.

Hermeneutics

3

Origins

The word "hermeneutics" comes from a Greek word meaning "to interpret." The word commemorated Hermes, messenger of the gods, who descended from Mount Olympus to interpret the will of Zeus to humankind. Known to the Romans as Mercury, he was depicted as a naked youth with a messenger's staff and winged sandals. In this form he symbolizes a messenger in many advertisements today.

The Greeks also had to interpret their own legends of the gods and, in particular, to explain why the immortals often behaved cruelly. So they developed a technique for interpreting texts and called it "hermeneutics." The technique enabled them to find contemporary equivalents for words and practices whose meaning had become obscure. Christian theologians used this technique to interpret the Scriptures, and judges used it when applying old laws to new cases.

In the nineteenth century some German philosophers, notably Wilhelm Dilthey, argued that interpretation itself, though not necessarily the use of the hermeneutic technique, actually is central to a much wider range of understanding. Not only canonical texts, they said, but all texts, from teaching manuals to literary classics, are interpreted. And so, they added, are human acts and products, such as the act of teaching and the institution of the school. To understand these things, they said, we interpret them. Dilthey and others called the philosophic study of understanding, considered as interpretive, "hermeneutic" philosophy.

What is the affinity, then, between texts and acts? How do we come to understand such seemingly different things in a similar way? And how does such understanding involve interpretation? According to Dilthey, an act (e.g., an act of teaching) is meaningful; hence, understanding it is like reading a text. In each case we aim to find out what authors or agents are seeking to accomplish. To do so, we take their place, assume their prejudices, look through their eyes—in short, identify with them. Then we are ready to intuit what the author sought to do. Dilthey called this entire process "empathetic understanding" (Verstehen). Verstehen includes interpretation because it involves recovering a meaning that is not immediately obvious. This meaning, said Dilthey, is identical with the author's or agent's intention.

Empathetic understanding, Dilthey maintained, is the true method of the human studies, including the human sciences.[1] Unlike the natural sciences, which examine phenomena from without, human studies (including the study of education) investigate human acts and products as "expressions" of the inner lives of their authors.[2] To understand such expressions, we must reconstruct what they meant to these authors. To under-

---

[1] The German word for human studies, Wissenschaften, denotes both the humanities (e.g., history, philosophy, literary criticism) and the human sciences (e.g., psychology, sociology, anthropology).

[2] Compare the analytic philosopher's distinction between explanations in terms of causes and explanations in terms of reasons (see Chapter 1, pp. 13–16). On some similarities between hermeneutic and analytic philosophy, see Roy J. Howard, Three Faces of Hermeneutics: An Introduction to Current Theories of Understanding (Berkeley and Los Angeles: University of California, 1982), ch. 1. Another good introduction to hermeneutic philosophy is David Couzens Hoy, The Critical Circle: Literature, History, and Philosophical Hermeneutics (Berkeley and Los Angeles: University of California, 1978).

stand a school, for example, we must ask, among other things, what those who participate in it intend it to achieve.

More recently, however, Martin Heidegger and Hans-Georg Gadamer have applied the term "hermeneutics" to a philosophy of human existence as a whole. Understanding, they argue, is more than a mental process. It is not just something we do but the way we are. We are beings who understand, and understanding underlies all our activities. Moreover, such understanding fundamentally is a process of interpretation. What do they mean by this?

Heidegger and Gadamer distinguish between "primordial" and "everyday" understanding. For Heidegger, as we have seen,[3] people are beings who seek to fulfill their possibilities. As a human being, he says, I regard what I encounter (people, processes, things) in the light of my purposes, authentic or otherwise. Of my very nature, I try to make sense of things. Thus, I live in the world "understandingly."[4] This basic disposition Heidegger calls "primordial" understanding. In what sense is this disposition interpretive? To *understand* something is to grasp its meaning or significance. To *interpret* something is to apprehend what it signifies for a certain standpoint or situation. According to Heidegger, I understand things in the light of my purposes, and hence from the standpoints or situations those purposes define. Thus, understanding at heart is interpretive. In fact, Gadamer often uses the term "interpretive understanding."

Consider the part played by interpretive understanding in teaching. I do not encounter my students as human beings and nothing more. I meet them as young people with different temperaments for whom I feel responsibility and affection. I can tell, for instance, from the stir in the room that the class looks forward to discussing a movie we have just seen, or from the slump in that boy's back that he has had enough algebra for the

---

[3]See Chapter 2, p. 34.

[4]Heidegger, says Gadamer, has shown that "understanding is not just one of the various possible behaviors of the subject, but the mode of being of [human] being which . . . includes the whole of its experience in the world." Hans-Georg Gadamer, "Foreward to the Second Edition," *Truth and Method* (New York: Continuum, 1975), p. xviii.

day. Similarly, in the classroom I encounter things not as objects merely but as charts, chairs, chalk, and so forth—articles that not only are used in teaching but are congenial to me. My school, my city, and the world itself are full of meaning for me. I cannot encounter them without interpreting them.

How does this philosophy affect my view of education generally? To answer this question, I first mention some hermeneutic themes and then introduce the philosophers themselves.[5] (1) In contemporary hermeneutics, education is like a conversation or game aimed at understanding. (2) Understanding a human act or product, and hence much learning, is like interpreting a text. (3) All interpretation occurs within a tradition. (4) The interpreter begins with a preliminary understanding of what he or she interprets. (5) Interpretation involves opening myself to a text (or its analogue) and questioning it. (6) I must interpret a text in the light of my situation.

Heidegger: The Revelation of Being

In *Being and Time* Heidegger launched existential phenomenology. In the same book he took the first steps toward the hermeneutic philosophy of his later years.[6] That philosophy is more concerned with "Being" than with human beings. (By "Being" Heidegger means Being in general as opposed to particular beings such as people, schools, and stars.) The greatest of our possibilities, says Heidegger, is to "attune" ourselves to Being. Only then can we fulfill ourselves completely. Yet through the ages, he holds, we have forgotten about Being, and

---

[5]I focus on philosophers rather than themes because each thinker speaks for himself. To reduce the ideas of these philosophers to variations on common themes would turn this philosophy from a movement of inquiry to a body of doctrine. However, in the Appraisal at the end of this chapter, I summarize the main ideas presented in this chapter and assess them.

[6]On Heidegger's philosophic range, see *Heidegger and Modern Philosophy*, ed. Michael Murray (New Haven: Yale University Press, 1978).

[7]"We do not *know* what 'Being' means. But already when we ask, 'What is Being?' we stand in an understanding of this 'is' without being able to determine conceptually what the 'is' means. We don't even know the horizon in which we are to grasp and pin down the meaning. *This average and vague*

as a result little definite can be said about it.[7] What scant knowledge we have of Being is contained mostly in the writings of the early Greek thinkers and of poets through time. These writings have to be interpreted, however, because we no longer share their authors' vision.

Heidegger approaches the nature of Being by reflecting on what he considers the fundamental question of philosophy: "Why is there anything rather than nothing?" That things exist, he says, is the most astonishing fact of all. Why astonishing? Because, on the face of it, things might just as well *not* have existed. By this I do not mean simply that you or I or this book might not have existed. I mean that there might never have been anything at all anywhere. Then what is this "is-ness," this ultimate quality of existence, that is present in everything and without which there is nothing?[8]

Let us look for the ultimate quality of existence in a school, for example. Since the school *exists,* we should be able to *find its existence,* just as we can find its location, its shape, and its structure. Let us inventory the school, check the buildings for safety, the rooms, the contents in the rooms, and even the staff and students who use them. If we stick to our task, we will locate and define everything in the school—except its existence. Why can't we find it? Why can't we trace the being or the "is-ness" of the school? Because, says Heidegger, existence or Being is not a thing at all. It is better understood as a "light" in which things are revealed and in which they appear to us as they actually are.[9]

This light, says Heidegger, is more precious to us than anything else, because without it there would be nothing, and we ourselves would not exist. It is our duty, then, to seek to respond to Being, to be aware of it, to live consciously in its presence. And it is the teacher's duty to bring home to students

---

understanding of Being is a fact." Martin Heidegger "Introduction" to *Being and Time,* in Heidegger's *Basic Writings,* ed. with an intro. by David Farrell Krell (New York: Harper & Row, 1977), p. 46.

[8]A good introduction to Heidegger's views on Being is George Steiner, *Martin Heidegger* (New York: Basic Books, 1979), ch. I.

[9]"Only this lighting grants and guarantees to us humans a passage to those beings that we ourselves are not, and access to the beings that we ourselves are. Thanks to this lighting, beings are unconcealed in certain changing degrees." *The Origin of the Work of Art,* in *Basic Writings,* p. 175.

that nothing in their lives matters more than their relation to Being.

In Heidegger's view, the early Greeks had a rapport with Being. They were open and responsive to the world. Plato, however, broke this rapport by seeking to explain the world through abstractions. Unlike the first philosophers, the pre-Socratics, who had asked about Being, Plato inquired into certain particular beings, the Forms, that he took to be the ultimate causes of things. Heidegger maintains that the history of thought since Plato is the story of how Being was forgotten. Instead of seeing things in their relation to Being, philosophers began to consider them as discrete objects in a world independent of the observer. Thus, human beings became detached and alienated from the world; they regarded it as something to be known and controlled; and philosophy paved the way for science and technology.[10] The will to control the world rather than receive from it—the "will to power"—has governed Western civilization ever since. This will to power now has "run amok" and "rules the world." Nature has become "a gigantic gasoline station, an energy source for modern technology and industry."[11]

For Heidegger, it is not science that reveals Being but literature. Great writers, and especially great poets, use words in their original senses and thus evoke the astonished response to Being that still is condensed within the primal words of the language. Long ago when the first bards chose some being (an oak, say, or a child) from the multitude of nameless things, and gave it a name, they captured that being in its singularity and hence in the light of Being itself.[12] Thus, as Heidegger puts it, "Poetry is the inaugural naming of Being and of the essence of all things."[13] Although language since has been devitalized by

---

[10]"The end of philosophy proves to be the triumph of the manipulable management of a scientific-technological world and of the social order proper to this world. The end of philosophy means the beginning of the world civilization based upon Western European thinking." *The End of Philosophy and the Task of Thinking,* in *Basic Writings,* p. 377.

[11]Martin Heidegger, *Discourse on Thinking,* trans. John M. Anderson and E. Hans Freund (New York: Harper & Row, 1966), p. 50.

[12]On Heidegger's view of the origin of language, see Theodore Kisiel, "Introduction," in Werner Marx *Heidegger and the Tradition,* trans. Theodore Kisiel (Evanston, Ill.: Northwestern University Press, 1970), pp. 3–14.

[13]"Hölderlin and the Essence of Poetry," in *Existence and Being,* ed. Werner Brock (Chicago: Regnery, 1962; Gateway Edition, 1962), p. 283.

technical and abstract uses, the poet still can tap its power to evoke Being and enhance life. Poetry, "the primitive language of a historical people,"[14] is the creative edge of language, the medium most able to reawaken the sense of Being in our time.[15] This power resides in language itself, however, rather than in the poet. *It is language that speaks through the poet rather than the poet through language.*

As a teacher, how can I help my students become aware of Being? First, says Heidegger, I must both practice and encourage "meditative" thinking. Such thinking often proceeds without logic or concepts.[16] It can allow things to appear as they are rather than in the forms the mind imposes on them.[17] Ultimately, it can let them appear in the light of Being. (Heidegger does not say that meditative thinking *will* have this effect, only that it *can.*) Such thinking may be difficult, because I must detach myself from practical concerns and subordinate my ego to the object of my thought. However, it is "natural" for me to do so, for insofar as I belong to Being, I potentially am responsive to it. As Heidegger says, "Anyone can follow the path of meditative thinking in his own manner and within his own limits. Why? Because man already is a *thinking*, that is, a *meditating* being."[18]

As a teacher, how do I practice meditative thinking? One way is to learn from things themselves. Before I plan a lesson or a course, I let the world I am going to present—ideas, facts, states of affairs—reveal itself to me.[19] I allow the geography of the United States to unfold to me; the characters of *David Copperfield* to speak to me; Newton's laws, and the orbits they govern, to unroll before me. The more open I am to the realities

---

[14]Ibid., p. 287.

[15]On Heidegger and poetry, see Benita A. Moore, "Hawthorne, Heidegger, and the Holy: The Uses of Literature," *Soundings*, **64**:2 (Summer 1981), 171–196.

[16]*Letter on Humanism*, in *Basic Writings*, p. 227. See also William Bruening, "Heidegger on Teaching," in *Philosophy of Education 1981: Proceedings of the Thirty-Seventh Annual Meeting of the Philosophy of Education Society* (Normal, Ill.: Philosophy of Education Society, 1982), pp. 233–240.

[17]"The meditative man is to experience the untrembling heart of unconcealment." *The End of Philosophy and the Task of Thinking*, p. 387.

[18]*Discourse on Thinking*, p. 47.

[19]Truth, says Heidegger, is "disclosure of beings." *On the Essence of Truth*, in *Basic Writings*, p. 129.

about which I teach, the more I respond to what is vital in them, the quality of existence itself.

How do I encourage meditative thinking? I ask my students to do what I have done myself—open themselves to what they are learning. Instead of deciding that the geography of the Sahara is not exciting enough, or that *David Copperfield* is too sentimental to take seriously, they let the landscape and the novel present themselves. Once the students have so opened themselves to a topic, they are less likely to misunderstand or reject it. They then can study it systematically—that is, think about it "calculatively."

"Calculative" thinking, says Heidegger, is "all thinking that plans and investigates," whether it uses numbers or not.[20] Such thinking always has a definite and specific purpose—to pass a test, prepare for a profession, draw up a syllabus. As a teacher, I must recognize that calculative thinking is both essential and justified. Calculation promotes the advance of knowledge, keeps the economy moving, earns a person a living. Most school learning is calculative.

At the same time, calculative thinking seeks to control ideas and things. It is the essence of science and technology. How, then, can I complement the calculative thinking of science with a meditative approach? According to Heidegger, I must help my students interpret science in the light of their everyday knowledge (or "preunderstanding") of the world. All of us, especially young children, are responsive to the look and feel of nature. We see that all of nature is not captured in the laws and theories of science. These describe only selected aspects of things. Hence we can appreciate that science is not necessarily the final truth about nature; instead, it is knowledge that works, in that it enables us to make the world more habitable.

According to Heidegger, we come upon the truth when things reveal themselves to us as they are. Instead of testing hypotheses about things, we then are receptive to them, listening and observing. The school, therefore, must complement classroom activity with the direct study and observation of nature. Important in this respect is laboratory work, since here—through the microscope and on the slide—the student can ob-

---

[20]*Discourse on Thinking*, p. 46.

serve the details of things as they actually are. In the field and in the laboratory students will make contact with the realities they consider intellectually. They will be closer to their true home, with the things themselves rather than with theories about them.

What forms of technology belong in the curriculum? Preeminently the crafts, because they preserve some of our old relation with Being. As Heidegger points out, a cabinetmaker's apprentice must learn more than the use of tools and the forms of furniture. He also must respond to "the different kinds of wood and to the shapes slumbering within wood—to wood as it enters into man's dwelling with all the hidden riches of nature."[21] Students must learn to work with wood, or metal, or leather, or with some material that is close to its natural condition and has been used through time. In this way they will labor congenially with nature, they will make things serve them while respecting their essential character, and they will renew their traditional tie with the earth. As a teacher, I must help my students become truly aware of different materials, so that their work is one of creation rather than mere exercise. I must remember that in passing on the crafts, I make it possible for these students to come closer to Being in future. In this capacity I become what Heidegger calls a "shepherd of Being."[22]

How do I teach literature? First, my students and I listen to the subject or theme of a work, not to the author. We do not ask what the author intended his original audience to feel, but what the work itself makes *us* feel *now*. As novelist D. H. Lawrence once put it, we "trust the tale," not "the teller." We also observe how the language of a work can make a subject that is unnoticed or taken for granted so rich that its very existence amazes us—as Keat's "Ode to Autumn," for instance, amazes us with the heartbeat of nature, with the "is-ness" of things:

And full-grown lambs loud bleat from hilly bourn:
Hedge-crickets sing; and now with treble soft
The red-breast whistles from a garden-croft,
And gathering swallows twitter in the skies.

---

[21]*What Calls for Thinking?* in *Basic Writings*, p. 355.

[22]*Letter on Humanism*, in *Basic Writings*, p. 221.

Finally, as a teacher I remember that in their meanings words carry the experience of a civilization, including its early insights into Being. Hence a great work of literature means far more than its author knew or intended. Insofar as its words still can evoke a trace of that original response to Being, those words can reveal whether the events depicted in the work, and their analogues in the world today, take us closer to or further from Being. My students and I therefore read such a work in the light of our own time in history. We find, for instance, that in its moments of peace *Moby Dick* conveys our affinity with Being in nature, and that in its scenes of slaughter it anticipates the despoliation of nature by global technology.

Critique   Heidegger is one of the most powerful and original philosophers of our century. His analysis of the Western drive to control nature and society will strike a chord in many teachers who are dissatisfied with the increasing regimentation of modern schooling and the overemphasis on calculative thinking. These teachers should not hestitate to adapt his insights to the educational needs of a technological society. For example, one of Heidegger's most relevant points is that the student is not a spectator of the world but lives understandingly in it. Educators could act on this insight and combine craftwork, which Heidegger recommends, with the study of science. Craftwork leads to science, in that the problems encountered in working with materials can be investigated scientifically. The student who wants to know why oak and pine are useful for different purposes can study the cell structure of plants and materials. Another Heideggerian insight is that literature is a source of vital truths. Literature should be studied for what it reveals about human beings and for its evocation of Being, as well as for its emotional appeal.

Nevertheless, the teacher should bear in mind the failings of this redoubtable thinker. For instance, he leads the student to wait for understanding rather than seek it; he encourages the student to listen to poetry and to allow Being to approach him in moments of meditative thinking. Since the nature of Being is not explicated, this approach can induce passive reverie and a mainly aesthetic response to life. Teachers should counter this tendency by encouraging students to be artistically creative (to paint, write, sing, and so forth). They also should provide opportunities for meditative thinking in structured disciplines and crafts.

Heidegger often writes enigmatically. How do I know when I am "open" to a text or topic? How do I judge whether a natural phenomenon or a historical event appears to me as it "really is"? If I cannot tell in my own case, how can I tell in the case of my students? To be sure, Heidegger's ideas are no less suggestive for lacking strict criteria of meaning. Nevertheless, teachers who apply them should make sure that his ideas suggest *some* criteria, and that they test these criteria in practice. In the case of a natural phenomenon, like the behavior of a frog, one criterion of a true appearance of the thing might be a clear vision of the whole along with a view of its parts. In the case of a historical event, like the signing of the Declaration of Independence, the teacher's initial criterion of a true appearance might be a set of detailed intuitions of the mental states of the key participants, provided that at least some of those intuitions are unexpected. (If all of them are expected, they will reflect the biases of the teacher rather than the event itself.)

A third failing, from an educator's point of view, is Heidegger's emphasis on Western philosophy as the root cause of global technology. Heidegger almost ignores such disciplines as economics, sociology, and political science. Yet these disciplines are indispensable as we seek to steer our technological society in directions we choose. It is not enough to extol rural life and await a revelation of Being. The school also should foster confidence in our ability to remake the world in which we find ourselves. Especially at the secondary school level, economics and other social studies should be given as much weight as art, literature, and history.

Gadamer: Dialogue Within a Tradition

Heidegger's daring philosophy stimulated a range of thinkers. Let us see how his student, Hans-Georg Gadamer, starting from certain Heideggerian insights, has come to focus on the process of understanding itself and its role in everyday life.[23]

For Gadamer, as for Heidegger, our greatest need is to attune ourselves to Being. Heidegger, however, came to have little faith in our present ability to do this. All we can manage, he said late

---

[23]"Philosophical hermeneutics takes as its task the opening up of the hermeneutical dimension in its full scope, showing its fundamental significance for our entire understanding of the world and thus for all the various forms in

in life, is to wait for Being to reveal itself in some new form.[24] Gadamer is more optimistic than Heidegger, more practical, more aware of the realities of educating. "What man needs," he declares, "is not only a persistent asking of ultimate questions, but the sense of what is feasible, and what is possible, what is correct, here and now."[25] And where can this sense be found? In the great texts of the Western tradition. These, says Gadamer, preserve insights into Being through which we can overcome the "nihilism and irrationality of our times."

Tradition, says Gadamer, makes me what I am. A tradition is a collection of ideas, beliefs, and practices that enables me to understand and deal with people, institutions, and things. Tradition is always present; I never can get completely outside it. Long before I reflect on these things, it tells me what a good parent is, an able teacher, a satisfactory school. For Gadamer, these givens of a tradition—these preconceptions—are the base of all understanding. Without them I could not question my ideas, for I would have none to question. Preconceptions as such, or the things I take for granted, do not fetter my mind but enable me to reflect. In Gadamer's words,[26]

They constitute the initial directedness of our whole ability to experience. They are biases of our openness to the world. They are simply conditions whereby we experience something —whereby what we en-

---

which this understanding manifests itself: from interhuman communication to the manipulation of society; from personal experience by the individual in society to the way in which he encounters society; and from the tradition as it is built of religion and law, art and philosophy, to the revolutionary consciousness that unhinges the tradition through emancipatory reflection." Hans-Georg Gadamer, *Philosophical Hermeneutics,* trans. and ed. David E. Linge (Berkeley and Los Angeles: University of California, 1970), p. 18.

[24]"'Only a God Can Save Us': The Spiegel Interview (1966)," in *Heidegger: The Man and the Thinker,* ed. Thomas Sheehan (Chicago: Precedent Publishing, 1981), pp. 45–72.

[25]"Foreword to the Second Edition," *Truth and Method,* p. xxv.

[26]*Philosophical Hermeneutics,* p. 9; and *Truth and Method,* p. 324. On Gadamer's view of tradition, see Linge, "Editor's Introduction," *Philosophical Hermeneutics.*

counter says something to us. . . . Thus to stand within a tradition does not limit the freedom of knowledge but makes it possible.

Does this mean that for Gadamer all preconceptions are justified, that I must accept tradition en bloc? Not at all. Gadamer distinguishes between "blind" preconceptions and those that "illuminate."[27] Nevertheless, he insists, tradition bequeaths us both forms of preconception, and at any given time we are unlikely to have one form without the other. How, then, do I recognize and overcome blind preconceptions and thus expand my mind? How, in a word, am I educated? By understanding things, says Gadamer. And the model for this is understanding a text (or its analogue). *Understanding texts is the heart of education.* However, Gadamer's idea of understanding texts is no ordinary one.

In his view, any text or event stands in a tradition formed by past interpretations that have been handed on. Neither I nor my students approach Shakespeare's *Hamlet* or the American Civil War with a completely open mind. Each of us has ideas about them that are the result of previous experience or study. Thus, the meaning of a text or event is not limited to its original significance. The text or event has a structure that each generation and each individual interprets afresh in the light of new personal insights and a new historical situation. Therefore, there is no limit to the process of interpretation, and each successful interpretation is different. In Gadamer's words,[28]

Not occasionally only, but always, the meaning of a text goes beyond its author. That is why understanding is not merely a reproduction, but always a productive attitude as well. . . . It is enough to say that we understand in a different way, if we understand at all.

Like Heidegger, Gadamer is a stimulating teacher, but one

---

[27]"The Problem of Historical Consciousness," in *Interpretive Social Science: A Reader*, ed. Paul Rabinow and William M. Sullivan (Berkeley and Los Angeles: University of California, 1979), p. 156.

[28]Ibid., p. 264.

who prefers discussion to the charismatic lecture. He is inspired by Plato's dialogues,[29] and especially by the fact that the participants are borne by their discussion to insights they had not anticipated. Teaching, for Gadamer, is dialogue within a tradition.[30] The teacher interprets the great acts and texts of a civilization. He or she is an interpreter of, and within, a tradition. The teacher's task, however, is not so much to transmit the tradition as to enable the student to interpret it, and thus to permit the tradition itself to continue. Although the teacher is an authority, his or her knowledge and skill are used to encourage students to think through what they interpret rather than merely absorb it.

The model for such teaching is dialogue, in which two or more speakers, all coming from their own limited point of view, reach an understanding they had not anticipated. Genuine dialogue allows the truth to appear and to be seen by each. As a teacher here, I obviously am ahead of my students, but I cannot foresee what insight will arise or when and how. The discussion has a momentum of its own. Each speaker risks himself, taking a position he has not staked out before. Gadamer contrasts this process with recitation, in which, he says, the student gives the teacher an expected answer. "Recitation knows what is coming and is closed to the sudden idea."[31] By contrast, the end of dialogue is both insight and discovery—discovery in the sense of "uncovering" the subject matter under discussion. What we discover (uncover), however, is not necessarily a preexistent proposition, but one of countless possible interpretations of a text or subject.

Dialogue proceeds through question and answer.[32] There are several reasons for this. First, according to Gadamer the subject or text itself is an answer to a question or questions. For example, a comprehensive history of the American War of Inde-

---

[29]For Gadamer's view of Plato's dialogues, see Hans-Georg Gadamer, *Dialogue and Dialectic: Eight Hermeneutical Studies on Plato* (New Haven: Yale University Press, 1980); and *Truth and Method*, pp. 425–433.

[30]On dialogue, see *Truth and Method*, esp. pp. 434–441.

[31]"To What Extent Does Language Reform Thought?" Supplement II, *Truth and Method*, p. 497.

[32]Gadamer calls this process "dialectic," "the art of conducting a real conversation." *Truth and Method*, p. 330.

pendence tells us why the war was fought, how it was fought, how it ended, and what its results were. Second, the students, out of their interest in the subject, ask these very questions, while I, their teacher, stimulate them to do so through questions of my own. Above all, I question them to elicit their "preconceptions"—the ideas they themselves bring to the subject.

Genuine dialogue presupposes a subject and a desire to understand it. Openness on both sides is essential. No one must come with his mind made up. In the give and take, each of us arrives at a new understanding. The students shed or qualify their preconceptions. For example, they come to realize that in the War of Independence the colonists were not all heroes and many were not at all opposed to rule by a distant king. I, in turn, correct my own preconceptions about the insights students will reveal during the discussion. An abandoned preconception frees the mind for a wider view. One's mental horizon expands. My students begin to see that great events generally have many causes, while I discover that particular boys and girls are even more complex and surprising than I had thought.

If the discussion is successful, our mental horizons converge. My students and I come to see the same elements or structure in the subject, even if each of us interprets them differently. We agree, for instance, that the War of Independence contained such and such events or had such and such causes, though we may differ in the importance we attach to them. Finally, insight comes, sought for but not determined. Now there occurs what Gadamer calls "the fusion of horizons."[33] As a result of discussion, each of us now brings a similar mind-set to the subject. We all see, for instance, that the War of Independence is a certain kind of war or that it largely is the result of a certain kind of cause. We may disagree, however, on particulars within this framework.

Successful dialogue changes both teacher and student. In Gadamer's words, "The participants part from one another as changed beings. The individual perspectives with which they entered upon the discussion have been transformed, and so they are transformed themselves."[34] As a teacher, I have seen a

---

[33] Ibid., pp. 273–274, 337.

[34] *Reason in the Age of Science*, trans. with an intro. by Frederick G. Lawrence (Cambridge, Mass.: M.I.T. Press, 1981), p. 110.

familiar subject in a new light. I feel that I may be getting somewhere with my students. They, too, may be changed in various ways. They may be more appreciative of history and more sophisticated about public affairs. Some of them may read more. Others may express themselves more fluently in class. Nevertheless, our insights are only tentative, since any subject is open to many interpretations and our own interpretation reflects our present horizons and our moment in history.

Students follow this same process of interpretation when they read a text or investigate a subject. They listen to the text, turning the written word into imagined speech. They allow the text to make its point, letting it encounter their own preconceptions (or present "horizon"). Instead of submitting to the text, students converse with it. They recognize that the text has something to give—not a determinate meaning but a possibility of interpretation that must be filled in and made relevant to the present. They endeavor to locate the question that the text addresses. The answer is the subject of the text, and it is this rather than the author's personal meaning that concerns students. By moving back and forth between their altering horizon and that of the text, students seek to locate the message of the text and make it personally meaningful.

Finally, in a striking analogy, Gadamer compares the process of understanding with a game. The game may be played by teacher and students together or by the student alone with the text. A game has its own rules. The player submits to the rules and becomes absorbed in the to-and-fro movement of the game. In fact, says Gadamer, we do not play the game as much as the game plays us. "The game is what holds the player to its spell, draws him into play, and keeps him there."[35] Similarly, we play with the text. Its structure corresponds to the rules of the game. Any number of persons can play, each abiding by the rules but reaching an individual result. This view of understanding requires that students both respect the text and make it mean something for themselves.

Critique   Gadamer's hermeneutics has much to offer the educator. As a model for teaching and learning, Gadamer's concept

---

[35]*Truth and Method*, p. 96.

of dialogue is broader and less demanding than Buber's. His notion of understanding as play also is fruitful. In this age of sports and video games students will be receptive to the idea of play in learning, and they may even add the element of winning. Every problem solved is a touchdown! Again, for Gadamer education is a gradual process with no harsh demands or sudden crises. Students mature by continually bringing their preconceptions to light and outgrowing them. Yet again, Gadamer gives students freedom to interpret. To understand a text, he says, is not to read off a determinate meaning but to recreate the text's significance for oneself.

But this philosophy also has certain shortcomings. For Gadamer, education always occurs within a tradition. As a teacher I can bring some elements of that tradition to consciousness, and thus in principle I can modify them; but there are others of which I will remain unaware. In practice this dependence on tradition may not seem too harmful, provided the educational process gradually is improved. On the other hand, if the tradition is profoundly conservative, some of the strongest psychological obstacles to change may not come to light. Gadamer offers me no way to overcome the deep limitations of my tradition.

Again, as Gadamer describes it, the quest for understanding tends to become receptive rather than critical. It treats the text as an authority to learn from rather than supersede. In my view, after we have understood a text, we should be ready to criticize it. In some cases we might improve on it. Gadamer, it is true, urges that interpretations of texts be supported by arguments, but he does not recognize sufficiently the importance of taking issue with the texts themselves. He seems averse to criticizing traditional authorities. Indeed, throughout his writing he especially upholds the works of classical humanists.

Also, in allowing the student freedom of interpretation, Gadamer undervalues the original work of creation. As a result, the student may not appreciate that the text expresses an individual vision and a deeply felt response to specific historical circumstances. In interpreting texts for one's time, the student may detach them from time altogether and thus lose sight of the real movement of history.

Finally, Gadamer does not tell us clearly enough how dialogue with a teacher or text changes the student's life. A dialogue can have many different effects. The student can become a better person, or take some action, or remember what he or she has learned, or engage in further study. In each case the student is changed in some way, but the concept of change embraces too much. Since Gadamer is imprecise, one step the teacher might take (after a successful dialogue) is to ask students what they think they can do with their newly acquired insight.

Ricoeur: Varieties of Interpretation

Paul Ricoeur has applied the hermeneutic view of understanding to many issues in the humanities and human sciences. Responsive to postwar French intellectual currents, he has brought structuralist[36] and psychoanalytic (Freudian) approaches within the hermeneutic tradition of Heidegger and Gadamer. Once a phenomenologist, he has continued to pay attention to the individual self. Unlike the phenomenologists, however, he believes that the self is formed largely by culture and that the cultural contribution to individual experience should be made explicit and evaluated rather than bracketed.[37] Ricoeur also is a seasoned educator. In 1970, he was Dean at Nanterre, just outside Paris, when the University was occupied by students and stormed by police in one of the most serious campus confrontations anywhere. Here we examine some hermeneutic themes in Ricoeur that illuminate education.

For Ricoeur, the core of education is the process by which students "appropriate the worlds" disclosed by texts to broaden themselves and their view of reality. (Texts here include analogues such as lectures, films, and TV programs.) To appropriate, says Ricoeur, is to "make one's own what initially was alien."[38] This does not mean that students impose themselves on a text

---

[36]For my discussion of structuralism, see pp. 85–86 and Chapter 4.

[37]See Paul Ricoeur "Phenomenology and Hermeneutics," *Hermeneutics and the Human Sciences: Essays on Language, Action, and Interpretation,* ed., trans., and introd. John B. Thompson (Cambridge: Cambridge University Press, 1981).

[38]"Appropriation," *Hermeneutics and the Human Sciences,* p. 185.

or that they put themselves in the author's mind. On the contrary, the student first "lets go" of him or herself to allow the text to reveal a world or subject beyond his or her limited horizon. Taking the part constructed for the reader, the student receives, "as in play, the self conferred by the work itself."[39] Clearly, the more imaginative the work, the more of his or her everyday self the student must surrender. A novel or a poem, for instance, will take most students further from the here and now of the classroom than a geometry text. Nevertheless, the same principle—"let the work play (unfold) itself"—applies in both cases. In Ricoeur's words, "To understand is not to project oneself into the text but to expose oneself to it; it is to receive a self enlarged by the appropriation of the proposed worlds which the interpretation unfolds."[40]

Differing somewhat from Gadamer, Ricoeur insists that the student should follow the lead of the text rather than play with it as an equal partner. It is the text that has the initiative and changes the student. As Ricoeur puts it, "Only the interpretation which satisfies the injunction of the text, which follows the arrow of meaning and endeavors to think in accordance with it, engenders a new *self*-understanding."[41] A deeply felt encounter with *Hamlet*, for example, may leave the student feeling more responsible for his or her own life. A concentrated reading of a chemistry text makes the student more aware that he or she is a material being. Nevertheless, not all students will be changed alike, since each responds according to his or her point of view, and all surrender only partly to the text.

Does the student become less critical by not imposing himself on the text? Is he more inclined to accept the world as it is? No, says Ricoeur. And here he advocates a "hermeneutics of suspicion," like that practiced by Marx, Nietzsche, and Freud.[42] This hermeneutics involves interpreting texts and their analogues in order to elicit the meanings they conceal rather than

---

[39] Ibid., p. 190.

[40] "Hermeneutics and the Critique of Ideology," *Hermeneutics and the Human Sciences*, p. 94.

[41] "Appropriation," pp. 192–193.

[42] Paul Ricoeur, *Freud and Philosophy: An Essay on Interpretation*, trans. Denis Savage (New Haven: Yale University Press, 1971).

those they offer. It seeks to uncover, for instance, the hidden forces and repressed desires that (according to Ricoeur) stamp many of our acts and beliefs. Clearly, however, many high school students lack the knowledge to interpret their reading or experience on these lines. How, then, does a hermeneutic education make students less susceptible to current orthodoxies?

According to Ricoeur, the reading of great texts tends to correct such orthodoxies in two ways. First, the text projects its own world and hence, in principle, a different perspective on the present. As Ricoeur puts it, "The power of the text to open a dimension of reality implies a recourse against any given reality and thereby the possibility of a critique of the real."[43] The greater the writer, the less he or she is circumscribed by history and the more he or she offers a later interpreter. Reading Shakespeare's tragedies, for example, makes students more aware of the corruption of power in their own time. Reading passages from Newton's *Principles of Natural Philosophy* shows them that a great scientific theory is not a straightforward representation of the world but an interpretation that is partly philosophic. Second, says Ricoeur, in opening themselves to a text, students shed some preconceptions that partly close their minds to other possibilities. In Ricoeur's words, "The appropriation of the proposed worlds offered by the text passes through the disappropriation of the self. The critique of *false consciousness* thus can become an integral part of hermeneutics."[44]

Ricoeur maintains that the mind is liberated from prejudice especially by works of literature and history. The historian seeks to preserve what should be remembered from the struggles of the past—and what is more memorable than the values by which people acted? Insofar as these values differ from our own, they show students other ways in which they can live today. Greek and medieval history, for example, teach us that people then strove for public honor rather than private wealth. Thus, says Ricoeur, "The 'true' histories of the past uncover the buried potentialities of the present."[45] Poets or novelists, on

---

[43]"Hermeneutics and the Critique of Ideology," p. 93.

[44]Ibid., pp. 94–95. People exhibit "false consciousness" when they hold the beliefs of their own social class without realizing it or entertain beliefs that express unconscious motives.

[45]"The Narrative Function," *Hermeneutics and the Human Sciences*, p. 245.

the other hand, ignore the complexities of actual events in order to highlight essential human nature. They proceed, as Ricoeur puts it, "directly to the universal, that is, to what a certain type of person probably or necessarily would do in a certain type of situation."[46] By disclosing the universal, literature helps students focus on essentials and interpret life around them less conventionally. For example, it helps them clarify their life purposes and intuit the true feelings behind the moods and inconsistencies of their parents, teachers, and friends.

What special import does Ricoeur's hermeneutics have for educational research? Let us focus on two points: Ricoeur's response to French structuralism and his use of the text as a model of human action. The essence of French structuralism is the view that certain systems—that is, wholes made of parts, such as texts, social institutions, and cultural practices—may be (1) treated as closed and independent of their surroundings and (2) explained solely by showing how their parts interact. For structuralism, the paradigm of a system is language itself, considered as a collection of verbal signs that are related to one another (as "teach" and "learn" are complementary terms) but not to the outside world (i.e., not to actual cases of teaching and learning).[47] This approach, which objectifies a system and ignores any significance it may have for an outsider, is the very opposite of hermeneutics, which insists that all systems must be interpreted. How does Ricoeur treat structuralism, and why does this treatment matter to educational research?

Ricoeur consistently has sought to enrich the hermeneutic tradition with contributions from other movements. Thus, instead of rejecting the structuralist approach, he shows how it can be used as one stage in a broader process of interpretation. He points out that structuralism tells us how a system works but not what the system means. It does not state what problem the system is intended to solve or what significance this solution can have for anyone else.[48] For example, suppose I explain how a school system works by specifying the interactions among the superintendents of schools, school boards, school

---

[46]Ibid., p. 296.

[47]French structuralism is discussed more fully in Chapter 4, pp. 99–100.

[48]"The Model of the Text: Meaningful Action Considered as a Text," *Hermeneutics and the Human Sciences*, p. 217.

principals, teachers, students, and others within the system. Have I understood the system? No, says Ricoeur. To understand the system, I must do more than explain the way it operates; I must ascertain what problem the system is intended to solve (or what question it is meant to answer), and what this solution can tell us about how people should be educated.

To interpret a school system fairly, I must refrain from conceiving it too fixedly from my own point of view. Here, says Ricoeur, a structuralist approach can help me by providing a technique for classifying the parts of the system and their interactions dispassionately. If I begin with a structuralist analysis, I am more likely to view the system in its own right. Nevertheless, the analysis will not tell me what the system means to the participants or what it can mean to an investigator from another country or generation.[49] What interpretive model should I use, then? Again, Ricoeur proposes the model of a text.

An institution, he says, signifies more than its founders or its participants are aware of.[50] A school system, for example, has a social significance that surpasses the everyday purposes of those who take part in it. Even members of a school board, meeting to discuss the annual plan, must ask themselves what the system is for. In doing so, they may neither list nor agree on all of the system's immediate objectives, let alone those for the next fifty years. Still less can they anticipate what possibilities an outsider might see in the system. It is this further, unnoticed significance that the researcher must "read."

Ricoeur does not specify a method for the educational researcher. What he proposes is an *orientation.* Do not, he says, approach the practices and institutions of education as though they were phenomena with no hidden significance. Instead, try to become aware of your own preunderstanding, and ask yourself what these practices and institutions mean to those involved in them, and what human possibilities they suggest to you and might suggest to others. In short, interpret them as

---

[49]Ibid., p. 220: "May we not say that in social science . . . we proceed . . . from surface interpretations to depth interpretation *through* structural analysis? But it is depth interpretation which gives meaning to the whole process."

[50]Ibid., p. 208: "Is it not a fundamental trait of the great works of culture to overcome the conditions of their social production, in the same way as a text develops new references and constitutes new worlds?"

though they were texts whose human significance in principle is inexhaustible. Here, like Heidegger and Gadamer, Ricoeur insists, against positivism,[51] that education and the human sciences have an approach of their own quite distinct from that of the natural sciences.

Critique   Ricoeur has sought to enrich hermeneutics with elements from other movements of thought. He also has sought to go beyond the position reached by Gadamer. Here one of his main contributions is the concept of "appropriation." The student, says Ricoeur, first opens himself to the actual meaning of the text and then makes that meaning his own. Ricoeur claims that appropriation is compatible with critical thinking, since, in appropriating the meaning of a text, the student must abandon some of his preconceptions and open himself to a different world and hence to a different possible perspective on the present.

Nevertheless, Ricoeur's claim is not altogether persuasive. The student may modify his preconceptions during his encounter with a text but reinstate them later. He may appreciate that the world of the text is different from the world around him, and even perhaps that it makes an implicit criticism of that world. But he may not feel moved to make that criticism himself. When reading *Gulliver's Travels*, for example, he may realize that in mocking the customs of the Lilliputians, Swift is satirizing social conformity everywhere. Yet this inference may remain intellectual. The student may not feel that the customs *he* knows are any the worse for this satire. It therefore would seem better for the student to do as Gadamer recommends and *re-create* the meaning of a text for himself. Then he is likely to be moved more deeply and hence to reinterpret his own world in the light of the experience.

Granted, by incorporating a structuralist perspective, Ricoeur has made the hermeneutic approach to social phenomena more objective and hence more useful to educational research. Nevertheless, his notion of the text as a model of

---

[51]On positivism, see Chapter 5. For an argument (different from Kuhn's) that the natural sciences are interpretive in their way and hence hermeneutic, see Stephen Toulmin, "The Construal of Reality: Criticism in Modern and Postmodern Science," *Critical Inquiry*, **9**:1 (September 1982), pp. 93–111.

actions and institutions needs to be developed in more detail. At the moment the model is mainly a metaphor. An institution resembles a text, says Ricoeur, in that it signifies more than its participants realize. True enough, but researchers also need guidelines indicating what textlike features to look for in an institution, so that predictions can be made and tested.

Ricoeur is not an easy author to understand. He is prolix and fond of abstractions. Yet the effort of reading him is well repaid. He has absorbed many influences and takes a broad view of his subject matter. Few contemporary philosophers can match his range. Let us hope that as he continues to examine how individuals and cultures come to understand themselves, he will propose a clearer, more precise role for the schools. If he does, he undoubtedly will deepen our conception of the educational process.

Kuhn: Hermeneutics and the Natural Sciences

Let us now consider a hermeneutic approach to the natural sciences that owes nothing to the Heideggerian form of hermeneutic philosophy. This is the approach of the American historian of science, Thomas S. Kuhn. His modern classic, *The Structure of Scientific Revolutions*, [52] has stimulated ideas not only in the history and philosophy of science but in many other fields, including education.

Kuhn tells how he came to hermeneutics. Originally a physicist, he used to regard the historian as a mere compiler of facts. In 1947, however, while preparing to lecture on seventeenth-century mechanics, he read Aristotle's theory of motion. At first the theory struck him as absurd, but then he decided that so great a thinker hardly could have made so many mistakes. Kuhn solved his problem when he realized that Aristotle could not be understood in twentieth-century terms. Instead, Kuhn had to recapture "out-of-date ways of reading out-of-date texts." [53] When he did so, Aristotle started to make sense. "I did

---

[52]Thomas S. Kuhn, *The Structure of Scientific Revolutions*, 2nd ed. (Chicago: University of Chicago Press, 1970).

not become an Aristotelian physicist as a result," he declares, "but I had to some extent learned to think like one. Thereafter I had few problems understanding why Aristotle had said what he did about motion or why his statements had been taken so seriously."[54]

Kuhn had discovered a method reminiscent of Dilthey's— put yourself in the author's mind and imagine what he sought to say. Kuhn formulates the method as follows:

When reading the works of an important thinker, look first for the apparent absurdities in the text and ask yourself how a sensible person could have written them. When you find an answer, . . . when those passages make sense, then you may find that more central passages, ones you previously thought you understood, have changed their meaning.[55]

This approach led Kuhn to his theory of the growth of science.[56]

Kuhn maintains that young scientists acquire the skills or know-how of their profession by working on variants of what generally is recognized as *the central, solved problem* in their field. Kuhn calls this solved problem a "paradigm" and its variants "exemplars."[57] The paradigm, he says, is the outstanding achievement in a field and hence the model to be imitated. It shows the researcher what facts to consider, what problems to choose, and what methods to use in solving them. An example of a paradigm is Galileo's solution to the problem of how to calculate the movement of a body along a slope. Galileo showed

---

[53]Thomas S. Kuhn, "Preface," *The Essential Tension: Selected Studies in Scientific Tradition and Change* (Chicago: University of Chicago Press, 1978), p. xiii.

[54]Ibid., p. xii.

[55]Ibid., p. xii.

[56]For a review and critique of current theories of scientific growth, see my *Science as a Human Endeavor* (New York: Columbia University Press, 1978), chs. 2 and 3.

[57]In response to charges of vagueness and ambiguity, Kuhn withdrew an earlier and broader conception of a paradigm. See Thomas S. Kuhn, "Preface," *The Essential Tension,* p. xix, and "Second Thoughts on Paradigms," in *The Structure of Scientific Theories,* ed. Frederick Suppe (Urbana, Ill.: University of Illinois Press, 1977), pp. 483–517.

that a ball rolling down an inclined plane resembles a swinging pendulum since (in the absence of friction) it gathers enough speed to return to the same height on any second incline. Galileo's solution was applied by later scientists to other problems in mechanics. Today, says Kuhn, such exemplary, solved problems are recorded in textbooks as standard exercises for the aspiring scientist.

The basic skills of a science belong to what Kuhn calls its "disciplinary matrix." They include skills in the use of instruments, experiments, mathematical formulas, and libraries. They are learned from practice, not from a book, and they cannot be spelled out. In Kuhn's words, they are "a mode of knowing that is less systematic or less analyzable than knowledge embedded in rules, laws, or criteria of identification."[58] As such, these skills form a "preunderstanding" of the field. In turn, they presuppose a range of more basic skills, such as those involved in moving and handling objects and judging distances—skills that belong to our everyday preunderstanding.

Kuhn distinguishes between "mature" and "immature" and between "normal" and "revolutionary" science. A mature science, he says, is dominated by a single paradigm—as physics, for instance, was dominated for 200 years by the Newtonian paradigm. An immature science, like biology before Darwin, is split between competing paradigms and hence makes little progress, since the adherents of each paradigm reject the findings of others. Normal science is research done in a mature discipline under a single paradigm. Normal science is highly efficient, because it focuses on problems that are known to be soluble and hence achieves results fast. As the price of this efficiency, however, it ignores any problems that look "different." In time, these problems accumulate until they threaten the paradigm and set off a "crisis." Then scientists search desperately for an alternative paradigm that will solve their problems. Either the established paradigm weathers the crisis or it is replaced by another, as the Newtonian paradigm was replaced by those of quantum mechanics and general relativity.

---

[58]*The Essential Tension*, p. 192. The disciplinary matrix also includes standards for judging, for example, that such and such constitutes a good experiment or a good paper.

For Kuhn, the adherents of rival paradigms not only hold different beliefs, they also see and do different things, and in this sense "practice their trades in different worlds."[59] During the sixteenth century, for example, a supporter of Ptolemy's geocentric theory literally saw the sun *rise* above the horizon to circle the earth. A Copernican, on the other hand, noticed that the earth had moved relative to the sun.

However, if rival scientists look at the world differently, how can they compare theories and decide which is best? According to Kuhn, each scientist must empathize with his or her opposite number and ask how the world looks from the other point of view. Each must seek to enter, in Diltheyan style, into the spirit of the opposing paradigm. Nevertheless, even when interpreted in this way, rival paradigms cannot be compared objectively, since different scientists value the standards of comparison—such as accuracy, range, and consistency—differently.[60] In the absence of an objective comparison one cannot say that one paradigm is any truer than another.[61] The scientist, then, always must look at the world in terms of a paradigm and its accompanying disciplinary matrix. Or, as previous hermeneuticists have stated, the scientist must think and act within a tradition. There is no fully objective point of view, and all points of view must be understood empathetically.

How is the scientist trained to work in a tradition? Kuhn maintains that most college science education is designed to turn out competent normal scientists. Until their last year of graduate work, students rely mainly on textbooks, which are written in the language, and according to the principles, of dominant paradigms. These texts largely ignore the history of science, including the circumstances in which a current paradigm was created. They give the impression that science is a body of established knowledge rather than a historical movement in which paradigms are challenged and overthrown.

---

[59]*The Structure of Scientific Revolutions*, p. 149.

[60]"Second Thoughts on Paradigms," p. 335.

[61]"We may . . . have to relinquish the notion, explicit or implicit, that changes of paradigms carry scientists . . . closer and closer to the truth" (*The Structure of Scientific Revolutions*, p. 169). Also: "As in political revolutions, so in paradigm choice—there is no standard higher than the assent of the scientific community" (ibid., p. 93).

Kuhn is ambivalent toward this education. On the one hand, he points out, it equips the scientist "almost perfectly" for "puzzle-solving" within a tradition. On the other, he says, it is more "rigid and narrow" than any preparation "except [that] perhaps in orthodox theology."[62] How, then, should science be taught to students some of whom may be headed for this system?

Although Kuhn himself does not answer this question, his views, as we have considered them, allow us to do so. First, a science education should start concretely, with observation and experimentation closely related to the child's own activities. This start will build a preunderstanding of science directly on the child's preunderstanding of the world. If this approach is combined with studies of key episodes from the history of science, such as Torricelli's discovery of the barometer or Wegener's theory of continental drift, it will show the child that science is not a collection of books but an ensemble of activities and discoveries. In the upper elementary grades children should begin the study of particular sciences, such as physics and biology, but again mixed with history and social thought to show that scientific knowledge does not accumulate of its own accord but is created in many different ways and under very different conditions. Throughout their school career students should be encouraged to reflect on science, to ask what difference it makes in their lives, and what purposes it has served in other times and places.

High school science, in turn, should be guided by the following principles: (1) Science should be taught as an activity rather than a body of knowledge. In physics, for example, mechanics should be presented not as a set of propositions but as a way of seeing the world and solving certain problems in it. (2) Students should be asked to regard themselves as apprentices in the important Newtonian research tradition, a tradition that is indispensable to a wide range of modern technologies, including that of space flight. (3) They should appreciate that, as apprentices, they are learning to use one of the most powerful methods of solving problems ever developed. The method involves visualizing and operating mentally on phenomena in motion. (4) To understand an unfamiliar research tradition such as that of Darwinian evolution, students should ask themselves how its

---

[62]Ibid., p. 166.

adherents view the world and what central problem or problems they seek to solve. (5) Students should realize that, although modern science solves more problems than the science of the past, it has reached no final truths. Since all paradigms rest on assumptions, none legitimately can claim to represent the world exactly as it is.

Finally, Kuhn states that research in education and throughout the human sciences is "immature." Why immature? Because it contains many schools of thought. The psychology of education, for example, is divided among the behaviorist, the cognitive-developmental, the humanist, and the information-processing schools. The sociology of education includes structuralist, Marxist, behaviorist, phenomenological, and systems-oriented approaches. Other areas of education are similarly crowded. Educational research will not be mature until it is guided by a single paradigm. Will this ever take place? Here considerable skepticism is justified. Since people feel so strongly and disagree so often about education (as about all human conduct), researchers surely will have to describe educational phenomena in valuational terms. And since values almost certainly will remain controversial, findings that are expressed in valuational terms are unlikely to command universal assent. Hence no single paradigm seems likely to be accepted.[63]

Critique   Kuhn has made two main contributions to hermeneutics. First, he has singled out the part played in science by the researcher's preunderstanding of his field, a preunderstanding formed as much by the researcher's practices as by his or her beliefs. Second, Kuhn has pointed out that to understand a new paradigm, scientists must imagine themselves using it. They must ask how the paradigm would highlight the world, what problems it would pick out, and how it would help them solve these problems. In other words, scientists first must interpret the new paradigm empathetically rather than try to approach it objectively. Both of Kuhn's points also are valid for educational research.

Kuhn claims that science grows through alternating phases

[63]See Charles Taylor, "Understanding in Human Science," *Review of Metaphysics*, **34**:1 (September 1980), 33–37.

of normal and revolutionary science. But is this true? Science, it would seem, is more revolutionary during normal phases than Kuhn allows, and there is more competition between rival theories. For example, during the nineteenth century Newtonian mechanics was challenged as a model for physics by the electromagnetic theories of Michael Faraday and James Clark Maxwell. For Kuhn, too, educational research is "immature" and hence "unprogressive" (in his sense). In fact, educators have found that Imre Lakatos' model of competing "research programs"—theories that guide research over a period of time— gives them more insight than Kuhn's ideas into the growth and decline of research traditions in education.[64] Lakatos' model states in more detail what aspects of a research tradition the student of education should look for, and what factors make such a tradition successful.

Kuhn also is a relativist. Theories cannot be compared objectively, he says, since the standards for comparing them are applied differently by different scientists. Hence we cannot say for certain that one theory is more true than another. Need this conclusion trouble the science teacher? In one sense, not too much, since Kuhn maintains that theories prove themselves over their rivals by solving more problems and hence accumulating more knowledge. Thus, the teacher may hold that, provided a theory does this, the student need not worry whether it ultimately is more true than another. In this case the question of ultimate truth is academic. However, Kuhn's relativism has more serious consequences if it is applied to intellectual traditions generally. If the teacher sees *all* research traditions as based on Kuhnian paradigms, he or she must maintain that all knowledge is relative. This is a defensible position, but the teacher should be clear that he or she has taken it.

---

[64]Lakatos presents this model in "Falsification and the Methodology of Scientific Research Programmes," in *Criticism and the Growth of Knowledge, Proceedings of the International Colloquium in the Philosophy of Science, 1965,* ed. Imre Lakatos and Alan Musgrave (Cambridge: Cambridge University Press, 1970), pp. 91–196; and "History of Science and Its Rational Reconstructions," in *PSA 1970: In Memory of Rudolf Carnap,* Boston Studies in the Philosophy of Science, vol. 8, ed. Roger C. Buck and Robert S. Cohen (Dordrecht, Holland: Reidel, 1971), pp. 91–136. For a summary and an evaluation of Lakatos' model, see my *Science as a Human Endeavor,* pp. 68–73.

Finally, will a Kuhnian science education encourage critical thinking? Kuhn points out that graduate science education today fosters normal rather than revolutionary science and hence conventional rather than radical thought.[65] With reservations Kuhn accepts this state of affairs. Nevertheless, it should be clear that in the public school an education based on Kuhnian theory undoubtedly will develop critical thinking. A Kuhnian teacher will encourage students to regard all paradigms as relative and to reconstruct in their imaginations the research styles of paradigms that are unfamiliar to them. Acquaintance with a range of paradigms and a readiness to identify with new styles of thought cannot but make students, at this stage in their careers, imaginative and critical rather than conformist. Kuhn surely would welcome this outcome.

Appraisal[66]

Hermeneutics is of interest, first, because it takes its model of understanding from the human studies rather than the natural sciences. Understanding, it says, is like reading a text (or studying its analogues) rather than observing an object. A text always has meaning, but since the author is absent, or dead, or from another culture, that meaning has to be interpreted for the present time. For hermeneutics, then, interpretation is the heart of understanding.

This view should be congenial to many teachers, since their role is to understand human beings and human creations, and develop this understanding in others. Teaching, says hermeneutics, is an art, not a science or a technology. As a teacher, I

---

[65]For an intense and informative exchange on Kuhn's view of science education, See Harvey Siegel, "Kuhn and Critical Thought," in *Philosophy of Education 1977: Proceedings of the Thirty-Third Annual Meeting of the Philosophy of Education Society,* ed. Ira S. Steinberg (Urbana, Ill.: Philosophy of Education Society, 1975), pp. 172–179; "Kuhn and Schwab on Science Texts and the Goals of Science Education," *Educational Theory,* **28**:4 (Fall 1978), 302–309; and "Rationality, Talking Dogs, and Forms of Life," *Educational Theory,* **30**:2 (Spring 1980), pp. 135–148; and Jon Fennel and Rudy Liveritte, "Kuhn, Education, and the Grounds of Rationality," *Educational Theory,* **29**:2 (Spring 1979), pp. 117–128.

[66]Analyses and criticisms in the body of the chapter are not necessarily repeated here.

must ask what my subject means to me and what it can mean to my students. I must introduce it when it potentially is within the "mental horizon" of my students, and I must help my students understand it for themselves. The core of this teaching-learning process is the reading and discussion of texts and their immediate analogues, such as pictures, demonstrations, and audiovisual presentations. In studying this process and others, educational researchers ask what the activities and institutions of education mean both to their participants and to the researchers themselves.

Second, according to hermeneutics, we begin with some preliminary understanding of a text or its analogue. Without this preunderstanding we have no idea what we are encountering and thus are unlikely to understand it. As a teacher, then, I ask my students to view a topic first in the light of their present knowledge and interests, and then to modify their attitudes in response to what the topic itself has to say to them. In this way they advance their mental horizons toward the horizon of the topic. This is the creative role of preunderstanding: not to resist the new and the alien but to expand the mind's horizon by admitting them.

Third, for the hermeneuticist the teaching-learning process is like a dialogue or game in which the participants are carried by something larger than themselves toward an insight they had not anticipated. A genuine discussion is not planned in advance. My students and I risk ourselves and speak spontaneously. In the process we discover something new about the subject and even about ourselves, and the knowledge changes us. Students also can "converse" with a text or project. They ask what questions the text is answering and listen to what the text says to them. In the game of understanding they move to and fro between their questions and the text's responses.

Fourth, regarding the approach to a text or its analogue, Dilthey tells the student to empathize with the author and ask what he or she sought to convey. Kuhn advises the student to place himself in the mind and behind the eyes of the user of a new paradigm. Most hermeneuticists, however, urge the student to bracket the author and let the text speak for itself. The fact of publication, they say, separates the text from its author and delivers it to an unlimited audience. Each text discloses a subject that the student should interpret for his own moment in history. The student should open himself to the text and ask what the text says to him. In this way he makes what is *in* the text his own. Ricoeur calls this process "appropriation"; for Gadamer, it is the "fusion of horizons." Most hermeneuticists maintain that literary and historical texts contain the most important truths for humankind. Kuhn, however, focuses on works of science that have created long-lasting paradigms.

Finally, hermeneuticists agree that understanding takes place within a tradition. Heidegger, for example, urges the school to preserve what remains of the ancient affinity with Being by fostering meditative thinking, traditional crafts, and the reading of great poets. Gadamer maintains that tradition stimulates rather than constrains creation. The teacher's task is to enable students to interpret great texts and achievements and remake them for their own time. In Gadamer's view, the student is a participant in tradition rather than its recipient. A Kuhnian teacher regards scientific traditions more prosaically as social institutions for channeling research. He or she advises science students to keep their minds open by recreating in their imaginations the research styles of older or less orthodox traditions than their own.

As a philosophy for education, however, current hermeneutics has several limitations. Since this movement of thought has arrived only recently from Continental Europe, its significance for education in the English-speaking world has only begun to be worked out. More importantly, there are major concerns in education to which this branch of philosophy seems to have limited relevance, except via the concept of preunderstanding. These areas include (among others) moral education, civic responsibility, personal health, and discipline.

Next, most hermeneuticists are unsympathetic to industrial civilization. Heidegger, for instance, wants to restore a pre-Socratic intimacy with Being through poetry, philosophy, and meditative thinking. But until the nature of Being is spelled out more fully, his program must remain too nebulous for the public school. Heidegger's practical advice to the school, again, has limited appeal. We must educate people to go back to the land, he says, and to preindustrial crafts. Gadamer maintains that, since we interpret texts in the light of the present, we always can modify the tradition we inherit. Nevertheless, the texts he admires are the classics of a culture. He does not recommend the study of texts that might stimulate the student to more radical critiques—works of contemporary literature, for example, or works in the human sciences. Ricoeur, it is true, has sought to transcend Gadamer's conservatism, yet his hermeneutics of suspicion—like that of Marx, Nietzsche, and Freud—will be suited only to advanced high school students.

One should note, that this distrust of modernity is not essential to hermeneutics. One can equally well imagine a hermeneutic curriculum that introduces the student to texts of other civilizations (e.g., Chinese and Indian) and to twentieth-century works (such as the poems of D. H. Lawrence, stories by Ernest Hemingway, and essays by Lewis Mumford, not to mention films and docudramas). Such a curriculum surely would tend to foster an open mind.

Hermeneutics also entails relativism. If students cannot transcend their tradition, they cannot tell whether it is better or worse than any other. This may not seem to matter much, provided they are educated to reflect on their tradition and be disposed to improve it. A conservative curriculum, for example, that promotes traditional moral and intellectual values may foster a resistance to decadence. On the other hand, the relativism implicit in a hermeneutically inspired eclectic curriculum—like the one outlined above—might lead the student to nihilism, the belief that nothing *profoundly* matters. If students are exposed to a range of cultures and contemporary works, with no traditional standards to show why these are more important than others, they may well come to believe that moral and intellectual principles are matters of personal taste.

I have mentioned some limitations of contemporary hermeneutics, but these should not be allowed to obscure its great promise for the understanding of education. There is no philosophy that does not face serious problems, for it is in the nature of philosophy to ask radical questions and hence to raise difficulties for itself. The wide horizons of hermeneutics can expand the thought and enrich the practice of every educator who finds its ideas attractive. Let us hope that many educators do so. In the meantime, I must present another broad and challenging movement with some roots in Continental thinking—the movement of Structuralism.

Structuralism

4

Introduction

In the humanities and the human sciences people have thought about structures for many years. Educationists, for instance, long have distinguished between the structure of a school system and its functions. As a distinct philosophy or movement of thought, however, structuralism began in the late 1950s. Its central claim is that society, culture, and the individual psyche contain *structures* that can be grasped objectively as opposed to interpreted from particular points of view.[1]

The essence of structure is internal coherence. A structure is a whole, an arrangement of parts that is complete in itself. A school's student body, for instance, is a whole. It is a group of people who have come together for the express purpose of getting an education. Because it is coherent, a structure tends to endure.

The parts of a structure are governed by laws or rules intrinsic to the structure, laws or rules which give them properties they do not

---

[1]A good introduction to the structuralist movement is Jean Piaget's *Structuralism,* trans. and ed. Chaninah Maschler (New York: Basic Books, 1970).

possess in isolation. In the case of a student body we do not know the relevant laws (although some sociologists have theorized about them). In the case of the number system the rules are known. Mathematical integers, for example, form a structure. They do not exist separately from one another; they are subject to rules (e.g., addition, subtraction, multiplication, division); and they possess properties (e.g., of forming groups, fields, rings) that do not belong to isolated numbers.

A structure is self-regulating. Its parts change, but in ways that do not violate the structure. For example, if we add or subtract any two whole numbers, we get another whole number, not a number outside the structure. Similarly, the rules of a language allow certain combinations of words but forbid others. The rules of English, for instance, permit the sentence, "Yesterday was a holiday for teachers," but reject, as not a sentence, the words "For a holiday was teachers yesterday."

Structures, says the structuralist, *exist everywhere: in the physical world, in living things, in the mind, in social life, in language, logic, and mathematics.* Some of the most important structures are present in everyday life, though not often observed—the structure of linguistic rules, for example, and the structure of relations among social classes. These structures shape the way we think and live. The researcher, therefore, must uncover these structures, and the philosopher must reflect on their significance, including their significance for education. Let us see how some philosopher-scientists are doing this.

Piaget: Intellectual Development

Although he is renowned for his work in child psychology, Jean Piaget (1896–1980) does not regard himself primarily as a psychologist. In his view, he is a biologist and philosopher who studies the origin and growth of intelligence from infancy to adulthood. Hence he calls himself a "genetic epistemologist"—literally, one who investigates the genesis of knowledge. Moreover, what interests him mainly is not this or that particular child—the "individual subject"—but rather the "epistemic subject," or the totality of intelligence traits common to all human subjects at the same stage of development.[2]

As a philosopher of the mind, Piaget advocates "genetic structuralism"—the thesis that the organism orders its experience by creating mental structures and applying them to experience. Piaget deduces the existence of these structures from his studies of individual children. For him, knowing is an active process in which the organism or individual interacts with the environment and transforms it in his mind with the aid of these structures. In Piaget's own words,[3]

To know an object is to act upon it and to transform it . . . . To know, therefore, is to assimilate reality into the structures of transformation, and these are the structures that intelligence constructs as a direct reflection of our actions.

Thus, Piaget places himself in opposition to (1) theories that treat the mind as a *tabula rasa,* or "blank tablet," that absorbs information without formally structuring it; (2) theories maintaining that the mind structures experience by means of ideas contained at birth;[4] (3) positivist theories relying on quantitative experimentation; and (4) functionalist theories, which argue that the best way to understand the mind is to observe what it does.

As a biologist, Piaget believes that intellectual growth is part of biological growth and governed by the same laws.[5] Thus, he calls psychology "the embryology of intelligence."[6] An organism grows, he says, by assimilating information from the environment and then accommodating itself to the environment in a process of "equilibration." (The same process—assimilation of the environment balanced by accommodation to it—also is

---

[2]Jean Piaget, *Genetic Epistemology,* trans. Eleanor Duckworth (New York: Columbia University Press, 1970). See also *Structuralism,* p. 139.

[3]Jean Piaget, *Science of Education and the Psychology of the Child,* trans. Derek Coltman (New York: Viking, 1970), p. 78.

[4]For Chomsky on "innate" ideas, see pp. 117–118.

[5]Jean Piaget, *Biology and Knowledge,* trans. Beatrix Walsh (Chicago: University of Chicago Press, 1971).

[6]Jean Piaget, "Autobiography," in *A History of Psychology in Autobiography,* ed. E. G. Boring, vol. 4 (New York: Russell and Russell, 1952), p. 245.

responsible for the evolution of species.) Equilibration, however, is not a static process. It is a striving for ever more inclusive states of equilibrium and hence for ever greater control over the environment. [7]

As part of equilibration, intellectual development involves the creation of progressively more elaborate mental structures. [8] This process of creation is genetically programmed; it is an instinctive response of the human organism to its surroundings. A structure here is a group of mental operations that are related to one another and represent physical actions. Addition and subtraction, for instance, are internalized versions of such physical actions as pushing objects together and then pulling them apart. By internalizing actions and coordinating their internalized versions in structures, children can do in their heads what before they had to do with their hands.

By virtue of forming a structure, the child comes to understand and apply a fundamental concept. [9] Different structures govern different concepts. Take the concept of *conservation* in its basic physical or mathematical sense. This concept means that something stays the same even in changed contexts, or, more precisely, that changes in properties irrelevant to the concept (position, shape, etc.) do not alter relevant properties (amount, length, number, etc.). A five-year-old, for example, has no concept of conservation with respect to amount. If you give him two tumblers, each half full of water, he will agree that there is the same amount of water in each. But if, before his eyes, you pour the water from one glass into a tall, narrow container, he will say that there is more water in the new glass than in the

[7]In Piaget's words, it is "a continual search for a better equilibrium," a search in which "fresh goals always arise from an attained equilibrium," and in which "each result remains pregnant with new progress." Jean Piaget, "Problems of Equilibration," in *The Essential Piaget*, ed. Howard Gruber and Jacques Vonèche (New York: Basic Books, 1977), p. 840. Cited by William E. Doll, Jr., "A Short Note on Haroutunian's View of Piaget's Biological Conception of Knowledge," *Educational Theory*, **31**:2 (Spring 1981), 190–191. See also Jean Piaget *The Development of Thought: Equilibration of Cognitive Structures*, trans. Arnold Rosin (New York: Viking, 1977).

[8]Jean Piaget, *The Origins of Intelligence in the Child*, trans. Margaret Cook (New York: International Universities Press, 1953).

[9]Jean Piaget, *The Child's Construction of Reality*, trans. Margaret Cook (New York: Basic Books, 1954).

old. Again, a child who does not understand conservation with respect to length will maintain that a necklace laid out in a straight line is longer than an identical necklace that lies in a circle.

Most children form the concept of conservation by the time they are eight. To do so, says Piaget, they have to be able to coordinate such mental operations as addition/subtraction, compensation, transitivity, identity, and reversibility.[10] The operation of *addition/subtraction* enables children to reason that if nothing is added to or taken from a substance, it stays the same. *Compensation* allows them to judge that a change in one dimension is balanced by a change in another—that as a rubberband is stretched, for example, it gets thinner. *Transitivity* tells them that if jar A holds as much water as jar B, and B as much as jar C, then A holds as much water as C. *Identity* informs them that if something isn't changed, it remains the same. Finally, *reversibility* enables them to undo any of these operations, once it has been performed, by turning it around and thus restoring the original state of affairs.

According to Piaget, a child's intelligence develops through the same sequence of stages,[11] each one marked by a characteristic mental structure and way of thinking. During the "sensorimotor" stage (from birth to 2 years) children explore their immediate surroundings with their bodies, pushing, pulling, and sucking things. By the end of this period they have laid the foundations of all the mental structures they later will need. During the "preoperational" stage (2 to 7 years) they begin to use words and mental images to represent actions and internalize them as thoughts. They still are egocentric, however, and do not take into account other points of view. During the period of "concrete operations" (7 to 11 or 12 years) they are capable of quite subtle mental acts, such as recognizing conservation, yet they reason best about objects at hand rather than abstractions. Finally, during the period of "formal operations" (from 11 or 12 to 14 or 15 years) they are able to think abstractly, and propose and test hypotheses about possible states of affairs.

---

[10]Jean Piaget, *The Psychology of the Child*, with Bärbel Inhelder, trans. Helen Weaver (New York: Basic Books, 1969).

[11]For a comprehensive discussion of the stages, see Margaret A. Boden, *Jean Piaget* (New York: Viking, 1980), pp. 23ff.

Piaget points out that these age brackets are only approximate. All children pass through the same stages, but at different rates. For example, to perform concrete operations a child must be capable of preoperational thinking, but not all children achieve this capability at the same age. As Piaget insists,[12]

It is . . . disastrous . . . to assume that a child has or has not reached a certain stage just because he is a certain age. The ages I have mentioned are only averages. Any child may be a year or so beyond or behind the average capabilities reached by most children his age.

Piaget also rejects accelerated learning. "Intellectual growth," he says, "contains its own rhythm, and speeding up cannot be continued indefinitely."[13] Premature teaching may lead to a purely verbal understanding of a topic with no real insight into what it means. Nevertheless, Piaget regards the stages as potentials rather than limitations. He writes:[14]

Too many people take the theory of stages to be simply a series of limitations. . . .The positive aspect is that as soon as each stage is reached, it offers new possibilities to the child. There are no "static" stages as such. Each is the fulfillment of something begun in the preceding one, and the beginning of something that will lead on to the next.

What causes intellectual growth? Primarily, says Piaget, the process of "equilibration," or the search for "optimal equilibrium." A mental structure is in equilibrium when it can integrate the information it assimilates, and the child can act on this information. For example, a child who wants to cross a crowded playground assimilates what he sees into his spatial structure, which then processes the information and gives him cues on how to proceed. A structure is out of equilibrium when it cannot process some anomalous information or some contradiction in the child's thoughts. Disequilibrium, however, often is a

---

[12]"Piaget Takes a Teacher's Look" (interview with Eleanor Duckworth), *Learning,* 2:2 (October 1973), 25.

[13]*Biology and Knowledge,* p. 21.

[14]"Piaget Takes a Teacher's Look," p. 25.

positive good, since it can stimulate the child to create a higher level structure to handle it. As Piaget puts it, "Any structure at all is going to create others by the possibilities it raises.[15] It follows that *active learning, or finding things out for oneself, should be at the heart of the educational process,* since it is most likely to lead to the creation of new structures.[16] Says Piaget, "We need pupils who are active, who learn early to find out by themselves, partly by their own spontaneous activity and partly through material set up for them.[17]

What does Piaget mean by finding things out for oneself? Does he mean that the students should discover everything for themselves without consulting their teachers? Clearly not, for Piaget says that some materials must be prepared for the students. Or does Piaget mean that all active learning should include some manual or motor activity? Again, no, for students may be as active in working out the proof of a theorem as they are in designing a laboratory experiment. In Piaget's words, "A student may be totally 'active,' in the sense of making a personal rediscovery of the truths to be acquired, even though this activity is being directed toward interior and abstract reflection."[18]

Partly through their own efforts, then, and partly with their teachers' help, students should *learn to learn.* This would include learning, for instance, what questions to ask about a poem they wish to appraise, what factors to consider as the possible causes of a historical event, and what qualities to strive for in formulating a scientific hypothesis. When students know how to learn, they can find things out for themselves. Moreover, they do not cease learning to learn, since as they acquire new kinds of knowledge, they may need to ask new types of

---

[15]Jean Piaget, in *Language and Learning: The Debate Between Jean Piaget and Noam Chomsky,* ed. Massimo Piattelli-Palmarini (Cambridge, Mass.: Harvard University Press, 1980), p. 157.

[16]See Piaget's *The Science of Education and the Psychology of the Child,* and *To Understand Is to Invent: The Future of Education,* trans. George-Anne Roberts (New York: Grossman, 1973).

[17]Quoted by Piaget's long-time research associate, Eleanor Duckworth, "Piaget Rediscovered," in *Piaget Rediscovered,* ed. R. E. Ripple and U. N. Rockcastle (Ithaca, N.Y.: Cornell University Press, 1964), p. 5.

[18]*The Science of Education,* p. 72.

questions and use new modes of inquiry. Thus learning to learn not only continues at school, it can continue for the rest of their lives.[19]

Spontaneous, practical activity is especially important in the early grades, where the child forms the prototypes of later logico-mathematical abilities. Here, says Piaget, heavy reliance on reading and writing actually can hinder the natural growth of intelligence. Before understanding can be internalized in words, it must exist in practical form. A young child who says "Two plus three equals five" or who does the sum in figures may know nothing about cardinal numbers or the equivalence of sets. The structures of ordering and classifying, necessary for mathematical understanding, are internalized from bodily activities, such as comparing, ordering, and sorting physical objects. In Piaget's words,[20]

As for teaching children concepts that they have not attained in their spontaneous development, it is completely useless. A British mathematician attempted to teach his five-year-old daughter the rudiments of set theory and conservation. He did the typical experiments of conservation with numbers. Then he gave the child two collections and she immediately said, those are two sets. But she couldn't count and she had no idea of conservation. . . .You cannot teach concepts verbally; you must use a method founded on activity.

How do I as a teacher help children grow intellectually? I do so primarily by providing materials and situations, appropriate to their level of development, that will stimulate them to rediscover and reconstruct knowledge for themselves, and thus to create higher-level structures. To set them thinking, I ask questions. To get *them* to question, I offer counterexamples. When students strike out on their own, I encourage them to go ahead, even if they make mistakes. With children under 12 especially, my role is to encourage, stimulate, and advise rather than simply to direct activity or impart information. In the later grades,

---

[19]*To Understand Is to Invent*, pp. 113–114.

[20]Elizabeth Hall, "A Conversation with Jean Piaget and Bärbel Inhelder," *Teacher Education Journal*, **22**:3 (March 1974), 30.

when students' minds are more formed, I can provide more exposition and more knowledge for them to master.

What does Piaget's theory say to curriculum designers? First, it tells them to provide materials that will stimulate the student always to move toward the next stage or substage of development. How is the curriculum designer to accomplish this task? Piaget supplies the answer:[21]

In the ideal situation, the questions the child asks himself and the reactions he discovers are always in the context of the possibilities opened by his findings at the preceding level. Of course, this requires materials in each area that encourage a progression. That is, once the child has answered the previous question, he will be likely to ask himself a new question.

The curriculum designer also should provide materials centering on problems that create conflicts in the minds of students and thus impel them to seek richer structures. These problems will include tasks that are suitable to the next structure (e.g., conservation tasks for the preoperational child). Such tasks stimulate the student to develop and coordinate the mental operations needed to perform them.

Second, Piaget's theory encourages the curriculum designer to produce materials that appeal simultaneously to students who are at different stages and operate on different levels within stages (e.g., students who recognize conservation of amount but not of length or weight). This calls for a multilevel curriculum consisting of (1) situations that can be experienced more deeply, or less, by different students, and (2) problems with varied solutions. For example, a session or chapter on the origins of the Industrial Revolution might focus on (1) technological inventions, (2) economic forces, and (3) population changes. The most advanced students probably would consider all three sets of factors, and the least advanced only the first set.

Critique   Piaget may be criticized on a number of counts. Too often he fails to design his observations and experiments care-

---

[21]"Piaget Takes a Teacher's Look," pp. 23–24.

fully enough to exclude alternative interpretations.[22] Again, although the sequence of stages by and large has been confirmed, the stages themselves are less distinct than he imagines. He tends to underestimate the competence of children at a given age. Most children, for instance, are born more coordinated than he claims.[23] They also are less egocentric. Piaget seems to underestimate children's competence as a result of questioning them too abstractly and questioning limited samples. Children generally think in a context, and several researchers have found that, when Piaget's tests are redesigned to embody situations more familiar to children, a far larger number of them answer correctly.[24]

Again, Piaget focuses on the individual (considered as representative, not unique) rather than the group and on cognitive rather than emotional development. Thus, his message to educators centers mostly on the acquisition of knowledge. He is inclined to undervalue the part played in intellectual development by language and personal relations, especially relations within the family.[25] He also tends to underestimate the contribution of formal schooling. For example, it has been found that concrete operations actually can be taught to children in the preoperational stage.[26] Again, although he advocates socialization as a way to reduce egocentrism, he fails for the most part to consider the pervasive influence exercised on children by their culture. Finally, his broad theory of development needs to be complemented by learning theories that pinpoint the effects of specific stimuli (such as cues, rewards, and punishments) on the general formation of mental structures.[27]

Finally, although Piaget's theory of equilibration has heuris-

---

[22]P. Bryant, *Perception and Understanding in Young Children: An Experimental Approach* (New York: Methuen, 1974).

[23]*The Competent Infant*, ed. W. Stone, H. T. Smith, and I. B. Murphy (London: Tavistock, 1974).

[24]Margaret Donaldson, *Children's Minds* (London: Fontana, 1978), p. 44.

[25]Boden, p. 159.

[26]Charles J. Brainerd, "Learning Research and Piagetian Theory," in *Alternatives to Piaget: Critical Essays on the Theory*, ed. Linda S. Siegel and Charles J. Brainerd (New York: Academic Press, 1978), pp. 69-110.

[27]Philip A. Cowan, *Piaget with Feeling: Cognitive, Social, and Emotional Dimensions* (New York: Holt, Rinehart and Winston, 1978), p. 323.

tic value, since it encourages psychologists to look at thought and action as self-regulative adaptations to the environment,[28] it needs to be clarified further if it is to be of more use to education.[29] For example, in his account of equilibration Piaget uses the term "accommodation" to mean both (1) the recourse of the organism to some structure it employed in the past and (2) the modification by the organism of a structure in current use. Thus, faced with a mathematical problem, the student may accommodate either by using a method that has served him before or by changing his present method. The latter response usually will be more creative. If the student radically changes his current method, he may well move toward a new stage or substage. If he uses an old method, he will not. The teacher, too, must perform two different tasks: help the student recognize when the old method still is applicable, and help him invent a method when it is not. The two responses, conservative and creative, need to be conceptualized separately and differently.

These criticisms, however, must be seen in the light of Piaget's achievements. At both observational and theoretical levels Piaget has contributed greatly to our understanding of intellectual development. His synthesis of philosophy, biology, psychology, and other branches of knowledge anticipates the interdisciplinary approach of current cognitive science. His work has stimulated much research and challenged many cherished educational beliefs, such as the alleged desirability of accelerated development and the presumed importance of early reading and writing. His work also was a source for the science programs and discovery learning theories of the 1960s. Again, despite his avowed interest in the universal "epistemic subject," Piaget's writings are filled with insight into, and affection for, particular children.

---

[28]Boden, pp. 161-162.

[29]Sophie Haroutunian, "Piaget: Adaptation and Equilibrium" [essay review of Piaget, *Biology and Knowledge*] *Harvard Educational Review*, **49**:1 (February 1979), 93-100; William E. Doll, Jr., "A Short Note," 189-192; and Sophie Haroutunian, "The Constraints of Explanatory Models, or: Even Piaget Can't Say Whatever He Likes," *Educational Theory*, **31**:2 (Spring 1981), 193-195. See also Christine Chaillé, review of Piaget's *The Development of Thought* and *The Grasp of Consciousness*, *Harvard Educational Review*, **49**:1 (February 1979), 101-105. For further comment on Piaget, see my *Logic and Language of Education* (New York: Wiley, 1966), pp. 90-98.

Kohlberg: The Development of Moral Thinking

Building on work done by Piaget in the early 1930s, Lawrence Kohlberg has proposed a theory of the development of moral thinking. Every individual, he says, passes through an "invariant sequence of stages." Each stage is marked by a distinctive mental structure, expressed in a special form of moral reasoning. Each stage, too, is morally more advanced than the preceding one.

Kohlberg identifies seven stages of moral development. These consist of three pairs of stages, representing "preconventional" moral thinking (stages 1 and 2), "conventional" moral thinking (stages 3 and 4), and "principled" moral thinking (stages 5 and 6), followed by a seventh stage of "religious" thinking.[30] During the preconventional stages children have no idea of moral rules or standards. For children in stage 1, the right thing to do is whatever avoids punishment, and in stage 2 it is whatever meets their immediate needs. During the conventional stages children regard morality as a set of social rules and expectations. In stage 3 (the "good boy—nice girl orientation") the right thing is to please and help others; in stage 4 (the "law and order orientation") it is to do one's duty and obey authority. During the principled stages, conventional morality is reassessed in the light of deeper moral values. In stage 5 a person believes that by and large the right thing is what promotes the general welfare. In stage 6 right action consists in following universal principles of justice and respect for others regarded as ends in themselves. In stage 7 the "religious orientation" combines these principles with a perspective on life's ultimate meaning.[31]

Each form of moral reasoning, says Kohlberg, is the product of a distinct cognitive structure, an "organized system of assumptions and rules about moral-conflict situations which give

---

[30]The six stages are set out in many of Kohlberg's writings. See, for example, the appendix to *The Philosophy of Moral Development: Moral Stages and the Idea of Justice* (San Francisco: Harper & Row, 1981), pp. 409-412. The seventh stage is presented in ch. 9 of this book.

[31]"Moral Development, Religious Thinking, and the Question of a Seventh Stage," ibid., p. 344.

such situations their meaning." Cognitive structures are not innate but result from the interaction of the human organism with its "social environment"—an environment consisting, for Kohlberg, of "opportunities . . . for role taking, for acting as if other entities are like the self but other than the self."[32] The function of moral reasoning is to resolve the conflicting claims of self and others.

There comes a time, however, when the form of reasoning produced by a certain structure no longer can perform this function. The individual then is out of "equilibrium" with his environment. As the individual strives to restore equilibrium, he or she may develop a new, more inclusive structure and hence a more adequate form of reasoning. The new structure is created by the twin processes of "differentiation" and "integration"—or, as Kohlberg puts it,[33]

a dual process of differentiating out of the situation new aspects not previously evident and a reintegration of all presently recognized aspects into a coherent whole which serves the same function as the previous structure but supersedes it by virtue of its more satisfactory state of equilibrium.

Kohlberg claims that his theory not only is psychological but "moral-philosophical." The theory states not just that people do in fact "prefer the highest stage of [moral] reasoning they comprehend," but also that this stage is "'objectively' preferable or more adequate" than its predecessor "by certain moral criteria.[34] What are these criteria? Kohlberg mentions, among others, the "formal" criteria of differentiation and integration.[35]

---

[32]Dwight Boyd and Lawrence Kohlberg, "The Is-Ought Problem: A Moral Perspective," *Zygon*, **8**:3-4 (September-December 1973), 361.

[33]Ibid., pp. 361-362.

[34]Lawrence Kohlberg, "The Claim to Moral Adequacy of a Highest Stage of Moral Judgment," *Journal of Philosophy*, **70**:18 (October 25, 1973), 633.

[35]Ibid., pp. 636-637. Kohlberg also states that "Moral thought . . . seems to behave like all other kinds of thought. Progress through the moral levels and stages is characterized by increasing differentiation and increasing integration, and hence is the same kind of progress that scientific theory represents." "Indoctrination Versus Relativity in Value Education," *Zygon*, **6**:4 (December, 1971), 304.

With each stage, he says, rights and duties alike become more differentiated and also more integrated. At stage 5, for instance, people are considered to have natural rights that society *ought* to respect. Hence, natural rights have become differentiated from socially awarded rights. Again, at stage 6, any right that a person possesses creates of itself a corresponding duty for another person. Here rights and duties are "completely correlative" and hence "better integrated" than at the previous stage, where duties are "what one has contracted to fulfill in order to have one's own rights respected."

What more does Kohlberg say to educators? He says that every child should be educated to attain the highest stage possible of moral reasoning. His program, he maintains, is both psychologically correct (since the child in fact prefers the higher stage)[36] and morally desirable (since the higher stage is morally better). His program also allegedly avoids the twin evils of moral indoctrination and moral relativism. It excludes indoctrination, because the higher stage already is latent in the child and needs only to be drawn out. In Kohlberg's words, "The child's preference for the next level of thought shows that it is greeted as already familiar, that it is felt to be a more adequate expression of that already within."[37] Finally, his program avoids moral relativism because the sequence of stages is universal.

What can I do as a teacher to stimulate moral growth? Kohlberg recommends that I facilitate class discussion of moral conflicts that students can resolve only by thinking at a stage higher than the one they are accustomed to.[38] If students come

---

[36]"Children . . . often comprehend the stage one higher than their own and occasionally two stages higher, although they cannot actively express these higher stages of thought. If they comprehend the stage one higher than their own, they tend to prefer it to their own." Lawrence Kohlberg, "Education for Justice: A Modern Statement of the Socratic View," *The Philosophy of Moral Development*, p. 46.

[37]Ibid.

[38]Lawrence Kohlberg and Elliott Turiel, "Moral Development and Moral Education," in *Psychology and Educational Practice*, ed. Gerald S. Lesser (New York: Scott, Foresman, 1971), pp. 410-465; Elliott Turiel, "Conflict and Transition in Adolescent Moral Development," *Child Development*, **45**(1974), 14-29; Paul Sullivan, "Moral Education for Adolescents," in *Moral Education: A First Generation of Research and Development*, ed. Ralph L. Mosher (New York: Praeger, 1980), pp. 166-170.

up against the limits of their current outlook (especially as they hear the counterarguments of other students), and if they feel the pull of a more enlightened outlook, they are more likely to move toward the new view. As a teacher I can assist discussion in two ways. First, I can present the moral conflict itself. Films (such as *The Godfather, Deliverance, On the Waterfront,* and *Serpico* for adolescents) can be very powerful stimuli to discussion. Second, I can sharpen the discussion by (1) supporting and clarifying those arguments that are a stage above the current lowest stage and, (2) when these arguments are understood, challenging that stage and clarifying the arguments of the next stage.

Kohlberg adds, however, that it is not enough to modify classroom practices, we also must reform the schools themselves. Schools, he says, must become "just" and "democratic" institutions in which students have a real voice in governing themselves.[39] Does Kohlberg believe that the experience of school democracy will stimulate stage 5 thinking? No. The experience is needed, he says, to give students at stage 4 the motivation and capacity to participate in the civic life of their communities. "The school," he maintains, "can offer a chance for experience in making a just community [that is] immeasurably easier, safer, and less frustrating than the experience of adult participation in society."[40] At the same time, he recognizes that the experience will not transfer readily to civic life unless the community itself becomes more participatory.

Critique   Kohlberg may be faulted in several respects.[41] First, he fails to prove that the sequence of his stages is progressive.[42]

---

[39]Lawrence Kohlberg, "High School Democracy and Educating for a Just Society," in *Moral Education,* pp. 20-57. For research reports on experiments in high school democracy, see ch. 3 and chs. 15-18 in the same book.

[40]Ibid., p. 35.

[41]Since I am interested in Kohlberg as a philosopher rather than a psychologist, I will not discuss the status of his empirical findings. For comprehensive comment by Kohlbergians on some of these findings, see *Moral Education.*

[42]As one critic has put it, "Kohlberg's philosophical machinery seems to me not always to engage effectively with the load of fact to which he wishes to hitch it." Richard G. Henson, "Correlativity and Reversibility," *Journal of Philosophy,* **70**:18 (October 25, 1973), 648.

He states that each stage is more structured than its predecessor and in this respect objectively better. To identify an increase in structure, he uses the criteria of "differentiation" and "integration," which, he claims, are "formal" and "content-independent." In his view, each criterion specifies a standard property that each stage can be shown to possess to a different degree.

Yet neither criterion is defined strictly enough to pick out such a property.[43] Thus, when Kohlberg says that stage 5 thinking is more "differentiated" than that of stage 4, because it separates natural from social rights, he fails to show that this separation represents a *degree* of anything. As he applies it to stage 5 thinking, "differentiation" *means* the separation of natural from social rights, and no more. It does *not* describe a standard property that this stage and others instantiate. Similarly, when applied to stage 6, "integration" means no more than the correlation of rights and duties. In short, Kohlberg's criteria are not spelled out clearly enough to denote anything more than the phenomena to which they are applied. Since they do not pick out properties independent of the phenomena, they cannot be used to evaluate these phenomena. Hence they do not show that each stage is more structured than the one preceding.

Second, Kohlberg's theory is refuted by his own data. After stage 4, he says, people question conventional morality and adopt a "social contract" morality. Yet his own evidence shows that at this point people go in many different directions. Some even regress to the egoism of stage 2. Thus, Kohlberg not only fails to show that stage 5 is *preferable* to stage 4, he also fails to show that it is *preferred*. Hence he is not entitled to claim that people will adopt stage 5 reasoning if they are exposed to it.[44]

Third, Kohlberg deals with only one, albeit central, aspect of morality—that of duty and obligation. He does not consider the teaching of rules and virtues, the cultivation of habits, or the projection of the consequences of one's actions. Yet unless rules and virtues are taught, how can students question the validity of the rules and virtues they follow and thus move upward

---

[43]See, for example, Israela Ettenberg Aron, "Moral Philosophy and Moral Education: A Critique of Kohlberg's Theory," *School Review,* **85**:2 (February 1977), 206-207.

[44]See Gilbert Harman, "Moral Relativism," *The New Republic,* 3,499 (February 3, 1982), 34–37.

through stages 2, 3, and 4? Yet again, since, as Kohlberg himself acknowledges, most members of our society do not get further than stage 4, would it not be wise to teach them the conventional morality expected of people at this stage? Unless we teach the basic moral code needed to maintain society, society surely will deteriorate.[45]

Kohlberg now in effect concedes a certain validity to this last charge, for in recent essays he has maintained that the goal of moral education should be, not the attainment of the fifth stage of principled moral thinking, but rather "a solid attainment of the fourth-stage commitment of being a good member of a community or a good citizen."[46] At the same time, however, his latest book[47] is a sustained plea for the pursuit of, and education in, principled moral reasoning. Kohlberg cannot consistently pursue the twin goals of moral indoctrination and the purportedly objective study of moral reasoning. If his program for developmental education is to continue to make progress, he must choose between these goals.[48]

Nevertheless, Kohlberg deserves our admiration for pursuing an ambitious research program that combines philosophic argument with empirical investigation.[49] His endeavor deserves to be imitated by other researchers who trivialize their studies

---

[45]See, for example, Cornel M. Hamm, "The Content of Moral Education, or In Defense of the 'Bag of Virtues'," *School Review*, **85**:2 (February 1977), 222ff.

[46]"High School Democracy and Educating for a Just Society," p. 28. See also "Educating for a Just Society: An Updated and Revised Statement," in *Moral Development, Moral Education, and Kohlberg: Basic Issues in Philosophy, Psychology, Religion, and Education*, ed. Brenda Munsey (Birmingham, Ala.: Religious Education Press, 1980), pp. 455-470.

[47]*The Philosophy of Moral Development.*

[48]See, for example, Alan L. Lockwood, "Bedding Down in Democratic High Schools" [review of *Moral Education*, ed. Ralph L. Mosher], *Harvard Educational Review*, **52**:2 (May 1982), 210–211. For further criticisms of Kohlberg, see Dennis M. Senchuk, "Contra-Kohlberg: A Philosophical Reinterpretation of Moral Development," *Educational Theory*, **31**:3-4 (Summer/Fall 1981), 259-273; Harvey Siegal, "Kohlberg, Moral Adequacy, and the Justification of Educational Interventions," ibid., 275-284; and Bill Puka, "Moral Vision: As Kohlberg Sees It" [review of *The Philosophy of Moral Development*], *Harvard Educational Review*, **53**:1 (February 1983), 68-73.

[49]For a critical review of Kohlberg's research program, see D. C. Phillips and Jennie Nicolayev, "Kohlbergian Moral Development: A Progressive or Degenerating Research Program?" *Educational Theory*, **28**:4 (Fall 1978), 286-301.

unwittingly by ignoring the philosophic assumptions on which they rest. Again, Kohlberg has done the cause of moral education a signal service by articulating and testing an alternative to the well-tried approaches of formal indoctrination and values clarification. In summary, notwithstanding the faults in his theory, Kohlberg has proved himself a worthy follower of Piaget, and one from whom much may still be expected.

Chomsky: The Structure of the Mind

Noam Chomsky is an outstanding linguist, an unusual philosopher, and a controversial spokesman on world affairs. I consider him here as a philosopher.[50]

Chomsky agrees with Piaget that the mind has its own structures for processing experience. Unlike Piaget, however, he insists that these structures are innate rather than constructed, and that they need only the slightest environmental trigger to develop.[51] Whereas Piaget picks out the dramatic, constructive achievements of childhood, such as the discoveries of the permanence of objects and the conservation of amount, Chomsky dwells on the abstract internal rules that he believes are responsible for the child's linguistic output. Where Piaget studies all forms of cognitive (or thinking) behavior, Chomsky focuses on language use. For Piaget, the capacity for language use develops in tandem with other cognitive capacities; for Chomsky, each faculty is *sui generis* and develops independently.

For our purposes the essence of Chomsky's theory may be stated as follows. (1) The human mind is a structure of substructures, each responsible for a distinct form of understanding or expression. (2) The mind is preprogrammed genetically, but this program, though it sets limits to the mind, also makes possible its achievements. (3) The substructure responsible for language use consists of a finite set of rules capable of generat-

---

[50]The philosophy of structuralism should not be confused with the American school of "structural linguistics," whose empirical, atheoretical approach to the study of language Chomsky rejected.

[51]See *Language and Learning,* ed. Piattelli-Palmarini, especially the Foreword by Howard Gardner.

ing an infinite number of different utterances, written and spo-
ken. (4) To develop a theory of language, one must ask what
basic rules need to be postulated to explain the observed features of language use.[52] I now will expand on these statements.

1.   According to Chomsky, the mind is a highly differentiated
system or structure. Like the body, it is a system of "organs" or
"faculties," one being the faculty for language use.[53] These faculties evolved gradually and now are biologically given. Each
faculty enables us[54] to accomplish a great deal on the basis of
relatively limited experience. The faculty for scientific thinking,
for example, enables us to construct and understand theories
that explain far more than the evidence available. The mathematical faculty allows us to comprehend and elaborate the
properties of numbers we have not counted. With the aid of the
music faculty we can create and appreciate works that are very
different from those we have heard before.

As a philosopher, Chomsky belongs to the tradition of the
Continental idealists René Descartes, Gottfried Leibnitz, and
Immanuel Kant. Like them, he believes that the mind is
equipped at birth with certain principles for organizing experience. Such principles dictate not the content but the general
form of experience—for example, that it will be the experience
of a world of persisting[55] persons and things located in defina-
ble space and time. For Kant, these principles incorporate such
basic concepts as "cause," "substance," and "quantity." For
Chomsky, they are the systems of rules underlying the different
mental organs or faculties. Like the philosophic idealists,
Chomsky insists that we know a great deal, independently of
experience, that experience can do little more than confirm.

---

[52]In this section I focus on Chomsky's main achievement, his theory of language. On other "organs" of the mind he has so far had little to say.

[53]"The Ideas of Noam Chomsky," in *Men of Ideas,* ed. Bryan Magee (New York:
Viking, 1978), pp. 215-217.

[54]By "us" here I mean the human being as such rather than this or that particular person. Clearly, not everyone can understand the general theory of relativity,
and at the time perhaps only one person could have created it. Nevertheless,
each of us has gifts, and each of us in our own way achieves far more than
experience alone, unorganized by mental structures, would allow us.

[55]"Persisting" is used here as opposed to "momentary" or "intermittent."

Most of this knowledge, such as our knowledge of the rules of language, is unconscious.[56] It is the mission of the human sciences, he says, to bring this knowledge to light, and the mission of philosophy to declare its significance for humankind.

2.   *Each of us,* holds Chomsky, *is programmed genetically to think in certain ways.* The basic structures of the mind reflect this programming. Whatever these structures will not accommodate remains closed to us; it cannot be understood or expressed. Does this genetic program fetter or free us then? It does both, says Chomsky, but mainly it frees us. Without it, we could do nothing that is distinctively human.[57] With it, we have civilization. For example, the rules of language prevent us from saying certain things, yet without those rules we could not utter a single sentence. This is not to deny that we might achieve more with other structures. Martians or other beings may have them; we ourselves may evolve them; yet these structures too will have their limits.

3.   *Governing the language faculty is a set of basic rules from which all permissible utterances in the language are generated.* Since these rules are too abstract to represent here, let us take a limited rule and show how it presupposes more basic rules. Consider the process of forming questions in English. It has been found that when a sentence[58] has a name in it, we generally can question that name. If I say, "I met Bill," I can ask, "Whom did I meet?" Similarly, if I say, "He thinks that he met Bill," I can ask, "Whom does he think he met?" And so on. So let us propose the rule: "To form a question, take the position in which a name can appear, put a word in it like 'Who' or 'Whom' or 'What,' and move the word to the front of the sentence." When we apply this rule, however, we find that, although it covers many utterances, in some cases it fails. Suppose I say, "He wonders who met Bill," and then I question "Bill." The

---

[56]For Chomsky, language "is a product of human intelligence, created anew in each individual by operations that lie far beyond the reach of will or consciousness." *Reflections on Language* (New York: Pantheon, 1975), p. 4.

[57]"The Ideas of Noam Chomsky," p. 214: "These achievements are possible for us precisely because of our rigid programming. Short of that, we would not be able to accomplish anything of the sort."

[58]A sentence is a grammatically self-contained unit of speech.

result is, "Whom does he wonder who met?" We know at once that this is not an English sentence, because it is ungrammatical. Is it totally meaningless, then? Not at all. If this string of words *were* a sentence, it would mean, "About whom does he wonder who met him?" So there must be some deeper rule of language that prevents us from uttering the words. Since there will be other rules too, it makes sense to ask how a theory of the English language, and indeed of language as such, might be constructed.

4. Since we know little as yet about the ways in which the rules of language are realized physically in the brain, we must theorize about a structure of rules we cannot observe. The facts of language, Chomsky says, are determined by two elements: the basic rules of language (which are determined genetically) and information from experience. If we can discern, in the facts of language, features that are absent from the input of experience, it is reasonable to suppose that these features result from the basic rules of language. We therefore ask: What basic rules must be at work if these features are to occur? If, for example, we find some particular rule at work in English, we investigate German and Japanese to see if it is at work there. If it is not, we seek to formulate some more inclusive rule that will account for features of all three languages. If it does so, we then see whether it is obeyed in the aboriginal languages of Australia and the Amazon. And so on. Eventually we propose a rule to cover certain features of all possible human languages. This rule will belong to the universal grammar, which all particular grammars realize.[59]

Let us now look at language more concretely. Chomsky maintains that language use is highly creative. Each of us, he says, can utter and understand an infinite number of sentences he never has heard or seen before. The sentence you are reading

---

[59]*Reflections on Language,* p. 29: "Let us define 'universal grammar' (UG) as the system of principles, conditions, and rules that are elements or properties of all human languages not merely by accident but by necessity—of course, I mean biological, not logical, necessity. Thus UG can be taken as expressing 'the essence of human language'. . . . UG will specify what language learning must achieve, if it takes place successfully. . . . Each human language will conform to UG; languages will differ in other, accidental properties."

now, or any sentence in any magazine, may be one you have not read before, yet you can recognize it as a grammatical English sentence. What enables you to do so? According to Chomsky, it is because what you possess are not the actual sentences of your language but *the system of rules for making sentences*. Most sentences we say or write we have not heard or seen before. We invent them spontaneously according to rules that we share with other speakers of the language. We cannot verbalize these rules, and no one has taught them to us. Yet they are the source of our amazing linguistic versatility.

Many of these rules are subtle and complex. To understand a sentence, for example, we often have to supply missing information. Thus, in the sentence, "Bill wants to play," there is no subject expressed for the verb "play," yet we know that the implied subject is Bill. Again, in the sentence, "Bill wants Betty to play," although there are now two nouns to consider, we know at once that Bill is the subject of "wants" and Betty of "play." This observation may seem obvious, yet further thought reveals that in order to understand the sentences, we must know just where to look for the intended subjects. In the sentences above we look to the noun most closely preceding the verb in question. But now take the contrasting sentences.

Bill told Betty to play the record.
Bill was told by Betty to play the record.

In the first, Betty is to play the record and, in the second, Bill. Although the nouns Bill and Betty occur in the same order in both sentences, the subject of "play" is understood differently. Here sentence structure (based on the voice of the main verb, active or passive) and not just word order, enables us to recognize the subjects of the verbs.

How do children handle such rules? According to Chomsky, they construct many themselves, reconstruct them as new evidence comes in, and eventually put together an internalized system of rules—a grammar[60]—that agrees with the facts of language. The basic rules they use in this task are innate; the

---

[60] A grammar is a system of rules that determine what a sentence is, what it means, and how it is to sound.

rest they create in response to the speech they hear around them.[61] Once they have made rules on the basis of what they have heard, they apply them as widely as possible. Often a child begins by using the correct forms of common *irregular* verbs. "It ran away," the child says, or "I went out," or "It broke." But then, after learning just a few *regular* past tenses (such as "walked" and "helped"), the child makes and applies a new rule. "It runned off," he or she declares, "I goed out," and "It breaked." In a relatively short time the child replaces the forms he or she has used with forms created according to a rule he or she has just abstracted.[62]

Language Education

By the time they enter school, most children have formed their basic grasp of the language. What activities will help them most to improve that grasp? Carol Chomsky suggests reading and listening to books read aloud.[63] Since written language is more complex than speech, children who read widely or have books read to them are exposed to more constructions that may be uncommon in their everyday conversation.[64] Throughout the elementary school, teachers should read to children and encourage them to read books as complicated as they are willing to try. For this purpose children's literature is more valuable than standard textbooks and materials. Children should read

---

[61]Noam Chomsky, *Language and Responsibility,* based on conversations with Mitsou Ronat, trans. John Viertel (New York: Pantheon, 1979), p. 98: "In a given linguistic community, children with very different experiences arrive at comparable grammars, indeed almost identical ones, so far as we know. . . . Each child has a different experience—but in the end the system is essentially the same. As a consequence we have to suppose that all children share the same internal constraints which characterize narrowly the grammar they are going to construct."

[62]Carol Chomsky, "Creativity and Innovation in Child Language," *Journal of Education,* **158**:2 (May 1976), 16. (Carol is Noam Chomsky's wife.)

[63]Ibid., pp. 17-21.

[64]For example, compound sentences, compound subjects, compound predicates, relative clauses, subordinate clauses found in different positions, adverbial phrases, complex structures (e.g., "I want Jim to keep his boots off the floor I've just cleaned," or "It was exciting to see so many people assembled in one place listening to a speaker tell them how to improve their health").

independently and for pleasure. The sooner they form their own tastes and choose their own books, the better. As Carol Chomsky puts it,[65]

In the long run what the child needs to learn to do, if he is to grow up into a reading adult, is to read for his own purposes. Whether it is for pleasure, or to find out about something, or for whatever reasons, it has to be out of internal motivation and not because someone else requires it of him.

Before they can read, says Carol Chomsky, most children can invent their own spellings. Spelling is a more concrete activity than reading, since the word to be spelled usually is known, whereas, in reading, the word to be pronounced first has to be identified. Children of 5 or 6 spell creatively, using letters according to their names or their sounds (if they know them). They represent words as they hear them (e.g., they may spell "see" as "c"). Then they start to write, not to perform a task, but to express themselves. As Carol Chomsky says, the child's "view of the written word is of something that belongs to him, a means of expressing what he perceives."[66] Some children produce a few sentences; others write entire stories.

Children who have written words their own way are at an advantage when they begin to read conventional spelling, since they are experienced in matching words and sounds. They have worked out their connections and are accustomed to thinking for themselves. In learning to read, they form hypotheses about the relation of spelling to pronunciation, alter these hypotheses as new evidence appears, and in due course produce a system of rules that fits the facts. In Carol Chomsky's words,[67]

This hypothesis construction is an active process, able to take the child far beyond the "rules" that can be offered him by the best of patterned, programmed, or linguistic approaches. The more the child is prepared to do for himself, the better off he is.

---

[65] Ibid., p. 21.

[66] Ibid., p. 24.

[67] Ibid., p. 23.

The school, then, should encourage children to write before they learn to read, and to create their own spellings before they write:[68]

Creativity . . . is the order of the day in children's handling of language. Their talent for innovation is a basic one. Our best efforts in teaching might well be directed toward providing a fertile environment in which this natural capacity can flourish.

After age 6, language learning proceeds at a slower rate until adulthood. Nevertheless, there seems to be a cutoff point in adolescence. It is well known that a child who starts learning a new language before adolescence is more likely to speak it with native fluency than one who starts learning it later. Similarly, there are elements of one's natural language that must be acquired, it seems, before adolescence if they are to be acquired at all.[69] It therefore is all the more important to stimulate language development during the early school years.

Critique   Having considered some merits of Noam Chomsky's theory, I now will raise several objections to it. First, the theory deals better with syntax than with semantics. Syntax tells us how words are put together to form sentences, and hence what combinations of words are meaningful. Semantics tells us what sentences mean. What a sentence means, Chomsky says, depends mostly on the sentence as such and hence remains by and large the same throughout the different contexts in which the sentence is used. Yet surely the meaning of a sentence pivots mainly on what the speaker is using the sentence for and hence on what speech act he is performing with it.[70] For example, the sentence, "It's a nice day," when uttered by one stu-

---

[68]Ibid., p. 24.

[69]Ibid., pp. 17ff. Carol Chomsky adds that by examining children's understanding of constructions through psycholinguistic experimentation, "it is possible to analyze children's linguistic progress into distinct stages of development. . . . The range of ages at each linguistic stage is considerable. In our data, for example, we identified five such stages." However, "the general pattern is one of gradual improvement with increase in age."

[70]On speech acts, see Chapter 1, p. 6.

dent, may mean that the day is fine, but when uttered by another, that it's too fine to waste in the classroom.

The function of speech acts, as we have seen, is to communicate. Virtually all utterances are acts of communication—acts in which we convey our thoughts to others and sometimes to ourselves. What we communicate hinges in large part on our intentions (whether to promise, warn, persuade, instruct, and so on) and on the social and linguistic rules governing the speech acts in which such intentions are expressed. What we *mean*, then, when we speak, depends not just on the dictionary meanings of the words we use but on what we are using these words to accomplish—that is, on the *point* of our utterance. Chomsky, however, plays down the use of language for communication and, therefore, does not adequately account for the meanings of utterances. John Searle puts the issue concisely:[71]

So long as we confine our research to syntax, where in fact most of Chomsky's work has been done, it is possible to conceal the limitations of [his] approach, because syntax can be studied as a formal system independently of its use. . . . But as soon as we attempt to account for meaning, for semantic competence, such a formalistic approach breaks down, because it cannot account for the fact that semantic competence is mostly a matter of knowing how to talk, i.e., how to perform speech acts.

In the investigation of language, therefore, the next move should be to combine the study of syntax with the study of speech acts. When this move is completed, Chomsky's theory will throw more light on teaching, which is a persistent, concentrated, formal attempt to communicate.

How does the capacity for language use develop? For Chomsky it is enough to say that the essential knowledge of linguistic rules is coded genetically. But this response is unsatisfactory on two counts. First, even if Chomsky is right, we still want to know precisely what cultural, physical and educational factors trigger the realization of particular linguistic potentials. Second, Chomsky discounts a great deal of empirical

---

[71]John Searle, "Chomsky's Revolution in Linguistics," *New York Review of Books,* **18**:12 (June 29, 1972), 23. (By "semantic competence" Searle means the rules governing the production of meaning.)

evidence to the effect that other cognitive capacities not only develop discontinuously but also incorporate information from the environment.[72] The linguistic capacity seems unlikely to be exceptional. In reply to this point, Chomsky reiterates his innatist thesis; he does not attempt to bridge the gap between his own and the interactionist (Piagetian) approach.[73]

A further objection is that Chomsky's theory treats the rules of grammar as though they were scientific laws. In fact, the rules of grammar must be more than generalizations that describe and predict a person's behavior—as the law of fall, for instance, describes and predicts the behavior of falling bodies. They must be rules that a person actually *follows,* and hence the content of the rules must *cause* his behavior. This causative role of rules can be shown by a simple example. If you explain my driving behavior by saying that I follow the rule, "Drive on the right-hand side of the road," the rule you cite is a statement not about my behavior but about a rule that I have internalized and that causes me to drive as I do.[74] Similarly, if you account for my language behavior by stating that I follow Chomsky's rules of syntax, the rules you quote are statements not about my behavior as such but about rules that I have either inherited or internalized and that cause me to speak and write in the ways I do.

Assuming, then, that rules cause the behavior they are said to describe and explain, how are we to determine whether the rules Chomsky proposes actually do cause the behavior he claims to explain? One way is to ask people whether they follow these rules and see if they agree. (If people have been following these rules unawares, they presumably should recognize the

---

[72]See especially Gardner's Foreword, p. xxvii, in *Language and Learning,* ed. Piattelli-Palmarini.

[73]For an attempt to bridge this gap, see Jean-Pierre Changeux, "Genetic Determinism and Epigenesis of the Neuronal Network: Is there a Biological Compromise between Chomsky and Piaget?" in *Learning and Language,* ed. Piattelli-Palmarini, ch. 8.

[74]John Searle, "Rules and Causation," *Behavioral and Brain Sciences,* 3:1 (March 1980), 37–38: "In the natural sciences hypotheses merely describe and explain; in the explanation of human behavior the rules *cause* the very behavior they describe and explain, and they don't explain the behavior unless they cause it. If the rule is one that people are actually following, then the content of the rule must function causally in the production of the very behavior that the rule explains."

rules when the latter are described to them.) If they disagree, Chomsky would seem to be wrong. True, there may be other tests we can run on his claim. However, he has not proposed any tests to verify that the rules he postulates actually function as rules at all.

Chomsky's notion of a language "organ" is no less ambiguous. An organ that consists of a grammar—an organ made up of rules—cannot govern my behavior in the sense that the heart and the eye "govern" my bodily processes. If my blood flows, it is not because I obey a rule of the heart. When I see things, it is not because I follow rules of the eye. The heart and the eye interact directly with other organs without the intervention of rules. An organ formed out of rules cannot do this. Granted, the brain may contain neuronal structures that correspond to the rules of language, just as it may contain a structure that corresponds to a highway code. Nevertheless, unlike the structures of the heart and the eye, these structures only affect my behavior through the intervention of my *mental representations* of the rules they embody.

For an educator it is disappointing that Chomsky says so little about the linguistic creativity expressed in verse, drama, novels, and essays. Chomsky would reply that the grammar he proposes makes this creativity possible. Perhaps it does, but only in the sense that it makes any permissible utterance possible. What we also would like to know are the rules, if there are any, that lead not just to utterances that are different but to those that are vitally and interestingly new. If we know these rules, we may well be able to take detailed, practical steps in the classroom to foster creative speech and writing.

In its present form Chomsky's theory may seem to be of limited value to education. Indeed, one might argue that if, in a linguistic environment, the language capacity develops fairly much of its own accord, it will need little help from schooling. More optimistically, one might derive from the theory the negative recommendation: Teach nothing that will tend to obstruct this development, or Allow children to follow their own linguistic inclinations. Carol Chomsky, it is true, makes a strong positive recommendation: Allow children to spell for themselves before they write and encourage them to write before

they read. However, as she herself admits, her reco_r
is based more on observation than theory.

Nevertheless, Carol Chomsky's recommenda
something very important about the Chomskyan endeav
that it is more than a theory, it is a *research program*. Not only has
the theory gone through many changes, it has generated a large
amount of research. Carol Chomsky's proposals may not have
been derived from the theory, but the theory encouraged her
observations and made her proposals possible. Because it highlights the linguistic inventiveness of the child, and because it
looks for exact rules to ground this inventiveness, Chomskyan
theory holds considerable potential for the study and practice of
education. Even Chomsky's sternest critics agree that he has
stimulated not only linguists but philosophers, human scientists, and educationists. He has challenged them to examine
more deeply the workings of language in their own fields.

Bourdieu and Bernstein: Class, Culture, and Educational Structure

Structuralists are everywhere in the human sciences. So far I
have discussed two structuralist psychologists and a linguist, all
of whom are likewise philosophers. I now will comment briefly
on two structuralist sociologists who are influencing educational thought.

Pierre Bourdieu is a French sociologist and philosopher interested in the nature and mutual relations of cultures, societies, and individuals. According to Bourdieu, structures arise
because people need order in their experience. All *particular*
structures, however, such as the structure of social classes or the
structure of academic disciplines, are arbitrary. They supply *an*
order, but not one that mirrors the world objectively or meets
universal human needs. Many structures reflect the interests of
the dominant social class, although most people, including
members of that class, are unaware of this. For Bourdieu, then,
the first task of the thinker—and the thinking teacher—is to
question social and cultural "reality," and to understand that
this reality is not natural but already structured.

Bourdieu is especially concerned with the mechanisms of "symbolic" (i.e., nonphysical) domination by which the social order is maintained—the principal mechanism being, for him, education. The educational process, he says, is a "communication system" between the social order and the individual.[75] The educational system "reproduces" and "legitimates" the social order by transmitting knowledge—"cultural capital"—that reflects the world view of the dominant class.[76] Schools are supposed to reward merit alone, regardless of a student's social origin, yet the knowledge they impart is geared mostly to those upper and middle class students who already possess the cultural and linguistic capital to appropriate it. Schools, then, do not reduce existing inequalities; they reinforce them. Teachers and students do not realize this, because they allegedly are unaware of the relations between the class structure and the educational structure.

We are enculturated first by our family and then by the school. Family enculturation produces what Bourdieu calls a "habitus," a system of modes of thinking, perceiving, and acting.[77] Since members of different social classes bring up their children differently, each class has its characteristic habitus, with individual variations. My particular habitus conditions my educational aspirations. Working-class students, for instance, tend to drop out of school because they do not think that further study will get them the better jobs for which their middle class peers are preparing. They also are weeded out by two other mechanisms, says Bourdieu, one being language. Teachers tend to use and encourage upper and middle class speech styles that are apt to alienate working class students from the subject matter being taught. The other mechanism is examinations, which

[75] Pierre Bourdieu and Jean-Claude Passeron, *Reproduction in Education, Society, and Culture,* trans. Richard Nice (London and Beverly Hills: Sage, 1977), p. 91.

[76] Ibid., p. 5: "All pedagogic action . . . is, objectively, symbolic violence insofar as it is the imposition of a cultural arbitrary by an arbitrary power." By "arbitrary" the authors mean "not . . . linked by any sort of *internal* relation to 'the nature of things' or any 'human nature'." "Cultural capital" comprises knowledge, style of thinking, and language.

[77] In Bourdieu's words, a "habitus" is a "generative, unifying principle of conducts and opinions" (ibid., p. 101).

reward the formal thought patterns and linguistic ease that belong to the upper class habitus.

Both in theory and detail Bourdieu illuminates the web of connections among class structure, "cultural capital," and education. Nevertheless, his work is flawed in several respects. His data are limited to the results of linguistic tests given only to humanities students at one French university. He focuses on a single culture—that of the "dominant class"—and he asserts, without adequate evidence, that students receive it passively. He ignores both the working class culture and the opposition of many working-class students to the culture that the school seeks to impose on them. He also takes too much for granted the stability of class and educational structures, both of which have been, and can be, considerably reformed. Finally, he underestimates the proportion of working class students who succeed academically. Were he to test American university students, for example, his results might reflect a "cultural capital" quite different from the one he writes about.

Like Bourdieu, British sociologist Basil Bernstein examines the "reproduction"[78] of the class structure through education, but focuses more closely on the school, regarded again as a communication system. The class structure is reproduced mainly through the school's "code" of control. In Bernstein's words: "Class relations generate, distribute, reproduce, and legitimate distinctive forms of communication, which transmit dominating and dominated codes." The school's codes have two main features: "classification," or the ordering of subject matter; and "framing," or student-teacher relations.[79]

Bernstein postulates four possible codes, categorized according to strong or weak classification and framing. However, he investigates only two of them: the "collection" code and the "integrated" code. The collection code is marked by strong clas-

---

[78]By "reproduction" Bernstein refers to the notion that class relations (1) are expressed in the curriculum and pedagogy of the school and (2) are absorbed by students and thus perpetuated.

[79]Basil Bernstein, "Codes, Modalities and the Process of Cultural Reproduction: A Model," in *Cultural and Economic Reproduction in Education: Essays on Class, Ideology and the State*, ed. Michael W. Apple (London and Boston: Routledge & Kegan Paul, 1982), pp. 304–305.

sification and strong framing. Subjects of study are clearly demarcated and generally traditional—for example, history and mathematics. The teacher is firmly in control. In the integrated code both classification and framing are weak. There are more mixed subjects, and the teacher's authority is more subtle and personal. These two codes socialize students differently. Students socialized in the integrated code, for example, are more socially and occupationally flexible. But both codes reflect middle class ways, and both alienate working-class students. Neither teachers nor students, Bernstein says, are aware of these codes. Why is this?

The codes originate outside the school.[80] The collection code is a mode of communication preferred by managers of physical production, who think in terms of hierarchies of knowledge, skills, and tasks. The integrated code is favored by managers of people, ideas, and symbols (as in personnel relations, public relations, and advertising). These managers tend to synthesize information and to prefer personal approaches. They manipulate ideas and persons rather than physical processes. The current movement within schools from a collection code toward an integrated code reflects a shift of power within the middle class from managers of production to managers of symbols and people.

Critique   Although Bernstein is less comprehensive than Bourdieu, he has given research a theory to explore. The theory, however, has certain weaknesses. Bernstein's categories, such as those of the two codes, tend to be polar opposites that do not interact. Hence he gives a somewhat static picture of the factors at work within the school. Again, Bernstein is highly abstract and (unlike the phenomenologists, for instance) rarely conveys how actual children confront, interpret, and sometimes reject the "cultural capital" transmitted in schools. Nor does he ask what actual groups control curriculum choice. Precisely whose cultural capital, for instance, is embodied in textbooks and TV programs? Precisely whose view of the economy, of social jus-

---

[80]"We see education as a fundamental reproducing and producing agency crucial to, but not in a correspondence relation with, the class regulation of the mode of production, and crucial to the class regulation of modes of social control." Ibid., p. 312.

tice, and of particular historic episodes is presented in class? Again, like Bourdieu, Bernstein concentrates on conflict within a class (in this case, the middle class) and pays little attention to conflict among classes. Nor does he point to social conflict within the school. For him, students on the whole do not resist the educational system but accept it and are molded by it.

Both Bernstein and Bourdieu claim that the abstractness of their theories actually is a virtue, since it separates the researcher decisively from an environment that he or she otherwise would take for granted. Yet they themselves, in the manner of most structuralists, are inclined to identify their own constructs with this environment. Bernstein treats his codes as real things. Bourdieu writes as though all his structures are actual (as opposed to hypothetical) entities. Both ignore important elements in the total process of education. The individual teacher and student, the particular classroom, and even the particular school system frequently are obscured rather than illuminated by the complicated theoretical machinery these sociologists introduce to explain them. Nevertheless, both theorists lead one to think afresh about the elusive links that bind culture, society, and education. Their message is particularly important to philosophers of education; it tells them that they must broaden their subject matter to embrace the structuring role of the culture of which they themselves are part.

Appraisal

As a philosophy, structuralism reflects on the fundamental nature of the human world—individual, cultural, and social—and the sciences which study it. Structuralism rejects the positivist assumption that the human sciences can generalize successfully about the world without radically questioning the way it appears to us. The human realm, including the realm of the school, is deceptive, says the structuralist, because to a much greater extent than the natural world, it already is structured by the mind. To understand the true character of the educational process, and of social and cultural phenomena generally, we must abstract from these phenomena and seek to grasp the underlying structures—both within the mind and outside it—that are responsible for them.

How are these structures formed? Here structuralists diverge. Some of them, such as Chomsky, maintain that the basic structures are innate. The rules of language and of mathematical thinking, for instance, are programmed genetically and, given an appropriate environment, develop more or less of their own accord. The task of education is to allow the child to study subjects in line with the natural growth of the mental structures related to them. Other structuralists, such as Piaget and Kohlberg, insist that children form structures gradually as they interact with their environment. Teachers should allow their students to learn actively so as to create these structures; they should also present materials that elicit mental operations belonging to the structures toward which the students are maturing. Still other structuralists, such as Bourdieu and Bernstein, argue that many structures are cultural, not natural. They are imposed on children by their schools and reflect the world view of the dominant social class.

Basic structures cannot be observed. According to Chomsky, the ground rules of language cannot be discovered by introspection, although eventually scientists may uncover the neuronal structures in the brain that correspond to them. Therefore, he says, we must *postulate* such rules and see whether their consequences can be observed in speech and writing. According to Piaget, the structures of rational thought must be *inferred* from the ways in which children solve problems and answer questions. Since basic structures are natural—being either innate (Chomsky) or biopsychical (Piaget)—the fact that they are unobserved poses a problem only to the scientist who seeks to discover them, not to the teacher who is allowing them to develop. The teacher's task is to encourage the behaviors in which these structures are thought to manifest themselves. For structuralists (such as Bernstein and Bourdieu) who hold that the important structures are cultural, the school is one of those social agencies that lead individuals to believe—mistakenly—that the structures they acquire are natural and immutable rather than reflections of the class system.

Fundamental structures are said to be objective and self-regulating. They are independent of individual human beings and tend to perpetuate themselves. Structuralists who believe in the "naturalness" of these structures welcome this state of affairs. Chomskyans maintain that the deep structures of the mind are the bases of our distinctively human capacities. Without them we could achieve nothing worthwhile. The school, then, must do whatever it can to encourage these structures to develop. Piaget and Kohlberg insist that the structures of intellectual and moral thinking are potentials, not limitations, and that the teacher's task is to facilitate, though not unduly hasten, the transition to ever more advanced structures. Those thinkers who stress the cultural origin of structures (Bernstein and Bourdieu) maintain that these structures tend to repress rather than release human potential. Teachers, administrators, students, all are unaware that they are products of the structures they absorb and perpetuate.

Nevertheless, like any philosophy or movement of thought, structuralism is inadequate in certain respects. Structuralists tend to be overly theoretical, believing that powerful ideas matter more than empirical data. Chomsky has been criticized by philosophers for underestimating the communicative (semantic) role of language, and by scientists for ignoring much experimental work on the brain. Piaget takes science more seriously and has conducted many experiments. Nevertheless he bases his findings on restricted samples of children and does not always design his research tightly enough to exclude alternative explanations of his results. Kohlberg has gathered data from several countries, but some of the data refute his theory; for example, they reveal that after the fourth stage, moral thinking no longer develops uniformly. Bourdieu, again, has tested his theory of education against the responses of a small group of students from a single university.

Structuralists are prone to emphasize general structures at the expense of individual human beings. Chomsky, for instance, does not propose a sequence of stages through which linguistic performance might develop. Even Piaget is interested more in the "epistemic" than in the individual subject—a theoretical bias that seems to have led him to decontextualize many of his test questions, making them more difficult for children to answer. Kohlberg is so committed to his sequence of stages that he has ignored data that clearly refute the order of the later ones. In Bourdieu, structures, and in Bernstein, codes, dominate teachers, students, and others. Both sociologists neglect the actual process of teacher-student interaction through which the social reality of the classroom is brought into being. Both underestimate the extent to which different individuals experience the educational process differently.

Structuralists also tend to elevate structures above human history and social conflict. For Chomsky, the mind's basic structures are laid down genetically. For Piaget, the structures evolve biologically, relatively unaffected by culture or society. Piaget does not inquire, for instance, whether primitive peoples once had, or whether Asians or Africans now have, mental structures different from Europeans. Kohlberg has not examined whether the stages of moral growth have changed in the United States over, say, the last century. Bourdieu's cultural constructs and Bernstein's codes remain largely static. In theory they respond to social change, but it is not shown by example how they do so. For Bourdieu and Bernstein, social conflict takes place only outside the school.

Structuralists tend to ignore instincts and emotions. Neither Chomsky nor Piaget inquires into the effects of emotional security and insecurity on the development of mental structures. This failure is especially surprising in Kohlberg, since moral issues are emotionally loaded and moral development clearly seems to require instinctual control. Neither Bourdieu nor Bernstein examines such issues as the extent to which the cultural conformity imposed by the school involves a repression of powerful instincts, and whether this repression is the same for students of all social classes. Educators who believe in the development of the whole child will be disappointed by the excessive focus of most structuralists on the intellectual and cognitive side of human nature.

Finally, many structuralist theories face conceptual difficulties. Chomsky assumes that the basic rules of language function like scientific laws and that mental organs behave like bodily ones. Such assumptions are problematic, if not untenable. Piaget's model of equilibration is too general to aid biologists and too imprecise to help teachers. Kohlberg's concepts of differentiation and integration are too unclear to serve as objective criteria of moral progress. Bourdieu and Bernstein maintain that the school is affected by social struggle, yet the concepts they apply to the school are inadequate to explain conflicts within the school. Bernstein's codes are polar opposites that do not interact to form other codes. The mechanisms that, according to Bourdieu, maintain the power of the dominant class within the school—linguistic style and examinations—are not connected to other mechanisms and hence are incapable, in Bourdieu's scheme, of entering into conflict with them.

Yet the virtues of structuralism outweigh its faults. Structuralist theories are ambitious and fruitful. They pose important questions (e.g., about the nature of the mind and society) and they stimulate major research programs. They combine philosophy with aspects of science and encourage the synthesis of disciplines. They aim at deep explanations, proposing unobserved and sometimes unobservable structures to account for a wide range of phenomena. They have brought about a renaissance of theory in the human sciences and have encouraged more theoretical approaches in educational research.

Structuralism offers educators more than theoretical understanding. It has generated a variety of healthy educational innovations. The Chomskyan program encourages teachers to let children master language by spelling, writing, and reading for themselves. The Piagetian program advocates letting children discover and reconstruct knowledge, while challenging them to extend their abilities. The Kohlbergian program for moral development is a valuable alternative to the authoritarian and the values-clarification approaches to moral education. The work of Bourdieu and Bernstein leads teachers to ask themselves whether they are imposing a socially biased world view on their students. All in all, structuralism brings to education a special blend of intellectual daring and practical relevance.

Positivism

5

Basic Characteristics

Contemporary positivism[1] began with the logical positivists, a group of scientifically minded philosophers who met regularly in Vienna between the two World Wars. The logical positivists proposed two doctrines that form the backbone of contemporary positivism. First, they said, all genuine knowledge is either scientific or logico-mathematical. All other claims to knowledge, such as those of theology or metaphysics, are only statements of belief and cannot be tested against the facts. Second, all the sciences share a common method: observe the facts, propose generalizations that relate facts to one another, formulate

---

[1]Positivism owes its name to the nineteenth-century French philosopher Auguste Comte. According to Comte, human thought had evolved from a theological stage, through a metaphysical stage, to its present "positive" or scientific stage. One could be "positive" (i.e., certain), he said, only about the findings of science. As sources of knowledge, theology, and metaphysics were unreliable and should be abandoned. Although the logical positivists agreed with Comte on a number of things, they were interested more in logic, language, and physics than in history or social science. See W. M. Simon, *European Positivism in the Nineteenth Century* (Ithaca, N.Y.: Cornell University Press, 1963).

theories to explain these generalizations, and test all generalizations and theories empirically.

The logical positivists were heavily criticized, however, especially for their so-called verification theory of meaning. According to this theory, a statement is meaningful only if it is either true in virtue of the meanings of its terms (like the statements of logic and mathematics[2]) or verifiable empirically (like the statements of science). Critics pointed out that if this theory were correct, it would exclude as meaningless all scientific laws and theories. A scientific law, they said, such as "Every action produces an equal and opposite reaction," cannot be verified empirically, because it covers an infinite number of cases, not all of which can be observed. A scientific theory cannot be verified empirically either, because as a rule it explains observable regularities by postulating as their causes the interactions of entities, such as elementary particles, which, again, cannot be observed.

The logical positivists also were criticized for claiming that all statements about psychical and social phenomena can be translated fully into statements about physical things and processes. Take such statements as "He thinks this class needs a better teacher" or "She doesn't like taking tests." Can these statements be translated without loss into ("reduced" to) statements about overt behavior or bodily processes, such as gland secretions and nerve firings? Not at present, because we do not know what the physical correlates of mental phenomena are. Could they be reduced to such statements at some time in the future? Only if it could be shown that mental states are no more than experiences of bodily states, for example, that what I call a thought is really the way I experience a certain state of my nervous system.

In response to these criticisms, the logical positivists modified their claims and renamed themselves "logical empiricists." Some moved to the United States, where they supported the attempts of many social scientists and educationists to use the methods of the natural sciences. The logical empiricists liberalized logical positivism in two main ways. First, they said, a

---

[2]For example, the statement, "$2 \times 2 = 4$," is true because of the meanings of the terms "2" and "4." If we know the meanings of the terms, we realize the statement is true. Thus, the statement is true by definition.

statement is empirically meaningful if it can be "confirmed" in most test cases (as opposed to "verified" in all possible cases.) For instance, a statement of a scientific law is meaningful if the law is found to hold when tested. Similarly, a scientific theory is meaningful if it yields predictions that are confirmed. Thus, it makes sense to speak of particles and their interactions because photographs taken in accelerators have provided evidence of them. Second, the logical empiricists declared that it is an open question whether the statements of the human sciences ultimately can be expressed in physicalist terms. Nevertheless, they maintained, it is heuristically profitable to assume they can be. Therefore, human scientists should strive for the same objectivity as physicists and biologists.

Positivism in Education

Positivism began to influence the philosophy of education in the early 1950s. Charles D. Hardie's *Truth and Fallacy in Educational Theory,* originally published in 1942,[3] became more widely known. It was followed by D. J. O'Connor's *An Introduction to the Philosophy of Education.*[4] Both authors criticized current educational theories as vague and unscientific and hence as mere expressions of opinion. Both urged philosophers of education to analyze language and concepts in a positivist manner. Both recommended that educational research become more scientific.

Hardie maintained that any genuine educational theory should have the same logical structure as a scientific theory. The theory should consist of (1) premises, (2) hypotheses logically deduced from them, and (3) a "dictionary" of statements defining key terms in the premises. What content should the theory have? Hardie stated that during the educational process the environment acts on "the original nature of man in such a way as to produce valuable changes in behavior."[5] He also stated

---

[3]In 1962, an American edition, with a preface and bibliography by James E. McClellan and B. Paul Komisar, was published by Teachers College, Columbia University.

[4](London: Routledge & Kegan Paul, 1957).

[5]*Truth and Fallacy* (1962), p. 73.

that human nature consists of both modifiable and unmodifiable characteristics. In addition to these propositions about education and human nature, he said, any theory should include statements about modifiable human characteristics and statements about which modifiable characteristics are desired or desirable.

Later, however, Hardie held that it is a mistake to model educational theories on theories in the physical sciences.[6] The essence of a physical theory, he said, "lies in the formal relations connecing the unobserved entities in the postulates." In current educational theories, on the other hand, the postulates, and hence the unobservable entities, remain unconnected. The theories, therefore, are "sterile." What, then, should educationists do? According to Hardie, they should analyze and clarify educational concepts, showing that all such concepts can be given meaning "in terms of what is publicly observable." Unobservable (i.e., mental) entities normally "have no place in educational theory." However, educational theories, modeled on those of the natural sciences, and yielding testable predictions, eventually will be constructed to explain aspects of the mind. "A beginning," he claimed, "has already been made with the factor theories of the mind, for there the postulated factors are linked by formal relations in a manner similar to that of [the] unobservable entities of physics."

Hardie also maintained that general philosophy says nothing meaningful about education, since its statements are neither empirically verifiable nor true in virtue of the meanings of their terms.[7] Philosophy of education as such should be replaced by such studies as "philosophy of curriculum," seen as the philosophic analysis of the concepts of language, mathematics, science, and history. Here, however, Hardie argued from the original, logical positivist theory of meaning, which (as we have seen) has been discredited.

In virtue of this theory of meaning Hardie also excluded ethics from educational philosophy. For the logical positivists,

---

[6]C. D. Hardie, "Reply to George L. Newsome, Jr.," *Studies in Philosophy and Education,* **3**:1 (Summer 1963), 97–98.

[7]C. D. Hardie, "The Philosophy of Education in a New Key," *Educational Theory,* **10**:4 (October 1960), 255–256.

ethical statements are merely expressions of personal feeling and hence of no philosophic interest. I would reply, however, and did, that the exclusion of ethics is unreasonable, since educational thought and practice constantly raise questions of value and policy.[8] Suppose a school board has to vote for or against the presence of police officers in schools. The board will need to weigh such moral principles as the rights of children, the freedom to teach and learn, and authority and control in an educational setting. Philosophers of education are obligated to reflect on the meaning of these principles, since without the clarity and perspective provided by philosophic reflection, the discussion of moral issues at all educational levels will tend to become biased and parochial.

Let us turn now to D. J. O'Connor. According to Israel Scheffler, O'Connor's theory is[9]

a cautious positivism . . . discernible in a qualified formulation of the verification theory of meaning, a sustained attack on metaphysics without attempt to define "metaphysics," a rejection of ethical cognitivism coupled with a recognition of the inadequacies of persuasive theories of ethics, and an assignment of place of honor to scientific as against other paradigms of thought.

What else should be said of O'Connor?

O'Connor's chief concern is the nature of educational theories and their relation to the human sciences. Most educational theories, O'Connor maintains, such as those of Pestalozzi, Froebel, and Montessori, have been no more than rationalizations of successful practice. These theories combine metaphysical claims (e.g., education is "improvement of the soul") with value judgments (e.g., "education according to nature") and statements derived from personal experience. Their main value lies in the practices they recommend. The theories are based, says O'Connor, on the working knowledge of human beings

---

[8]See my "Reply to 'The Philosophy of Education in a New Key' by C. D. Hardie (University of Tasmania)," *Educational Theory*, 12:2 (April 1962), 99–101.

[9]Israel Scheffler, *Reason and Teaching* (Indianapolis: Bobbs-Merrill, 1973), p. 160. By "ethical cognitivism" Scheffler refers to the view that moral judgments are meaningful statements, not merely expressions of feeling (as the logical positivists claimed).

that teachers, like other people, acquire through experience. Such knowledge met the needs of educators until modern times. Now that more is demanded of education, everyday practical knowledge of human nature is an "inadequate theoretical basis [for education] and needs to be supplemented or replaced by the sciences of man."[10]

At the very least, according to O'Connor, the human sciences make our working knowledge of human nature exact and systematic, and they back it with evidence. In some cases they provide new knowledge. Psychology, for instance, provides "well-confirmed hypotheses" about intelligence, perception, learning, motivation, and other matters, and it enables us to make changes in education that can be expected to work. O'Connor calls these hypotheses "genuine scientific theories," though (as he points out) they describe a narrower range of facts, and describe them less exactly, than the theories of the physical sciences.[11] Now that educationists need precise knowledge, he says, only science-based hypotheses deserve the name of "theories." In the case of other intellectual constructs the name "theory" is a "courtesy title."

In reply, I grant that O'Connor is partly correct in his statement that the human sciences "tighten up" everyday knowledge. However, he overestimates their current contribution to education. Instead of "a body of established hypotheses" we find a host of competing hypotheses none of which predicts outcomes with sufficient accuracy. Most of these hypotheses, narrow in scope and imprecise in language, are better regarded as models or generalizations than as theories. Indeed, O'Connor's own account of learning theories refutes the claim he makes for them. If "crucial experiments . . . are still needed . . . to decide between one theory or another," how can these theories be "established hypotheses that enable us to predict the outcome of their application and to explain the processes that we are trying to control"?[12] In summary, for the present at least,

---

[10]*Introduction to the Philosophy of Education*, p. 97.

[11]Ibid., p. 110: "There are several theories of learning all of which seem to be compatible with most of the known facts without being necessitated by them. Not one of them fits the facts so perfectly as to exclude all its rivals."

[12]Ibid., pp. 109–110.

the term "theory" in education deserves to be used in its traditional sense. It can be applied in O'Connor's sense only in the unlikely event that the study of education becomes fully scientific.

Positivism in Educational Research

Positivism has made deep inroads into educational research. *If I am a researcher guided by positivist principles, I seek data that can be verified by any suitably qualified investigator anywhere in the world.* If I observe a lesson, say, or a staff meeting, the data I record must be free of personal interpretation. My observations must match those that any trained investigator, in my place, would record. If possible, my data should be quantitative, but this is not essential. Some empirical findings may be characterized by "degree terms" (e.g., weak, moderate, strong) rather than numbers.

My next step is to generalize from the data, to propose a hypothesis stating that under similar (specified) circumstances, similar states of affairs will be observed. Unlike the phenomenologist, then, I do not carry out case studies of particular teachers or schools. Unlike the hermeneuticist, I do not ask what my data signify about human nature. Unlike the structuralist, I do not postulate an abstract structure and deduce its logical consequences. Instead, I imitate the physicist and the biologist. I propose generalizations about observable patterns, or regularities, in the educational process—generalizations that can be tested rigorously through the observations and experiments of other researchers.

My last step is to construct a theory by deducing a number of generalizations from some higher-level hypothesis. The hypothesis explains why the observed regularities occur and thus brings within a single intellectual scheme a range of facts not previously connected. In many fields of educational research this step is not yet posssible, since there are few, if any, tested generalizations available. Nevertheless, it is an ideal toward which research should strive.[13]

---

[13] An alternative to this step, recommended by many positivists, is to construct a model. This is a group of hypotheses about certain regularities that may occur but for which there is as yet limited evidence. A model is more limited and

The positivist approach to educational research is open to at least three objections. First, positivists assume that educational phenomena, such as teacher-student interactions, have the same meaning for everyone. They play down the fact that each class of students sees these interactions differently, and that each student in a class interprets them in his or her own way. Second, some positivists (e.g., some behaviorists) tend to ignore the inner (psychic) life. Others conceive it as a system of variables (such as memory, motivation, and conscience) which interact not only with one another but also with other variables that are independent of the individual but produce their effects on him or her. Thus, the positivist regards the individual student or teacher as the object not only of external stimuli but also of his or her mental processes. Third, in regarding the world of the school as objective ("out there") rather than continually created by those who participate in it, the positivist is inclined to treat this world as part of the natural order of things. For the positivist, the world of the school is to be described and explained "as is." The positivist does not conceive of ways in which it could be different.

Notwithstanding these criticisms, the positivist approach has been fruitful in some areas of educational research. Today three movements in particular exemplify this approach: behaviorism, cognitive science, and systems analysis. I now examine the philosophic principles of these movements rather than their research achievements.

Behaviorism: B. F. Skinner

Behaviorism was launched during the early 1900s by Ivan Pavlov in Russia and by James B. Watson in the United States. *Its central claim is that, if we want to understand behavior, we should study only its observable, and preferably measurable, aspects.* Behavior here is taken to mean the response of the human

---

tentative than a theory. Its purpose is to guide and stimulate research in a field (such as school organization or teaching styles) by suggesting possible relations between factors.

organism to stimuli mainly from the environment. Behaviorists tend to ignore mental phenomena, such as thinking and dreaming, on the grounds that they cannot be observed. Some behaviorists, however, infer from their experiments that variables, such as motivation, memory, and purpose, intervene between stimulus and response and produce effects on the organism.

Today's leading behaviorist is Burrhus F. Skinner, psychologist, philosopher, and educator. As a philosopher, Skinner is an empiricist, a mechanist, a determinist, and, in some moods, a materialist. As an *empiricist*, Skinner believes that all knowledge comes either immediately, or (in the case of mathematics) ultimately, from sense experience. As a *mechanist*, Skinner holds that behavior is externally caused rather than spontaneously initiated. Behavior is a response to a stimulus rather than the expression of a freely chosen intention. As a *determinist*, Skinner declares that *all* behavior is determined, partly by external stimuli and partly by the past history and present state of the organism. "Students," for instance, "are not literally free when they have been freed from their teachers. They then simply come under the control of other conditions" (e.g., their immediate interests or those of their peers).[14] As an *intermittent materialist*, Skinner maintains sometimes that there are no mental processes, and sometimes that, even if there *are* mental processes, they are of no interest to current science, since they can be neither observed nor controlled. Thus, on the one hand he says, "I see no evidence of an inner world of mental life relative either to an analysis of behavior as a function of environmental forces or to the physiology of the nervous system." And on the other, "No one doubts that behavior involves internal processes; the question is how well they can be known through introspection."[15]

The proper purpose of the human sciences, says Skinner, is to predict and control human behavior. Control is to be exer-

---

[14]B. F. Skinner, *Reflections on Behaviorism and Society* (Englewood Cliffs, N.J.: Prentice-Hall, 1978), p. 143. (This is a collection of Skinner's recent essays.)

[15]Ibid., p. 111. See also: "Psychologists should recognize that with proper techniques one can see learning take place, not in some inner recess removed from the observable performance of the organism, but as a change in that performance itself." B. F. Skinner, *Cumulative Record* (New York: Appleton-Century-Crofts, 1959), p. 252.

cised, however, not on human beings directly but on their environment. Since behavior is a response to the environment, changed environmental stimuli will lead to changed behavior. As Skinner puts it,[16] a science of behavior

turns to the environment—the environment that has produced the genetic endowment of the species through natural selection and that now shapes and maintains the repertoire of the individual through another selective process called "operant conditioning." By analyzing these two roles of the environment we can begin to understand behavior and, by changing behavior, to modify it.

What is "this selective process called 'operant conditioning'"? Skinner distinguishes between "involuntary responses," such as salivation,[17] and "operant responses." An operant response is one that is made for the sake of a reward associated with the response. A pigeon, for example, may learn that, if it pecks at a certain color or presses a bar, it receives a pellet of food. Similarly, much human behavior is operant. As a teacher, for example, I use a certain text year after year because I am rewarded by the ease with which my students learn from it. I insist on punctuality, not primarily because it is a virtue, but because I have found that my class goes more smoothly when it is not interrupted by latecomers. My students too are happy to be on time because they know that, if they are, I will dismiss them the moment the bell rings.

Skinner applied his notion of operant response to education. The teacher's task, he said, is to design the student's environment to encourage operant behavior—in this case, learning—that is in the student's and society's interest. As Skinner puts it, the teacher "acts upon the behavior of the student, and he does so by changing the verbal or nonverbal environment in which the student lives."[18]

Why is the teacher justified in changing the student's environment? Skinner gives us two reasons. (1) The world, he says, is a poor teacher. "The physical environment teaches awk-

---

[16]*Reflections,* p. 85.

[17]As Pavlov showed, when a dog has associated the smell of meat with the ringing of a bell, it will salivate at the sound of the bell alone.

[18]*Reflections,* p. 134.

ward behavior as readily as skilled; the social environment teaches aggression and competition as well as good will and cooperation."[19] (2) The students' own interests are too fleeting to include what they will need to know later in life. The teacher, then, must "contrive conditions"[20] under which students will learn what it is in their long term interest to know. Students are to be molded for their own good. This means that "the teacher should improve his control over the student rather than abandon it. The free school is no school at all." True, some teachers may not be good judges of their students' long-term interests. They tend to teach what comes easily to them. Nevertheless, says Skinner, this fact should not stop educators from spelling out what they believe students need to know. This task, he says, is not so hard to perform. "Suppose," he says,[21]

we undertake to prepare the student to produce his own share of the goods he will consume and the services he will use, to get on well with his fellows, and to enjoy his life. In doing so are we imposing our values on someone else? No, we are merely choosing a set of specifications which, so far as we can tell, will at some time in the future prove valuable to the student and his culture. Who is any more likely to be right?

How is the teacher to bring about learning? Skinner proposes two methods: "contingency management" and "programmed instruction." Contingency management is the careful use of positive reinforcement, or reward, as opposed to "aversive control." In Skinner's view, aversive controls—corporal punishment, low grades, notes to parents, visits to the principal—generally have undesirable consequences, such as apathy, truancy, and vandalism. Positive reinforcement, on the other hand, leads students to do what is right for themselves and others, and produces no backlash.[22] The essence of positive reinforcement is "responding to the student's successes rather

---

[19]Ibid., p. 153.

[20]Ibid., p. 145.

[21]Ibid., p. 147.

[22]"Positive reinforcement has a strengthening effect not only upon the behavior of the individual, but also upon the culture, by creating a world from which people are not likely to defect and which they are likely to defend, promote, and improve." Ibid., p. 11.

than his failures."[23] Instead of criticizing students, the teacher tells them what they are doing right.

Skinner mentions a variety of positive reinforcers ranging from "credit-point systems" to expressions of teacher and peer approval. To be effective, he says, these and other methods must reward progress promptly and consistently. The longer students must wait for their reward, the less they are affected by it. The most successful reinforcers, however, are those that are intrinsic to what the students are doing.[24] They do not lie in praise of teacher or peers but in the satisfactions of learning itself. In Skinner's view, work as such should be rewarding. However, much of what is learned in schools is not of immediate interest to many students. To supplement the limited natural (or intrinsic) satisfaction gained from learning this material, Skinner recommends adding the extrinsic satisfaction of knowing that one is doing well. This, says Skinner, is the special contribution of programmed instruction.

In a Skinnerian program, whether presented by text, teaching machine, or computer, the learning process is divided into the smallest steps possible. Each step is reinforced, in that students see that what they have just learned helps them take the next step. Thus, the program maximizes the frequency of reinforcement and minimizes the likelihood of error. To deter incorrect responses and to ensure that the learner makes (rather than merely recognizes) the correct response, the program excludes multiple-choice questions. It also includes "cues" or "prompts" to make the right answer more accessible. Students not only learn, but because they see that they are making progress, they want to learn. In Skinner's words, "Operant conditioning is a matter of 'acquisition' and 'motivation,' and signs of progress through a program are for most students a highly reinforcing consequence."[25] In addition, the program allows students to learn at their own pace, makes final examinations unnecessary, and releases the teacher from tedious drill, making time for more personal exchanges.

---

[23]Ibid., p. 145.

[24]Ibid., p. 11: "Behavior is most expeditiously shaped and maintained by its natural consequences."

[25]Ibid., p. 136.

In Skinner's view, positive reinforcement should be practiced on a societal scale. The culture itself should be redesigned
by reinforcing the right behavior from infancy onward. The
reason for this is that "people are not in any scientific sense free
or responsible for their achievements." On the contrary, they
are made by their environments. Under conditions of positive
reinforcement they can be made to "*feel* free and worthy,"[26] but
the feeling arises from the reinforcement received rather than
from an inner autonomy. What behavior should be reinforced?
Any behavior, says Skinner, that aids the survival of the culture
and the species. Good and bad, respectively, are what promote
and retard cultural and species survival. In his own words:[27]

*Men and women have never faced a greater threat to the future of
their species. There is much to be done and done quickly, and nothing
less than the active prosecution of a science of behavior will suffice.*

Critique   No thinker considered in this book has been criticized more harshly and by more people than B. F. Skinner. First,
it is said, he generalizes too crudely from the laboratory animal
to the human student and, as a result, many of his statements
are faulty. For Skinner, a reinforcer is an environmental stimulus that tends to increase the probability, frequency, or intensity of the behavior that follows it. In a laboratory, such
stimuli—clicks, smells, tastes—are readily identifiable, but
where are their counterparts in the classroom? Here each student interprets stimuli according to his or her present state and
past experience, and a reinforcer has only as much influence as
he or she allows it. Human learners are too complex, and their
environment is too uncontrolled, for Skinner's generalizations
to be valid.

Skinner's programmed materials work best with young
children and slow learners. To other learners their stimulus
value is questionable. Most students tend to be irritated by having to answer short questions. Knowing that they have answered such questions correctly does not necessarily encourage
them to answer more of them. Skinner also overestimates the

---

[26]Ibid., p. 125.

[27]Ibid., p. 55.

value of immediate reinforcement. Students will work diligently for months and years to master a musical instrument, pass an exam, enter a career. The goal itself, no matter how distant, is their chief spur. Moreover, students tend to disregard or reject information they believe to be false. They may make the correct responses and complete the program, but they do not necessarily accept it or learn from it.

Again, Skinner's belief that human beings are wholly determined by their environments is unconvincing. Skinner fails to recognize a qualitative distinction between habitual behavior and chosen, purposive action. On entering the classroom, for example, I may clean the chalkboard unthinkingly and out of habit. But when a student who has persistently interrupted the class makes one more unnecessary wisecrack, I face a clear choice—ignore him, ask him to keep quiet, or send him to the principal. Whatever action I take is chosen deliberately, and I am responsible for it. Skinner may reply that I choose in accordance with my character, which is the result of my previous environments, and hence that my character (and those environments) determine my action. But in my act of choosing, I am only *influenced* by my character, not determined by it. Moreover, I can, and often do, rise above my character—and overcome my environment. Suppose I am an obliging person and inclined to let people get away with things, yet for once I decide to take a stand and call this student to account for his or her actions. How am I still determined by my past?

Skinner wants education to advance the culture and the species. Yet it is doubtful whether the human beings his schools are likely to produce will do this. Skinner's students are largely passive; they are used to getting the right answers; they do as they have been conditioned to do. But the natural world and the course of events constantly surprise us. They are not always on our side and have to be dealt with. For this we need people who confront the world and seek to change it—people who have ideas of their own, not just ideas that the world has put into them. We need people who are environment-shapers, not environment-shaped.

Skinner's notion of cultural advancement is also suspect on other grounds. There are many qualities that may advance the culture and, arguably, the species—for instance, tolerance, civic participation, and payment of debts—and just as many ways to foster them through education. Which of these qualities we choose will depend on our values. But the planners of Skinner's utopia, those who reinforce the population's behavior—through education, propaganda, or whatever means—will choose what qualities to foster in the light of *their* values. What right do they have to impose their choices on the rest of us? Skinner assumes that the practice of positive reinforcement automatically will improve us and produce good candidates for the planner's role. But the mere fact that people happen to be "improving" is not in itself going to create agreement between us and the planners on what qualities to foster in society's behalf. Supose this "improvement" leads to greater independent-mindedness and a greater taste for debate? In this case, we will be even further from agreement.

These criticisms, however, must be weighed against Skinner's positive achievements.[28] His theory of operant conditioning is a decided advance over earlier behaviorist theories. After finding a way to control the behavior of organisms wihtout manipulating the behavior itself, Skinner produced findings and techniques (e.g., programmed materials) of value to educators, who normally are not allowed to manipulate students directly. Whatever the final verdict on Skinner's scientific findings, his techniques for enhancing learning have proved useful, and they have been improved by testing. Granted, there are dangers in his ideal of a society educated through positive reinforcement. Nevertheless, his plea for planning is more relevant to educators now, in a time of confusion and diminishing resources, than when it first was sounded. One Skinnerian recommendation, much discussed and adopted widely, is the use of behavioral objectives to guide and evaluate learning and instruction.

---

[28]For favorable evaluations of Skinner, see Mary Jane McCue Aschner, "The Planned Man: Skinner," in *The Educated Man: Studies in the History of Educational Thought*, ed. Paul Nash, Andreas M. Kazamias, and Henry J. Perkinson (London: Wiley, 1965), pp. 389–421; and James McClellan, "B. F. Skinner's Philosophy of Human Nature: A Sympathetic Criticism," *Toward an Effective Critique of American Education: Studies in the Educational Thought of James Bryant Conant, Theodore Brameld, Jacques Barzun, B. F. Skinner and Paul Goodman* (Philadelphia: Lippincott, 1968), ch. 5.

Behavioral (Instructional) Objectives[29]

Nowhere is the influence of behaviorism on instruction more evident than in the behavioral objectives movement. During the 1920s with the assistance of Edward L. Thorndike, and during the 1970s under the stimulus of Skinner, groups of educators sought to replace the long-range instructional goals characteristic of education with short-range objectives specifying "overt responses." These responses may be verbal (as in learning to write or say something) or bodily (as in learning to type or swim). Advocates claim that if teachers know exactly what they want students to learn, and how they want them to learn it, students will learn with minimum time and effort. Behavioral objectives can be stated precisely, and the behaviors required can be measured exactly. Hence, it is said, behavioral objectives are an efficient way to help students learn, to gauge how much they learn, and to hold teachers accountable for the learning they bring about.

How is a behavioral objective constructed?[30] First, the teacher chooses an overall goal for a course. If the course is in science, the teacher may choose the goal, "Teaching students to think scientifically." He or she then selects a series of particular objectives for the student to meet in order to develop this capacity. These objectives will consist of observable performances, such as "Propose and test hypotheses relating plant growth to environmental variables." The rationale behind the movement may be stated in four theses.[31]

1. Learning is assumed to be a change in behavior, and it is testable in terms of performance. Students learn the causes of

---

[29]"Instructional" now is the preferred term, since the educational process is intended to produce learning rather than behavior in general. Here, however, I use "behavioral," since I wish to stress the debt to behaviorism.

[30]See Robert Mager, *Preparing Instructional Objectives* (Belmont, Calif.: Fearon, 1962); and Robert M. Gagné, "Behavioral Objectives? Yes," *Educational Leadership*, **19** (February 1972), 394–397.

[31]See George L. Newsome, "Instructional Behaviorism: A Critique," in *Philosophy of Education 1974: Proceedings of the Thirtieth Annual Meeting of the Philosophy of Education Society*, ed. Michael J. Parsons (Edwardsville, Ill.: Philosophy of Education Society, 1974), pp. 336–340.

inflation, say, and show that they have done so by reciting them or writing them out.

2. Courses should have clearly expressed behavioral objectives, stating both the content to be learned and the method of instruction. Without such objectives there is no sound basis for choosing appropriate content and methods, and there is no way to evaluate courses accurately and efficiently.

3. Behavioral objectives imply behavioral criteria for judging the quality of teaching, learning, and subject matter. Instructional methods, content to be learned, and student learning, all are to be stated in terms of observable performances. Teachers' objectives in explaining certain items, and the objectives their students are to attain in order to understand these items, may be stated as follows: After L (number of) lessons, X percent of the students will solve correctly N (number of) problems in M minutes.

4. Instruction and content are related to behavioral objectives as means to ends or as input to output. The student's performance is the end, and the content and instruction are the means used to produce it. The end then is used to judge the success of the means. Content and instruction also are the input leading to the student's output. The input-output model is taken from business and industry, and is justified in the name of (measurable) efficiency.[32] To increase sales and profits, a firm identifies attainable objectives, develops a strategy to reach them, and evaluates the performance of those appointed to achieve them. The objectives motivate and guide managers and improve performance all round.

Critique   Like many endeavors that seek to improve instruction, the behavioral objectives movement has been roundly criticized. For one thing, the use of behavioral objectives, in my view, leads to too much control.[33] Granted, teachers can be held more strictly accountable, learning can be evaluated more relia-

---

[32]See Raymond E. Callahan, *Education and the Cult of Efficiency* (Chicago: University of Chicago Press, 1962).

[33]See my "Behavioral Objectives? No," *Educational Leadership,* **19** (February 1972), 398.

bly, and adults can perceive their children's achievements more accurately—but only if teaching and learning are rigorously circumscribed. The educational process is controlled more tightly at the cost of giving everyone in the system less freedom of choice. Behaviorists want this outcome because they believe that people really are less free than they think. This belief, however, resists empirical proof. Freedom is not something that can be measured in such a way as to confirm the desirability of teaching according to behaviorist principles.

Behavioral objectives have other unfavorable effects. (1) They tend to trivialize learning, since only the more superficial aspects of comprehension generally can be stated in terms of observable performances. To understand the causes of inflation or racial discrimination, it is not enough to be able to state them out loud or write them down. One also must be able to say (for example) why these causes had the effects they did and what might have happened if one or other of the causes had been absent. (2) Behavioral objectives prevent teachers from taking advantage of unexpected learning opportunities that arise during instruction.[34] Suppose a student asks a question that throws new light on a subject or expresses some unanticipated difficulty that other students are experiencing. The teacher who remains loyal to his or her limited objectives has little time to cope with the unexpected challenge. (3) Behavioral objectives may hinder the personal growth of students and teachers. Students are less encouraged to learn in ways that make sense to them or to follow up ideas of their own. They become less independent, less creative. They may also feel the urge to rebel, openly or silently, against the system. So may their teachers.

Although behavioral objectives are capable of having the effects I have described, there still are good grounds for using clearly stated, delimited objectives for certain kinds of learning. The school is responsible for ensuring that all students learn the basic intellectual skills. To meet this responsibility, it would do well to provide a schedule of clearly stated objectives for all students to attain, together with adequate instruments for measuring what is attained. In my view, these objectives should be

---

[34]Leonard Waks, "Re-Examining the Validity of Arguments Against Behavioral Goals," *Educational Theory;* **29**:2 (Spring 1973), 140.

"specified" rather than "behavioral."[35] The school should choose or specify them according to its own educational priorities, and mainly for those subjects it considers basic for all students. In the case of other subjects, teachers themselves should specify objectives both for the individual student and for groups of students. They should be guided by their own educational principles and the abilities and choices of their students.

Cognitive Science[36]

Other scientists in the positivist tradition are studying the human mind as an information-processing system. Under this approach, mental processes and structures—such as the processes by which children acquire new facts and skills, and the structures in which they represent and organize their knowledge—are modeled by means of computer programs, which then are run through computers for researchers to observe the results. The working of the computer is held to simulate the working of the mind. The operations performed by the computer are taken to represent mental processes. In the words of Ulric Neisser, an early advocate of this approach, "The task of a psychologist trying to understand human cognition is analogous to that of a man trying to discover how a computer has been programmed."[37]

Cognitive science, with its exclusive focus on the mind, may seem a far cry from behaviorism, but it is no less positivist in spirit. For the cognitive scientist, the mind is a system of interacting parts and processes, and it is studied in isolation from the self to which it belongs. The system is like a machine. Every interaction, like every interaction in the computer that simulates it, is governed by the program on which the system runs. One studies, not the person thinking, but the mind that thinks—according to rules.

How is a computer used to model the mind? A computer handles symbols. It can accept, store, modify, examine, con-

---

[35]"Behavioral Objectives? No," pp. 399–400.

[36]"Cognitive" refers to those aspects of mental life concerned with the acquisition of knowledge.

[37]Ulric Neisser, *Cognitive Psychology* (New York: Appleton-Century-Crofts, 1967), p. 6.

struct, interpret, and transmit them. A program is a set of instructions (or rules) telling a computer how to handle symbols. Now the mind itself, through such processes as perception, learning, and decision-making, also may be said to handle symbols. To get a computer to simulate these processes, I design a program telling the computer to perform operations that correspond to those I postulate as occurring in the mind. Thus, the program states the rules by which I think the mind works. I then examine whether the computer produces results similar to those I would have expected from an actual mind, and whether it performs any operations, permitted by the program, that I actually had not foreseen. These may parallel processes in the mind itself.

Human information processing originally was believed to take place in a succession of independent stages. Now it is regarded as a complex system of interacting cognitive operations, including those involved in interpretation, attention, perception, memory, comprehension, and action. Information is received by a sense receptor and then encoded and processed in a limited-capacity working memory. The information is interpreted and organized by using a range of skills—attention, rehearsal, encoding, comparison with previous information, and higher level or metacognitive operations—and either deployed immediately or stored in long-term memory.

What do cognitive scientists say to education? They confirm Kant's theory that the mind organizes and transforms its experience. The young mind, they say, is active, exploratory, and astonishingly intricate. *To a large extent children choose what they will perceive.* "Anticipatory schemata . . . prepare the perceiver to accept certain kinds of information rather than others and thus control the activity of looking."[38]

Perception and all other forms of information processing depend on a wide range of cognitive procedures and on data structures organized for recall. Many procedures interlock, in that two or more contain each other as parts. So do data structures. They are said to be "mutually recursive." This means that, contrary to mainstream behaviorism, *the data and procedures involved in learning a subject sometimes cannot be broken*

---

[38]Ulric Neisser, *Cognition and Reality* (San Francisco: Freeman, 1976), p. 20.

*down into independent atomic units but must be defined in relation to
one another.* In studying a subject, children may have to learn
many interrelated things side by side, accepting confusion, cor-
recting earlier learning in the light of later knowledge, and
gradually putting together an interlocking structure in their
minds. Much learning is neither cumulative nor linear. Rather,
it is creative and complex, calling for coordination, a global
view, and toleration of ambiguity and mistakes.[39]

Cognitive scientists focus on the inner processes of learning
rather than on the outcomes of instruction. For them, the prime
aim of instruction is to foster the processes that will produce
certain kinds of results. This may involve inculcating the required cognitive skills, or getting students to use cognitive
skills that they have acquired, or allowing skills they have mastered to function automatically. Researchers seek to identify
cognitive skills and to design instructional techniques for elicit-
ing and presenting them. Three classes of skills are regarded as
especially important: attention, memory, and "metalearning,"
the latter defined as "an individual's awareness, knowledge,
and use of the monitoring of cognitive goals, experiences, and
actions for the purpose of increasing understanding and reten-
tion of learned material."[40]

What strategies does cognitive science propose for problem
solving? Here the contrast with behaviorism is striking. The
behaviorist, interested in outcomes, specifies rules for solving
problems in particular subject areas. The cognitive scientist, on
the other hand, investigates the similar cognitive processes involved in solving a variety of problems.

Cognitive scientists have identified several types of problems, such as those of arrangement, transformation, and insight.
Arrangement problems include anagrams and other problems that
can be solved simply by reordering the basic elements.[41]

---

[39]See, for example, Aaron Sloman, *The Computer Revolution in Philosophy: Philosophy, Science, and Models of Mind* (Brighton, England: Harvester, 1978), ch. 9.

[40]Michael J. Brezin, "Cognitive Monitoring: From Learning Theory to Instructional Applications," *Educational Communication and Technology,* 28:4 (Winter
1980), 230.

[41]See, for example, J. G. Greeno, "Nature of Problem-Solving Abilities," in
Handbook of Learning and Cognitive Processes (Vol. 5), ed. W. K. Estes (Hillsdale,
N.J.: Erlbaum, 1978), pp. 239–270.

Transformation problems, which include logical exercises or puzzles, are solved by redefining the initial situation as a state of affairs in which a goal has to be achieved, and then finding a means to achieve it. *Insight* problems, involving analogies and generalizations from instances, require two skills in particular for their solution. These are (1) representing the problem schematically, and (2) identifying relations among the problem elements and recombining the elements into new patterns.

Consider insight problems. Here the crucial step, according to the cognitive scientist,[42] is to reformulate the problem, sometimes by dropping a traditional assumption. Take this example:

If a standard-sized cigarette can be rolled out of six standard-sized cigarette butts, how many cigarettes can be made and smoked *from 36 butts?*

The assumption to be overcome is that this problem can be solved in one move, giving the answer "6." In fact a second move is required, for the six cigarettes that are smoked yield the butts for one more cigarette. After trying to solve this problem, the student may be given the solution and the assumption to be overcome, and advised to reconstruct the problem without narrowing his or her focus.

Critique   Cognitive science may be criticized philosophically on at least two grounds. First, it assumes that the mind is a mechanism, a system of distinct parts whose interactions comprise the mind's activity. This assumption is justified neither by neurophysiology (which cognitive scientists tend to ignore) nor by common experience. The assumption is made to support the claim that computer programs are adequate representations of the mind. But computer programs do not capture what occurs in the experience of self-directed thought. When I direct my own thinking, I do not tell my mind to do certain things; I do those things myself *with* or *in* my mind. I now am identified with my mind, so that the mind at this point cannot be a separate mechanism. Granted, to explain other forms of thinking—

---

[42]Frank W. Wicker et al., "Problem-Reformulation Training and Visualization Training with Insight Problems," *Journal of Educational Psychology,* **70**:3 (June 1978), 372–377.

unconscious thinking, reverie, thoughts that occur to me—one might propose the existence of a semi-independent mechanism. Yet in these cases the thought-processes appear alogical and quite unlike the instructions given to computers. Thus, the concept of mind assumed by cognitive science is likely to make the student seem less independent, less the controller of his or her thoughts, and a less unified being than he or she really is. The concept also seems likely to separate logical from other types of thinking, and even to separate logical thinking from the student's general intellectual and emotional development.

The mind, then, is not a mechanism pure and simple. It is not a computer program either, for the reason that a computer, unlike the mind, manipulates symbols without understanding them.[43] The instructions given to a computer—move one square to the right, print a one, erase a zero—do not mean anything to the computer. Indeed, I myself could perform these operations without understanding them. Rational thinking, then, cannot be identified with following a program, for I cannot think rationally unless I understand what I am thinking. Philosopher John Searle clinches the argument:[44]

No formal program by itself is sufficient for understanding, because it would always be possible in principle for an agent to go through the steps in the program and to still not have the relevant understanding.

These criticisms, however, do not alter the fact that cognitive science is yielding many valuable insights and steering research in desirable directions. Cognitive science is to be saluted for taking researchers back into the mind and for stressing the active nature of thought. Cognitive science also seeks to do justice to the global, exploratory, to-and-fro movement of the mind in learning many kinds of subject matter. Again, this approach emphasizes the extraordinarily intricate and varied processes involved in mastering even simple things. All in all,

---

[43]Not all cognitive scientists claim that the mind actually is equivalent to a program. Some maintain, instead, that it is useful to study certain mental processes *as though* they were programmed.

[44]John Searle, "The Myth of the Computer," *New York Review of Books*, 29:7 (April 29, 1982), 5.

cognitive science is a healthy riposte to approaches that ignore or oversimplify the mind; and its many models of thinking are a fertile stimulus to instructional design.

Systems Engineering

We come now to a third positivist approach to educational research and practice. *Systems engineering is the analysis and design of alternative solutions to a wide variety of problems.* A "system" is a collection of interacting parts forming a whole. A nation's schools and colleges, a single school, a class of students, and an individual student, all are said to be systems. A "problem" is an unsatisfactory state of a system. To solve the problem requires a systems "analyst" and a systems "designer," or else the same person taking both parts. The analyst identifies the parts of the system and their relations and specifies the parts that can be controlled. The designer then models the system, represents the model on a computer program, and simulates alternative states of the system ("scenarios") to see which is most satisfactory.

Systems engineering is well suited to solving certain problems in schools. In fact, the principles of systems engineering, if not the actual procedures, can be followed by teachers themselves. Let's suppose a teacher plans a course. Her students now are the system, and their current knowledge, interests, and abilities are the present state of the system. The system will be "satisfactory" when her students have acquired the knowledge she wishes to teach them. How can she move the system most effectively from its present state to a satisfactory one? She can analyze each student's state of preparedness, and then design a sequence of lessons covering the knowledge her students need to acquire and a sequence of content items and instructional acts that will enable them to acquire it.[45]

---

[45] Professionals construct a curricular program in three stages: definition, development, and evaluation. (Walter A. Wittich and Charles F. Schuller, *Instructional Technology: Its Nature and Use,* 6th ed. [New York: Harper & Row, 1979], p. 310.) First, analysts determine the students' state of preparedness and the school's resources, propose a tentative program, and create a team to design it. Then designers choose instructional objectives, draw up an instructional sequence (or prototype), and specify how it is to be tested. Finally, the prototype is tested and then revised in the light of findings.

Systems analysis also enables us to conceive and evaluate the school as a production system that receives inputs, processes them, and yields outputs. Among the inputs are teachers, equipment, space, and books. The system processes these inputs by organizing them in various ways to yield outputs. The outputs range from the services provided by the school, through the results of these services, to the returns made to the individual students and society. The *services* include instruction, guidance, and transportation; the *results,* student academic achievement and the ability to socialize; the *returns,* fulfillment in life and contributions to the economy. How does systems analysis improve on other forms of evaluation? It allows us to view a cross section of the system in the present moment and to pay equal attention to *all* phases of the production process.

Critique   Systems analysis and design are pervaded by the philosophy of positivism. The school is treated as a composite of interacting variables rather than as the sum total of practices sustained by the individuals who participate in it. Students and teachers are seen as the objects of largely external forces, not as actors who partly construct the social world around them as they go about fulfilling their own purposes. Their inner lives are not considered. Little attempt is made to ask them how they see the school and the society it is said to serve. Nor do systems engineers ask themselves whether the school might fulfill purposes other than those it currently is held to serve. Above all, the purpose of their work is not to promote the self-expression and self-fulfillment of teachers and students but rather to bring about more efficient teaching and learning.[46]

Systems-designed instructional programs also make little allowance for individual differences. Their subject matter is well organized, but it is adapted to only a few, broadly conceived learning styles. Moreover, the responsibility of teachers is diminished, since content and methods of instruction are chosen

---

[46]For a criticism of the systems approach, see George Katsiaficas "The Limits to Systems Analysis," paper presented at the 1982 Western Regional Conference of the Comparative and International Education Society (Stanford University, October 22, 1982.)

and sequenced for them. Their role largely is to deliver the package.[47]

What are the prospects, then, for systems-designed schools—schools specially created to educate students with maximum efficiency to their full potential? These schools face three serious obstacles. First, educators and the public must agree on specific objectives for these schools, an agreement that will be hard to attain. Second, systems designers must simulate the educational process accurately. This involves calculating precisely the interaction of scores of variables, many of which cannot be isolated. How, for example, are the designers to assign values to the learning process, when researchers themselves (e.g., behaviorists, cognitive scientists, humanistic psychologists) cannot agree on the nature of learning? Third, designers must specify optimum instructional inputs; yet research still has to prove that one instructional medium is superior to another for any single purpose.

Nevertheless, there is much to be said in favor of the systems approach. It provides instructional programs and media combinations beyond the ability of the teacher to create. As knowledge of behavior grows, these programs surely can be tailored more closely to individual needs. The prospects for systems-designed schools also are brighter than many critics have claimed. In some cases (e.g., in experimental schools and small communities) educators and the public do agree on the goals of schooling. If not all the relevant variables are known, limited systems can be designed and modified in the light of experience. Finally, why not combine systems analysis with phenomenological research in order to plan schools that answer more closely to the needs of those who actually use them?

Appraisal

Positivists maintain that all genuine knowledge is scientific and should be sought with the methods of the natural sciences. Positivist doctrines have important consequences for the way we study human beings and the lessons we draw for educational thought and practice.

---

[47]See also Chapter 6, pp. 188–189.

First, these doctrines limit considerably what is thought worth studying in human beings. Behaviorists, for instance, maintain that the crucial feature of learning is its outcome in some observable, preferably measurable, performance. Some behaviorists such as Skinner, insist that learning *is* this performance and nothing more. With this approach, the actual process of thinking, of inner search and debate, is minimized or ignored entirely. Instructional programs break down learning into tiny steps, while the behavioral objectives movement targets the instructional process at small-scale performances. For its part, cognitive science, focusing on mental processes, seems a more promising approach to the study of learning and the design of instruction. Yet cognitive science limits thinking to logical and mathematical operations that can be simulated on computers. The more creative phases of thought (as in artistic invention and scientific discovery) are treated in highly simplified fashion.

Second, positivists hold that all human behavior is fully determined. For them, human beings never are free agents in the full sense but always the objects of internal and external forces, such as genetic endowment, upbringing, and schooling. In the behaviorist view, education is a process of shaping people to society's specifications. The teacher or the instructional program shapes students by presenting them with readily understood information and by reinforcing (rewarding) each step of learning. The behavioral objectives movement details these steps throughout the entire educational process. Systems engineering takes this procedure a stage further, since it designs entire courses of study. Note that these courses are made for teachers and students in the name of efficiency; they are not made in the interest of self-determined teaching and learning. Finally, cognitive science regards the mind as almost entirely mechanical, a system of parts interacting according to logico-mathematical rules, rather than as an aspect of a self that can make unique decisions.[48]

---

[48]Behaviorists like Edward C. Tolman who treat purposes as intervening variables also operate with a mechanical model of the mind, since they regard purposive behavior as the contingent effect of other variables (including mental ones) rather than as action that is logically (and hence necessarily) linked to its informing purposes. See Chapter 1, pp. 14–16.

Like physicists, positivist researchers are more interested in correlations and trends than individual cases. To uncover these correlations, they isolate variables (such as a teacher's use of praise or the number of student-initiated responses in a lesson) and then seek to measure the effects of certain variables on others. The intention is to confirm or falsify hypotheses, and eventually to unify hypotheses in a theory from which predictions can be made that are relevant to educational planning and practice. Teachers and students are regarded, not as unique individuals for whom education is a means to realize a personal aspiration, but as bearers of standard properties (motivation, readiness, and the like), who differ from one another only in degree and behave according to knowable laws. Education is seen, in systems analysis, for example, as the processing of large numbers of people rather than as the interplay of individuals seeking meaning in their lives.

Positivists believe that schooling essentially is a predetermined process to which teachers and students adapt, not one they create. As people grow up, they absorb certain ideas about schooling—for instance, that it is inevitable, that it is run by adults, and that it consists in the transmission and absorption of knowledge. Because people hold these views in common, positivists assume that the process of schooling in effect is the same thing for all people and independent of the individual's perceptions. But, in fact, individuals and groups, students, teachers, and administrators, often see the process of schooling differently. In the classroom, for instance, as teacher and students get to know one another, their attitudes toward learning and instruction, and even toward life itself, tend to change. What we call schooling, then, is not a single phenomenon that people willy-nilly see in the same way, but rather many different phenomena that depend on individual attitudes and perceptions and different environments.

For the positivist, the prime purpose of educational research is to enable us to predict and control the process of schooling. For example, if we discover the laws that govern learning, we will know what variables to manipulate in order to bring learning about. Thus, much educational research clearly is practical in intent. Researchers test hypotheses to the effect that one instructional method will lead to higher student achievement than another, or that a certain administrative style will produce some desired objective more efficiently than another. Nevertheless, I must point out that scientific evidence that such and such a method leads to higher student performance than any other does not in itself necessitate the value judgment that the method should be adopted. We have to decide whether the method is worth adopting in principle and, if so, whether its effectiveness in certain respects is not offset in others. For example, if cognitive science were to single out the most efficient method of teaching problem solving, it would not necessarily follow that teachers should use this method. If we believe that teaching is an art, we may be inclined to say that teachers should be allowed to use whatever method they find most congenial.

The behaviorist especially maintains that certain forms of learning brought about under controlled conditions in the laboratory can and ought to be brought about under controlled conditions in the classroom. But because something can be done, it does not follow that it should be. The issue is a moral one, and it has to be settled according to the values prevailing in a particular school or community. Skinnerian behaviorists inform us that education, and society as a whole, should be planned by the most "culturally evolved" people, who will use positive reinforcement for the best evolutionary purposes. Just how this in fact would happen is uncertain, for there is no consensus as to who the most culturally evolved people are. Moreover, since cultural evolution itself is capable of following several different paths, there certainly will be disagreement over which path to take.

Nevertheless, positivist research in general has achieved many signal results: instructional programs, behavioral objectives, computer models of thinking, and systems-designed courses. Some of these have proved more limited in application than their advocates hoped for. Programs and behavioral objectives, for instance, have been found suitable almost exclusively for instruction in basic intellectual skills. However, their precise design is a tribute to the strict quantitative accuracy that positivists seek in their research. The potential for control inherent in the positivist search for the laws of the educational process also can be seen as a virtue. Surely, any increase in our power to change (and hence potentially improve) education is desirable. Once we have this power, it is up to us to decide whether and how to use it.

Marxism

Relevant Themes

No philosophy has had a greater impact on contemporary life and thought than Marxism. It is the official doctrine of a third of the world's nations and an inspiration to social and political movements in many others. It also has attracted scholars in a range of fields, including education. In this introduction I present five Marxist themes that are central to the discussion of education today: (1) historical materialism, (2) class struggle, (3) the role of the state, (4) alienation and liberation, and (5) the role of education.

1. *Historical materialism is the thesis that social and cultural change results from economic change.*[1] Marx explains this as follows. Work, he says, is a distinctively human activity. Only human beings act on the world and change it deliberately. In doing so, they enter into certain social relations. Some people

---

[1] "Historical" materialism must be distinguished from the broader doctrine of "dialectical" materialism, which states that nature and society develop through the creation and resolution of internal contradictions.

hire others, some oversee others, and so on. These "relations of production," together with the "forces of production" (labor power, technology, raw materials), form the "economic base" of society. On this base, which constantly changes, there rises a "superstructure"[2] of laws, customs, cultural achievements, and so forth. The economic base largely shapes the society and culture it supports and hence the thinking of individual men and women. In Marx's words, "The mode of production of material life conditions the general process of social, political, and intellectual life."[3]

2.   *History is made by social classes rather than by individuals:* *"The history of all hitherto existing societies is the history of class struggles."*[4] For Marx, individuals are the product of their class, which forms their morality, tastes, and conduct. To understand individuals, we first must understand classes. The ruling class controls the economy, an oppressed class provides the labor, and often there are other classes. Class conflict is inevitable, declares Marx. During the Industrial Revolution, for instance, the rising capitalist class, which owned the mills and mines, seized economic and later political power from the aristocracy. Now, under capitalist production, managers organize the work process for the sake of profit rather than in the interest of workers. The inherent conflict between management and workers will be resolved only when workers themselves control the work process and create a new society.

3.   *The state apparatus—the judiciary, civil service, schools, armed forces, police—all serve the ruling class, not the general welfare.* The capitalist class uses this apparatus to keep the workers from organizing against their employers. Police break up strikes; judges convict strike leaders; verdicts reflect capitalist bias. In Marx's words, "The executive of the modern state is but a committee for managing the common affairs of the whole bour-

---

[2]A superstructure is an entity based on a more fundamental one, in this case an economic base.

[3]Karl Marx, Preface, *A Contribution to the Critique of Political Economy*, ed. with an introd. by Maurice Dobbs (New York: International Publishers, 1970), pp. 20–21.

[4]*The Manifesto of the Communist Party,* in Karl Marx and Friedrich Engels, *Basic Writings on Politics and Philosophy*, ed. Lewis S. Feuer (Garden City, NY: Doubleday Anchor, 1959), p. 7.

geoisie."[5] Since the state apparatus is used against them, the workers have no alternative but to seize it themselves. The class war must be "fought to a finish."

4. *The workers are "alienated" from their work, yet the "productive forces" developed by capitalism could be employed to create a truly humane society.* Human beings naturally want to make full use of their powers and surround themselves with their creations. Under capitalism they can do neither. Because the work process is divided, workers use only some of their powers. Because the means of production are owned by a few, the workers must sell their labor, and what they produce is taken from them and sold to others. Yet since nature largely has been mastered by modern industry, it is now possible to abolish the division of labor and private ownership of the means of production. In their place, we should create a society in which each person works to fulfill himself rather than make a profit for someone else.[6]

5. *Under capitalism people are educated unequally, and only the capitalist class gets a satisfactory education. However, education can be made a powerful force for social reconstruction.* Believing in the importance of work, Marx maintained that children should hold jobs as well as attend school. "An early combination of productive labor with education," he said, "[is] one of the most potent means for a transformation of present-day society."[7] With the coming of full-time education, Marxists muted this call. Lenin pointed out that under socialism schools must teach knowledge discovered in capitalist societies.[8] This knowledge is not bad in itself but misapplied. It should be used to enlighten

---

[5]*Ibid.*, p. 9. A "bourgeois" is one whose social behavior and political views are influenced by private property interests.

[6]Michael C. Smith, "A Contribution to the Study of Karl Marx's Theory of Education," and Ralph C. Page, "Education Before and After the Revolution," in *Philosophy of Education 1981: Proceedings of the Thirty-Seventh Annual Meeting of the Philosophy of Education Society,* ed. Daniel R. DeNicola (Normal, Ill.: Philosophy of Education Society, 1982), pp. 199–206, 207–210.

[7]Karl Marx, *Critique of the Gotha Program* (Peking: Foreign Language Press, 1972), p. 32. See also Robin Small, "Work, Play and School in Marx's Views on Education," *Journal of Educational Thought,* 16:3 (December 1982), 161–173.

[8]Nikolai Lenin, *On Socialist Ideology and Culture* (Moscow: Progress Publishers, 1978), pp. 142–144.

the masses and build a just society. Whereas capitalist schools, said Lenin, train people to fit into the capitalist system, socialist schools "must develop the whole person." Modern Marxists examine ways in which schools inculcate the skills, values, and attitudes needed under capitalism. The class system, division of labor, and division of knowledge, all are preserved and perpetuated by the schools. Modern Marxists call this process the "reproduction" of existing social, economic, and cultural forms.

Contemporary Marxism takes two main directions. One line of thought, springing from Marx's earlier, more "humanist" writings, insists on the relative autonomy of the sociocultural superstructure (including education) and gives more scope to individual freedom. The other line of thought, stemming from Marx's later writings (e.g., *Capital*), pays more attention to the effects of the economic base. I examine the humanist line in the work of the Critical Theorists.

Critical Theorists: Marcuse and Habermas

The Critical Theorists came together in Frankfurt, Germany, in the 1920s and were called the Frankfurt School. During the next decade most of them left for the United States. Their influence grew slowly but reached a peak during the late sixties and early seventies, when the writings of Herbert Marcuse seized the imagination of leftist students and intellectuals the world over. Today, mainly through the disciplinary syntheses of Jürgen Habermas, a new generation of Critical Theorists has become a force in many academic fields such as history, sociology, and education.

Critical Theorists condemn Soviet communism and Western capitalism alike. One system produced Stalin, they say, the other Hitler. Critical Theorists blame traditional Marxists for believing that economic forces are inexorable and for focusing on economic growth at the expense of individual freedom. At the same time, however, they denounce capitalism for using wealth to create more wealth rather than to free individuals from subservience to the industrial machine. For Critical Theorists, a revitalized Marxism, having abandoned the doctrine of economic determinism, must show people how to see through the machinations of capitalism and start working for a more rational society *now*.

Marcuse

According to Marcuse, the situation in the advanced capitalist nations is not even prerevolutionary.[9] In these nations the individual has been reduced by industry and the media to a consumer of goods. Individuals think they are free but, in reality, they are "atomized," "isolated," and "subject to anomie." They live in order to work, in order to earn money, in order to buy things. Unfortunately, says Marcuse, no social class or ethnic group rejects this one-dimensional way of life. The schools themselves, by inculcating conventional values, actually reinforce it.

How can the situation be changed? Only through the creation or appearance of a new personality type that can conceive of a different way of life and thus can reject the limited possibilities of a consumer society. Marcuse writes:[10]

Self-determination will be real to the extent to which the masses have been dissolved into individuals liberated from all propaganda, indoctrination, and manipulation, capable of knowing and comprehending the facts and reviewing the alternatives. In other words, society would be rational and free to the extent to which it is organized, sustained, and reproduced by an essentially new historical Subject.

What agency, what event, can bring this new personality type into being?

Not, at present, the public schools, since they are subject to the decisions of local and state boards, and hence serve the society that must be changed. Nor, thus far, the free schools and open classrooms,[11] which have been inspired by a theory of

---

[9]Dialogue with Bryan Magee, in *Men of Ideas*, ed. Bryan Magee (New York: Viking, 1979), p. 64.

[10]Herbert Marcuse, *One-Dimensional Man: Studies in the Ideology of Advanced Industrial Society* (Boston: Beacon, 1964), p. 252.

[11]See Chapter 7, pp. 203–209.

teaching as "love" and "care" rather than by a philosophy of society that would make teachers and students social critics and thoughtful creators of a new way to live.[12] *The change must start with individual teachers.* What can they do?

First, teachers can use civics courses to stimulate students to examine their own and their parents' ways of life and to imagine possible alternatives. They can encourage students to grapple with such questions as, Why do their parents work in particular occupations? What is the purpose of work? What do they, and what do their parents, spend their money on? What kinds of lives do they want? Would they be willing to live differently? How ought they to interpret what is said by government officials and corporation executives? Do these officials and executives have interests other than those they express? Is what is said to be good for students always good for them? And so on. Such questions can turn the potential consumer into a potential analyst of school and society.

Second, teachers can use art, music, and literature to reveal the human instincts and emotions that are repressed by the imperatives of work and consumption. The arts, says Marcuse, show us spontaneous human nature at odds with society. They are an "accusation of existing society, but on the other hand . . . the promise of liberation." In the works of Shakespeare and Hawthorne, in the sculptures of Michelangelo, in the symphonies of Beethoven and Brahms, the students can feel displayed on a larger scale the same vitality that is latent in themselves. In these works they will find the human energies and aspirations that can be expressed spontaneously by all in a nonrepressive society. In Marcuse's words,[13]

Against all fetishism of the productive forces, against the continued enslavement of individuals by the objective conditions (which remain those of domination), art represents the ultimate goal of all revolutions: the freedom and happiness of the individual.

And elsewhere,[14]

---

[12]See Evelina Orteza y Miranda, review of Richard A. Brosio, *The Frankfurt School, Journal of Educational Thought*, **16**:2 (August 1982), 133–134.

[13]Dialogue with Bryan Magee, pp. 69–70.

[14]Herbert Marcuse, *The Aesthetic Dimension: Toward a Critique of Marxist Aesthetics* (Boston: Beacon, 1978), p. xi.

*A work of art can be called revolutionary, if . . . it represents, in the
exemplary fate of individuals, the prevailing unfreedom and the re-
belling forces, thus breaking through the mystified (and petrified)
social reality, and opening the horizon of change (liberation).*

Marcuse regards college students as potential "catalysts" of
social change. Students cannot replace the working class as the
main revolutionary force, he says, but they can raise issues and
develop lifestyles that bring the established order into question.
Because of their intellectual training and their freedom from
full-time work, they have time and energy to create enclaves of
rational, spontaneous living within the consumer society. In
Marcuse's words,[15]

*They are educational groups, mainly engaged in political, but not
only political, education. Their main task is the development of consciousness—trying to counteract the management and control of consciousness by the established power structure; to project in theory
and practice the possibilities of change.*

Finally, women teachers, says Marcuse, are an example to
students of the specifically feminine qualities—such as non-
violence, nurturance, and emotional strength—that are under-
valued in most societies.[16] Women teachers should regard
themselves as role models for both sexes. If girls prize the feminine qualities, and if boys develop them in addition to the more
masculine virtues, a new generation will begin to moderate the
callousness and brutality of adult male-dominated societies.

Critique   Marcuse makes at least two fundamental errors.
First, he underestimates the freedom that exists under advanced capitalism. People are free to live, work, study, and
worship fairly much as they please; to elect political representatives; and to choose their own occupations and lifestyles. The
vast range of consumer opportunities and satisfactions is an
invitation and a challenge more than an entrapment. Marcuse's
notion of untrammelled instinctual satisfaction is too vague

---

[15]Dialogue with Bryan Magee, p. 72.

[16]Ibid., p. 71.

and general to offer a plausible alternative to the relatively free and individualist society we live in.

Second, there is little that individual teachers can do on Marcusean or any other lines to bring about decisive social change. As I have said elsewhere,[17] teachers can do much to open the minds of their students, so that they may enter the adult world capable of appraising it and seeking to change it. By persuasion and example, teachers can lead their students to adopt more informed attitudes than those of many people in today's society. Indeed, it is their duty to liberate students from prejudice as much as possible. But there is a good deal of difference between opening students' minds and encouraging students to question social arrangements from a Marxist perspective. The first course makes society more decent and enlightened, the second indoctrinates people.

Public school teachers in any case do not control public education; the people and their government do. Even if teachers as a body were to agree on a program of large-scale social reform (and in the United States this is most unlikely), they would exercise very little influence on government or public opinion generally, since they represent no single social class and possess insufficient political or economic power. It may be said that a *nationwide* strike of teachers would be a very effective weapon against any government. So it might. Yet relatively few teachers are likely to strike solely for the right to teach reform or revolution. Teachers are more politically active today than at any time in history, but as a body they have shown little taste for radical social change.

In light of these criticisms, what does Marcuse still offer education? He offers a view of human beings and society that is provocative, insightful at times, and pedagogically challenging. Marcuse combines a deep faith in the intrinsic powers of individuals with a powerful indictment of the society that represses these powers. For Marcuse, human beings naturally are joyful, creative, and erotic. By encouraging critical reflection on consumer values, an appreciation of the life-enhancing power of art, and more gentleness in men, teachers can help their stu-

---

[17]"The Impact of Culture," in *Foundations of Education*, ed. George F. Kneller (New York: Wiley, 1971), p. 73.

dents develop qualities that surely are of value in
society. Provided teachers fulfill their other import;
sibilities (for instance, to impart disciplined kno
could be worth their while critically to try these Marcusean
approaches.

Habermas

Jürgen Habermas may well be the most eclectic of modern
Marxists. He criticizes, especially, the determinist strain in
Marxist thinking. Individuals cannot be free, he says, if ultimately they are conditioned by the economic base of society.
Therefore, he argues, since we believe in the possibility of individual freedom, we must postulate that communication ("symbolic interaction") is more important than production. That is,
people can engage in production only because they can communicate with one another.[18] Habermas, then, combines Marxism
with many other approaches, such as speech act theory (from
analytic philosophy), hermeneutics, Piagetian-Kohlbergian de-
velopmentalism, Chomskyan linguistics, and psychoanalysis.
One product of this eclecticism is his theory of the three
"knowledge-constitutive interests."

Rooted in human nature, says Habermas, these three "interests" not only make culture and society possible, they also direct our search for knowledge. They are (1) a "technical" interest
in prediction and control,[19] (2) a "practical" interest in mutual
understanding and consensus, and (3) an "emancipatory" interest in personal and social independence. These interests guide,
or should guide, the natural sciences, the social sciences, and
psychoanalysis, respectively; and they enter respectively into

[18]Jürgen Habermas, *Knowledge and Human Interests* (London: Heinemann, 1972).
For an authoritative introduction to Habermas' thought, see Raymond Geuss,
The Idea of a Critical Theory: Habermas and the Frankfurt School (Cambridge
University Press 1981).

[19]Thus Habermas emphatically rejects the positivist view that scientific knowledge is objective and independent of human interests. He criticizes especially
the positivist approach to the human sciences, on the grounds that it leads to
the control and manipulation of people. "The capacity for *control*," he writes,
"made possible by the empirical sciences is not to be confused with the capacity
for *enlightened action*." Jürgen Habermas, *Toward a Rational Society: Student Pro-
test, Science, and Politics*, trans. Jeremy J. Shapiro (Boston: Beacon, 1970), p. 56.

the activities of work, human relations, and "self-reflection" (i.e., reflection aimed at self-understanding). They therefore should direct the choice of school subjects, activities, and teaching methods. To this end, *"The developers of new pedagogical methods for curricula in . . . schools should go back to the philosophic presuppositions of the different fields of study themselves."* [20] For example, they might consider the nature of language (in both its innate and its acquired aspects), the interpretive character of historical understanding, and the nature of knowledge in science and mathematics as contrasted with knowledge in the humanities. Philosophic reflection will clarify the relation between schooling and the three interests.

For Habermas, the curriculum should give as much weight to history and the social sciences as it does to the natural sciences. Physics and biology, for instance, are not more true than other branches of knowledge but, instead, are those branches that enable us to predict and control nature. History and the social sciences, on the other hand, are interpretive (or hermeneutic) disciplines. Students should study history hermeneutically for the light it can throw on the present and the future. When they discuss the Mexican-American War, for instance, or the idea of Manifest Destiny, they should ask whether there are parallels in current American policy and, if so, what should be done about them. In studying literature (considered as knowledge of human beings) and the social sciences, they should ask not only what they think of other people—Camus's Stranger, say, or the Pueblo Indians—but more importantly what these people thought of themselves and how they saw the world. The students' next step is to ask how this knowledge can help them understand individuals and society better. When have they seen someone act arbitrarily like Camus's Stranger? How rational is this behavior, and when (if ever) might it be justified? How does the Pueblo Indian's attitude to nature differ from that of a present-day farmer or surveyor? What can they learn from the Indian?

According to Habermas, the school should encourage independent, critical thinking through class discussion. His first model for independent thinking was psychoanalysis, in which

---

[20] Ibid., p. 8 (italics added).

the client comes to understand and take responsibility for him or herself through conversation with a therapist. Clearly, however, the teacher cannot act as a therapist, let alone one for an entire class of students. Nevertheless, there is a group parallel to the therapeutic situation in what Habermas calls an "ideal speech situation." Here each person has an equal chance, and is equally encouraged, to speak, and the resulting consensus depends solely on the cogency of what is said, not on the authority or the social class of the speaker. In his own words, "The 'force' of the argument is the only permissible compulsion, whereas the cooperative search for truth is the only permissible motive."[21]

However, Habermas readily concedes that open discussion, though much to be desired, is not always appropriate. If the teacher has to impart a body of worthwhile knowledge, the class cannot spend too much time in discussion and the search for consensus. Nevertheless, because the school withdraws students from the "systematically distorted communication" of the workplace and the mass media, it should encourage them to look with some detachment at the values and practices of society. As Habermas puts it,[22]

The traditional patterns of socialization, which till now were ensconced as natural in the cultural tradition, are set free by . . . the planning of school curricula according to cultural policy, and rendered accessible to general practical discourse.

To reconcile the claims of both subject matter and open discussion, teachers should seek class consensus on the knowledge they present. In addition to asking particular students whether they understand the presentation, they should ask the class as a whole whether they agree with it, and whether they see where it leads.

Critique   Habermas' conception of the three interests is faulty, oversimplified, and inadequate as a guide to curriculum planning. Not all science, for instance, is guided by an interest in

---

[21]*Knowledge and Human Interests*, p. 363.

[22]Jürgen Habermas, *Theory and Practice* (London: Heinemann, 1974), p. 26.

prediction and control. The speculative motive is equally important. The general theory of relativity, for example, which is likely to underwrite any technology to exploit black holes, originally was created by Einstein primarily for the sake of understanding. Again, it is hard to see how psychoanalysis, as a branch of inquiry, is more intellectually emancipatory than any established discipline, such as philosophy, that reflects on its own foundations. As a therapy, psychoanalysis may free some clients from unconscious compulsions but it does not include reflection on psychoanalytic inquiry itself.

Next, Habermas' ideal speech situation seems hardly suited, even as an ideal, to most secondary, let alone primary, schools. Since the teacher must present knowledge and maintain discipline, he or she is both "an" authority and "in" authority,[23] and hence not the "equal" of other speakers. Furthermore, if not all students behave equally well, not all deserve an equal chance to speak. A wisecracking troublemaker hardly is entitled to the same discussion privileges as a serious contributor. Finally, although teachers naturally will try to get all students to understand the knowledge they present, it would be unreasonable, and possibly unproductive, for them always to seek class consensus on the truth of that knowledge. Consensus is a valid test of (provisional) truth in the natural sciences, where there are precise tests and expert practitioners, but these conditions do not hold in the schoolroom.

Nevertheless, there is much to say in favor of Habermas. Emancipation, prediction and control, and understanding and communication *are* the interests of knowledge, even if they are less strictly separated than Habermas suggests. Knowledge should be presented to enable students to satisfy those interests. History, for instance, should be taught not as a means of discovering laws and predicting the future, but as a way of understanding particular events, periods, and movements of thought, and learning from them how to handle the present. Physics should be presented as both theoretical and practical knowledge. The student should be invited to contrast the attitudes to science of, say, Francis Bacon and Albert Einstein.[24]

---

[23]See Chapter 1, pp. 7–9.

[24]Briefly, for Bacon, the purpose of science was to discover knowledge that could be used to master nature. For Einstein, it was to discover the ultimate order, and hence beauty, of nature.

Moreover, Habermas' notion of an ideal speech s considered as a partial goal, can make at least two contr to education. First, the more students know of a subject, the less they may need to be taught, and hence they and their teacher can become more equal discussants. Second, although class consensus may not establish truth, it may be an important step toward reaching it. Class consensus on the *value* of educational experiences is even more desirable, since it is likely to be based on wider thought and sharper questioning than the individual student alone is likely to achieve. All in all, Habermas' eclecticism is a refreshing contrast to the narrower approaches of many of his contemporaries. Whether or not one accepts his special brand of Marxism, Habermas is to be honored for his achievement in the art of philosophic synthesis.

Structural Marxism: Bowles and Gintis

"Structural" Marxists differ from "humanist" Marxists in three main ways. (1) Whereas humanist Marxists are interested in the possibilities for individual freedom in a given society, structural Marxists emphasize the extent to which individuals are molded by their class and limited by a class-structured society. (2) For humanists, the social and cultural superstructure, including education, is semi-independent and capable of influencing the economic base. For structuralists, the superstructure largely is conditioned by the economic base. (3) Humanists believe it is possible to hasten the revolution by making changes in the superstructure (e.g., by increasing working-class consciousness).[25] Structuralists maintain that the revolution may have to wait until the antagonism between labor and capitalists has reached a crisis.

One of the most forceful expressions of the structuralist view is Herbert Bowles and Samuel Gintis' *Schooling in Capitalist America*. According to these authors, *social relations within education correspond to those in the economic system*. In education, they declare, "Power is organized along vertical lines of authority from administration to faculty to student body; students

---

[25]The Italian humanist Marxist, Antonio Gramsci, advocated using adult education to create a working-class culture that would rival the dominant culture and would prepare the masses to take control of society.

have a degree of control over their curriculum comparable to that of the worker over the content of his job." Moreover, *changes in the social organization of work lead to changes in the social organization of the school.* In the nineteenth century, for example, universal primary education came about largely because factory owners wanted a disciplined work force. In the twentieth century, universal secondary education, vocational education, and the use of standardized tests all followed on the need of burgeoning corporations for more skilled workers. Nevertheless, say Bowles and Gintis, "though the school system has effectively served the interests of profit and stability, it has hardly been a finely tuned instrument of manipulation in the hands of socially dominant groups."[26] For example, schools still harbor student rebels and "misfits" as well as quite a few politically discontented teachers.

In Bowles and Gintis' view, *the educational system not only reflects, but also reproduces and legitimates, the division of labor in the workplace.* Here they agree with the French structural Marxist, Louis Althusser, according to whom the school takes children from every class and "drums into them . . . a certain amount of 'know-how' wrapped in the ruling ideology [English, math, science, literature] or simply the ruling ideology in its pure state [civics]." At sixteen or so, "a huge mass of children are 'ejected into production'; these are the workers and peasants." Later, another group "spills out" to fill the white-collar positions and the lower ranks of management. Finally, from the educational summit there emerge the capitalists, top managers, civil servants, politicians, and intellectuals.[27] Thus,

---

[26]Herbert Bowles and Samuel Gintis, *Schooling in Capitalist America*, (New York: Basic Books, 1976), p. 12 especially.

[27]Louis Althusser, *Lenin and Philosophy, and Other Essays* (New York: Monthly Review, 1971), p. 155. Another French structural Marxist, Nicos Poulantzas (born in Greece), agrees that the educational system reproduces the mental-manual division of labor in a capitalist society. However, he argues that elements in the superstructure—such as the schools, the churches, and the media—are more independent of the economic base than Marxists like Bowles and Gintis would claim, and that these elements respond to different and often conflicting groups within (and also outside) the capitalist class. Nevertheless, like Bowles and Gintis, and like Althusser, Poulantzas regards individuals as basically the instruments of larger economic and sociocultural forces. His main works are *Classes in Contemporary Capitalism*, trans. David Fernbach (London: New Left

the educational system stratifies the young for the benefit of the capitalist economy.

The educational system, say Bowles and Gintis, *reproduces the division of labor by fostering different personality types that fit different levels in the occupational structure.* In the hierarchy of a business enterprise the lowest levels require a rule-following personality type; the middle levels, dependability in the absence of continuous supervision; and the higher levels, a personality type that internalizes the norms of the enterprise and hence is capable of leadership. Similarly, at what Bowles and Gintis call the "lower levels" of the educational system, the high schools, especially in working-class areas, "tend to severely limit and channel the activities of the students"; at the middle levels, community colleges supervise students less and permit more independent activity; and at the top, four-year colleges expect the student to internalize educational norms rather than depend on supervision.[28]

The educational system also legitimates the division of labor "through the ostensibly meritocratic manner by which it rewards and promotes students, and allocates them to distinct positions in the occupational hierarchy."[29] Since all students supposedly are given the same opportunity to excel, an individual student's success in school, and hence his or her value to an employer, is said to depend solely on ability. Yet in actuality, say Bowles and Gintis, what the schools reward is not ability as such but just those personality traits required by the capitalist economy, such as perseverance, obedience, and reliability. They continue: "The only significant penalized traits are precisely those which are incompatible with conformity to the hierarchical division of labor—creativity, independence, and aggressivity."[30] Thus, they say, the legitimation that takes place is spurious.

Bowles and Gintis maintain that under capitalism the school

Books, 1975) and *State, Power, Socialism,* trans. Patrick Camiller (London: New Left Books, 1978). For an introduction to Poulantzas, see H. Svi Shapiro, "Education and the State in Capitalist Society: Aspects of the Sociology of Nicos Poulantzas," *Harvard Educational Review* 50:3 (August 1980), 321–331.

[28]Op. cit., p. 132.

[29]Ibid., p. 11 (italics added). "Allocates" here means "prepares for." The educational system does not assign students to actual jobs.

[30]Ibid., p. 136.

cannot fulfill the three main functions assigned to it. These are to integrate youth into the economy, promote equality, and foster personal development. Since the workplace is repressive (rewarding conformism rather than creativity) and inegalitarian (locking people into certain job levels), the school cannot prepare young people for the job market without limiting both their personal development and their chances in life. Thus, the "integrative" function is fulfilled at the expense of the other two. As the authors say,[31]

The educational system serves—through the correspondence of its social relations with those of economic life—to reproduce economic inequality and distort personal development. Thus under corporate capitalism, the objectives of liberal educational reform are contradictory: It is precisely because of its role as producer of an alienated and stratified labor force that the educational system has developed its repressive and unequal structure.

Nevertheless, say Bowles and Gintis, the schools are only partly to blame for the harm they do. *It is capitalism itself that distorts the educational process.* "The roots of repression and inequality lie in the structure and functioning of the capitalist economy." Capitalism "cannot solve the problems it creates." It cannot create a nonrepressive, egalitarian society because it needs an unequal, repressed workforce. To humanize education, we must humanize society, and to do that we must abolish capitalism. In the authors' words, "Capitalism is an irrational system, standing in the way of further social progress. It must be replaced."[32]

Bowles and Gintis do not present a formal program of educational reconstruction. Instead, they urge "revolutionary educators" to (1) press for the control of schools and colleges by students, teachers, parents, and other community members; (2) work for a system of "economic democracy" in which all people do their fair share of the unwanted but socially necessary jobs; (3) ally with other members of the working class to create "a

---

[31]Ibid., p. 48.
[32]Ibid., pp. 49, 274–275.

unified class consciousness"; and (4) combine a "long-range vision" with attention to immediate goals such as free classrooms, open enrollment, and adequate financial aid for needy students.[33]

Critique   What are we to say in response to Bowles and Gintis? First, they assume that students and educators are more passive than they really are. As I have pointed out,[34] students do not simply absorb standardized views of school and society; to some extent they form their own. Second, contrary to Bowles and Gintis, most teachers try hard to treat their students equally (as they legally are required to do) and most succeed in doing so. Third, Bowles and Gintis treat the school pretty much as a black box. They sidestep actual student-teacher interactions, and though they quote statistics by the score, they omit phenomenological studies of the school. They even ignore the curriculum. For instance, they do not ask how the economics taught in schools affects young people's views of the economy or the job market.

There are other deficiencies. In spite of occasional disclaimers, Bowles and Gintis play down the effects, on education and the economy, of changes in the superstructure. In particular, they minimize the effects of educational reforms undertaken by educators themselves. For example, they claim without argument that, despite their merits, none of the educational reforms begun in the 1960s, such as free schools, alternative schools, and community control, are capable of addressing the major problems facing U.S. society today.[35] Moreover, their own advice to "revolutionary educators" looks most unpromising. Even if they produced a precise theory or program showing how the working class could win control of society, which they do not, few American teachers would act on it. The overwhelming majority show no interest in forging a working-class consciousness.

---

[33]Ibid., pp. 287–288.

[34]See Chapter 2, pp. 57, 58. For an argument that Bowles and Gintis' data do not support their conclusions, see Michael R. Olneck and David B. Bills, "What Makes Sammy Run? An Empirical Assessment of the Bowles-Gintis Correspondence Theory," *American Journal of Education*, **89**:1 (November 1980), 27–61.

[35]Ibid., p. 263.

Bowles and Gintis also are mistaken in their claim that the schools cannot help serving the capitalist system, for in fact they can, and often do, cut their contribution to the system in several ways. Schools can abolish tracking, which channels working-class youth toward lower levels of the economy. Government and other agencies can distribute financial resources more fairly among schools and thus help equalize educational opportunity. Young people can be encouraged to examine why hierarchical relations are appropriate in the schools but not necessarily elsewhere. Arguably, the capitalist system might take these changes in its stride. A much more serious blow would be a decision by the schools to teach the young to question the system itself, a course of action that some teachers have not hesitated to take.

Nevertheless, for all its flaws, Bowles and Gintis' book is a Marxist classic. It probes deeply and uncompromisingly into the American educational system. The authors argue clearly, if not always cogently, for economic determinism and back their thesis with a wealth of material. Subsequent Marxist thought in the United States has sought to qualify the authors' thesis rather than refute it. Among the leading representatives of this more recent approach is Michael Apple.

Neo-Humanist Marxism: Apple

Writing in the tradition of humanist Marxism, Michael Apple incorporates the structuralist perspective of Bowles and Gintis within a more subtle and comprehensive analysis of the role of the school in capitalist society. Apple agrees with Bowles and Gintis that the school produces a stratified student body for a stratified workplace. Nevertheless, he argues, the school is more than a reflection of the economy; it is a site in which the economy, the state, and the culture are linked in many, and sometimes conflicting, ways. More fundamentally, since the economy, state, and culture themselves are sites of class conflict and compromise, the school is an arena in which the different classes struggle with and adjust to one another as part of a much wider process of interaction. As Apple puts it, "The school mediates and transforms an array of economic, political, and cultural pressures from competing classes and class segments."[36]

How does Apple argue for this view? Basically, he advances five theses. (1) The school not only prepares the young for the capitalist economy, it also transmits the culture of the corporate class (capital owners and upper management). That is, it "reproduces" the social order not only economically but culturally. (2) In addition to distributing knowledge as part of the reproductive process, the educational system "produces" the "technical/administrative" knowledge needed for capital accumulation (i.e., to maintain and increase profits). (3) Far from being absorbed passively, the reproductive process is accepted in part ("mediated"), contested, and at times rejected by some groups of students. (4) The school is an arm of the state, which employs it to promote and "legitimate" the process of capital accumulation. For instance, the state encourages the school to use prepackaged curricular materials, which embody ideologies of "possessive individualism" and management control conducive to work and consumption in capitalist society. (5) The use of the school in the interests of the corporate class also offers opportunities to resist those interests. Let us consider these theses.

1.   In order to run the economy at a profit, Apple asserts, the corporate class needs the compliance of other classes. To gain this compliance, it seeks to make its culture—its way of thought and life—prevail throughout society. Hence Apple calls this culture a "hegemony" (a form of control).[37] At the core of this

---

[36]Michael Apple, *Education and Power* (Boston and London: Routledge & Kegan Paul, 1982), p. 139.

[37]The notion of hegemony was introduced by Gramsci. See Antonio Gramsci *Selections from the Prison Notebooks* (New York: International Publishers, 1971); also Harold Entwistle, *Antonio Gramsci: Conservative Schooling for Radical Politics* (Boston and London: Routledge & Kegan Paul, 1979); and Michael Welton, "Gramsci's Contribution to the Analysis of Public Education Knowledge," and Don Dawson, "Educational Hegemony and the Phenomenology of Community Participation," *Journal of Educational Thought* 16:3 (December 1982), 140–149 and 150–160, respectively. According to Gramsci, the ruling class dominates subordinate classes by leading them to accept its culture—including its morality, customs, and institutionalized rules of behavior—so that this culture seems to be common sense. Thus, class rule is exercised through apparent popular consensus.

The literature on *ideology* is vast. One of the best treatments is Geuss, op. cit., ch. 1. For our purposes, however, ideology may be defined as a world view

hegemony is an "ideology" (a world view and system of values). Apple stresses three elements in this ideology: the view that progress depends on science and industry; the belief that society should enable individuals of differing abilities to "maximize their chances of attainment in a competitive market"; and the belief that the good life consists in producing and consuming goods and services as an individual.[38] How is this ideology reproduced in the curriculum?

According to Apple, the first two elements are expressed in the preference for structured subjects whose content can be organized in order of increasing difficulty and pursued at different levels by students of different abilities.[39] Some of these subjects, such as science and mathematics, serve industry directly.

The third element, "possessive individualism," is expressed, says Apple, in the use of prepackaged materials. These are held to "individualize" learning in several ways. Students work alone at their own speed and have little overt contact with one another or with their teacher. Knowledge is broken down into individual items and skills, to be mastered sequentially. "The mark of a good pupil," declares Apple, "is the possession and accumulation of vast quantities of skills in the service of technical interests." In the larger society, too, "people consume as isolated individuals. Their worth is determined by the possession of material goods or . . . of technical skills." Nevertheless, learning is individualized only to a limited extent, for the content, the answers, and the standards of evaluation are specified minutely by the manufacturers of the materials. In the workplace, too, individualism, especially as it is experienced by "the new petty bourgeoisie—those groups who make up middle management and technical occupations [including education]" and believe most strongly in possessive individualism— is not "individual autonomy, where a person . . . controls his or her destiny" but "a careerist individualism, . . . geared towards

---

and value system that are embodied in social practices and that seek to maintain or change the status quo.

[38]Michael W. Apple, *Ideology and Curriculum* (Boston and London: Routledge & Kegan Paul, 1979), p. 80; *Education and Power,* pp. 44, 122, 152–155.

[39]*Ideology and Curriculum,* pp. 37–38.

organizational mobility and advancement by following technical rules."[40]

2.   Mainly through the universities, says Apple, the educational system produces the technical/administrative knowledge
that is used "to create new techniques for production, for patent
monopolies, for the stimulation of needs and markets, and for
the division and control of labor." The schools use this knowledge "as a complex filter to sort out students according to their
prospective places in a hierarchical market." Students who are
identified as able to produce important amounts of this knowledge are steered toward professional and white-collar work,
while other students are directed toward service and manual
labor. Because of the extensive division between mental and
manual work, and because technical/administrative knowledge
is used and produced by relatively few people, "to a large extent
workers are ultimately excluded from the knowledge necessary
for both understanding and directing important aspects of the
production process."[41]

3.   However, says Apple, not all students submit passively to
the reproductive process. Drawing on several Marxist studies
which "enter the school and see it at first hand,"[42] Apple points
out that, especially in working-class areas, many students
"work the system," doing the required minimum but otherwise
"goofing off." Some students, he says, go further; they pay little
attention to the teacher and "join an informal group to counter
the official activities of the school."[43]

Yet, as Apple emphasizes, this "lived cultural response" is a
contradictory one, for the youngsters "both participate in and at
least partially reproduce the hegemonic ideologies" they oppose. Those youngsters who reject the school's program in

---

[40]*Education and Power,* p. 154.

[41]Ibid., pp. 51–52.

[42]Ibid., ch. 4. These studies are Paul Willis, *Learning to Labor: How Working Class
Kids Get Working Class Jobs* (New York: Columbia University, 1981); Robert Ever-
hart, *The In-Between Years: Student Life in a Junior High School* (Santa Barbara,
Calif.: Graduate School of Education, University of California, 1979); and An-
gela McRobbie, "Working Class Girls and the Culture of Femininity," in *Women
Take Issue,* ed. Women's Studies Group (London: Hutchinson, 1978), pp. 96–108.

[43]*Education and Power,* p. 101.

favor of "physicality and masculınity" embrace the life of manual labor for which the school has destined them. In due course, they become workers who "have some semblance of power on the shop-floor, but . . . who ultimately employ categories and distinctions that at root are aspects of the ideological hegemony required by the economy." Similarly, those students who manipulate the system, getting acceptable grades *and* goofing off, in effect rehearse the "social relations" that govern most blue-collar and low-level white-collar jobs anyway. "For," as Apple puts it, "the maintenance of some power and autonomy on the shop-floor or in an office does not necessarily challenge the needs of capital *if the minimum requirements of production are usually met.*"[44]

4.   Apple also looks at the school as part of the state's apparatus. The state, he says, is tightening its grip on teachers by encouraging the private sector to produce prepackaged curricular materials and advising or compelling school districts to buy them. In this way the state assists in capital accumulation, by making the "production process" in schools more efficient, and legitimates its own activity, by appealing simultaneously to a wide array of classes and interest groups. Prepackaged materials meet the need of administrators for accountability and control, the need of teachers for something "practical" to use with students, the concern of parents for a "quality education" that works, the interest of the new petty bourgeoisie in "individualization," and so forth. Thus, "the logic of capital" is "mediated" by the fact, among other things, that the school is a state apparatus. As a result, the logic of capital enters the school "in partial, distorted, or coded ways," one of which is "the encoding of technical control into the very basis of the curricular form itself."[45] What is this control and how is it coded?

Apple points out that—in the case of these materials—content, tests, teacher activities, and student responses all are prespecified, sometimes down to the exact words that teacher and students are to use. Control is built into the materials themselves; it is taken from the teacher by the manufacturer. Thus, teachers become "deskilled." Skills that once were thought es-

---

[44]Ibid., pp. 106, 103, 108.

[45]Ibid., p. 149 (italics deleted).

sential to the craft of teaching—setting curricular goals, choosing content, designing lessons and instructional strategies, individualizing instruction, and the like—are lost. The teacher executes what someone else has planned. At the same time, in workshops and courses and at teacher training institutions, teachers are taught behavior modification techniques and classroom management strategies "for better controlling students." This "reskilling," says Apple, involves the replacement of curricular and pedagogic skills with "the skills and ideological visions of management."[46]

Are teachers simply accepting this process? No, replies Apple. "The creation of the kind of ideological hegemony 'caused' by the increasing introduction of technical control is not 'naturally' pre-ordained. It is something that is won or lost in particular struggles." Culture, the economy, and the state are "inherently contradictory," and "if these contradictions are lived out in the school itself by students and teachers, then the range of possible actions is expanded considerably." Thus, the growth of technical control "creates contradictory effects and provides a potential for successful political work." On the one hand, teachers consult less and less about curricular matters. On the other hand, as teachers become unattached individuals, the pressure for unionization may increase, especially as teachers see other state workers in a similar plight. However, Apple warns that growing technical control makes cooperative action increasingly difficult.[47]

5. How can Marxist educators resist "the logic of capital"? Apple mentions various forms of action. Teachers, for example, can counter the emphasis on individualized instruction by focusing, where possible, on joint activity, on reports, papers, inquiry, class plays, art, and so on. They can demystify the "great man" theory of history and science by stressing "the contributions of groups of real working people acting together." Apple also recommends (a) proposing socialist alternatives that will appeal to working people as well as activists; (b) forming coalitions with other state workers; and (c) "highlighting the experience of women, . . . making [a feminist perspective] an

---

[46]Ibid., pp. 146, 147.

[47]Ibid., pp. 156, 165–166, 162, 159.

integral part of one's analyses and action." Nevertheless, Apple is hardly optimistic. Reconstruction is "possible," he declares, but "not easy." In the main he emphasizes supporting and coordinating particular attempts at resistance. The task of Marxists, he says, is to find these attempts: "We need somehow to give life to the resistances, the struggles."[48]

Critique   Apple is vulnerable on several counts. First, he uses key terms loosely. What, for example, does the school "reproduce"? Sometimes Apple says the school reproduces social class relations; sometimes he says it reproduces culture; sometimes, the division of labor. Perhaps he believes it reproduces all three. If so, why does he refer repeatedly to "cultural and economic," but never to "social class," reproduction? This inconsistency is especially striking in a Marxist, who presumably believes that social classes are more basic than culture. Moreover, even from Apple's perspective, the school itself cannot reproduce the division of labor but only the psychological predispositions for it. To take another example, "ideology" and "hegemony" are distinct terms, yet Apple often uses the phrase "ideological hegemony." Does this phrase mean hegemony exercised through ideology alone, or that part of hegemony exercised through ideology, or what? Again, "culture" is a key term for Apple, yet he also lists it *in addition to* norms, values, and cultural dispositions. What, then, does culture actually comprise?

Apple repeatedly uses, but does not define, the term "logic of capital." Is this term merely a metaphor meaning a strong tendency of capital? If so, how strong is the tendency when it so often is "mediated"? For Apple, to be sure, capital is "contradictory" and therefore may appear to be (in Marxist terms) a logically necessary dialectical process—that is, one that proceeds by generating and overcoming contradictory states of affairs.[49]

---

[48]Ibid., pp. 164, 176, 162.

[49]Marxists maintain that certain social phenomena contain contradictions akin to logical contradictions. History progresses, say Marxists, as one phenomenon or group of phenomena (the thesis) gives rise to its opposite (antithesis), and the two then are resolved in a higher synthesis. For example, capitalism will be overthrown and replaced by the dictatorship of the proletariat, which will be

Yet, for Apple, culture, the economy, and the state are also contradictory in their effects. Are they "logics," then? And if they are, what elements of our collective life are not "logics"? The social sphere seems too random and unpredictable to contain so much logical necessity. In summary, this careless use of words weakens Apple's case, for sometimes one does not know whether he is describing realities or pursuing the associations of his Marxist terminology.

Apple also misuses some of his ideas. Take his thesis that the schools produce technical/administrative knowledge that cycles through the economy and then returns to the school in the form of prepackaged materials. In fact, the schools do *not* produce such knowledge; other agencies do. True, Apple says at times that universities produce it, but he also states that they produce only "part" of it, and he insists that it *"re*enters" the primary and secondary schools, which implies that some at least begins there. Here Apple maintains the symmetry of his idea (that knowledge is produced by schools and returns to them) at the price of distorting the facts. He also says that schools stratify students for mental or manual work according to the probability that they will produce "important" quantities of this knowledge later. But most mental workers will use this knowledge rather than produce it, much less produce it in volume.

Apple's notion of "contradictions" (i.e., logical incompatibilities) is both mistaken and ambiguous. It is not clear whether culture, the economy, the state, and other social formations are contradictory in themselves or in their effects, or both. Nor is it clear what the contradiction amounts to. For example, Apple says that technical control has contradictory effects because isolating teachers may encourage them to unionize. Yet how much of a contradiction is present when one outcome *may* occur? And what more is involved in contradiction here than the claim that one *possible* state of affairs (teacher unionization) may offset an *actual* state of affairs (teacher isolation)? Again, Apple often asserts the existence of contradictions without demonstrating them, as when he says that there is a contradiction

---

succeeded by the final synthesis of the classless society. Marx took the notion of a logic proceeding via contradictions from Hegel, who called it "dialectic." Unlike Hegel, he applied it primarily to economic and social history rather than the history of ideas.

between the school's production of technical/administrative knowledge and its ideology of equality and social mobility, and that contradictions in education make socialist action possible.[50] In short, the notion of contradiction is misused when it is applied repeatedly to mere possibilities and to trends that are beneficial or adverse to certain interests.

Again, Apple exaggerates the part played by social classes in American education. In a few European countries, notwithstanding decades of reform, class differences persist, and European Marxists make much of them. In the United States, however, the divisions are more on ethnic and racial than on class lines. Surprisingly, Apple pays little attention to the differing educational experiences and expectations of blacks, Latinos, Asian Americans, and others for whom the dominant culture is not middle class but white.

Finally, although Apple mentions a range of strategies for Marxist educators, they are briefly sketched and belong to no grand design. Apple does not examine in detail how Marxist educators might exploit any of the contradictions he believes he has uncovered. In particular, he fails to show how teachers might reach out to disaffected students, respecting their hostility to a narrowly conceived individualism, and persuading them to look critically at the division of labor itself.

On the credit side, however, Apple has moved beyond the reductive Marxism of Bowles and Gintis to become an important critic of American education. He seeks to trace the complex interplay between the school and many other institutions and forces, such as the market, the state, the social classes, and "ideologies" like possessive individualism. He combines a structural insight into the workings of the capitalist system with a phenomenological sensitivity to the everyday realities of school life. This is especially evident in his account of the impact of prepackaged materials. In addition, Apple highlights what previous Marxist theorists largely had missed—the resistance of some students and teachers to the program and culture of the school.

Apple invites us to look for the pressure of class interests where we had not expected them, and thus makes us more self-

---

[50]*Education and Power*, pp. 58, 165–166.

critical as educators. Although a committed Marxist, he is not doctrinaire and seeks to learn from his mistakes. He uses other writers' works creatively, focusing a wide range of Marxist and allied scholarship on critical points in the educational system, such as resistance and technical control.[51] Finally, without minimizing the difficulties they face, he proposes steps that Marxist educators can take to improve education as they see it.

Appraisal

The history of Marxism is full of passionate disagreements over fundamentals as well as tactics. Most Marxists, it is true, acknowledge a common core of doctrines centered on historical materialism, class struggle, the state, alienation and liberation, and the role of education. Yet different Marxists develop these doctrines differently. Today, in the capitalist West, Marxist thought takes two main directions, humanist and structural. Humanist Marxists believe in individual freedom (as they define it) and the relative autonomy of the sociocultural superstructure. Structural Marxists largely submerge the individual in the class and emphasize the dominance of the economic base. However, both groups share some common limitations.

Most Marxists, in the United States at least, tend to underestimate the intellectual awareness of their fellow citizens. Marcuse thinks that Americans are one-dimensional consumers whose mental horizons are limited by the TV set and the supermarket. A minority may be. Yet most parents sincerely and actively seek the health, education, and welfare of their children. Bowles and Gintis declare that the capitalist system is so irrational that, until it is abolished, our schools cannot seriously be reformed. Yet they submit no blueprint of the society they envision. Apple blames earlier curriculum makers for imposing American "middle-class" culture on the children of immigrants.[52] What other culture does he expect our schools to im-

---

[51]See, for example, *Education and Power*, ch. 1. See also Apple's Introduction to *Cultural and Economic Reproduction in Education: Essays on Class, Ideology and the State*, ed. Apple (Boston and London: Routledge & Kegan Paul, 1982).

[52]*Ideology and Curriculum*, p. 68.

part? Most immigrants came, and still come, to the United States anxious to share in our middle-class culture and, above all, to gain the same privilege for their children.

Marxist thinkers focus on social classes, yet today in most industrial nations, with extensive educational and welfare programs, social-class lines matter much less in public education. In the United States, the split is between races more than classes, and what the "oppressed" really want is not less capitalism but more entrée to it. It is unfortunate that Marxists have not analyzed in more detail what different racial groups expect from American schools and what they actually experience in them.

Marxists as a whole still need to pay more attention to interactions and, in particular, conflicts, inside the school. Phenomenologists, studying the school, generally look for student-teacher negotiation rather than conflict. Structural Marxists focus on external, socioeconomic forces acting on the school. Until recently even humanist Marxists treated students as the collective object of the reproductive process. Apple's analyses of resistance and reproduction at work in the group are a step in the right direction.

Marxist educationists overestimate the potential radicalism of American teachers. Most teachers regard themselves as professionals, not workers or social reformers. Culturally, at least, they tend to be conservative; they transmit the heritage and respect community values. If they criticize new trends, such as the increasing use of instructional technology, they do so generally from a pedagogical rather than a political standpoint. Marxist proposals for teacher action are likely to founder not only on this conservatism but also on the self-interest of the profession as a whole. I say "self-interest" because, under present conditions, most teachers are aware that any radical social action by the profession is likely to antagonize both the public and the government while promising them little or no spiritual or material reward.

Marxism also may be said to conflict with the Western tradition of personal responsibility and self-reliance. Marxism shifts the blame for many acts from the individual to the class and ultimately to the economic system. Thus, Bowles and Gintis do not condemn the school as such for its role in stratifying American youth for the work place. Most teachers and administrators mean well, but they are in bondage to the capitalist system without realizing it. Similarly, Apple refuses to blame kindergarten teachers for accustoming young children to the demands of "work."[53] Most of these teachers are humane and caring, he says, and simply do not realize the consequences of their actions. I would reply that most teachers do realize the consequences of their actions, though not necessarily in Marxist terms. It is the duty of all teachers in a free society to reflect constantly on their actions, because they are responsible for consequences they could have foreseen if they had reflected long or deeply enough. Moreover, in any enlightened democracy public schools are organized and administered not by social classes but by individuals or their representatives. This is because schools are part of a political system that maximizes individual freedom, provided the individual is willing to use that freedom for the good of society as well as for his or her personal advancement.

In all fairness Marxist educationists ought to point out that in Marxist-oriented countries, too, education reproduces the social structure, in this case one dominated by the ruling party rather than by a corporate class. Marxist school systems indoctrinate more rigorously than democratic ones, since, in the United States especially, democracy is expected to accommodate various cultures and value systems. Marxist schools also steer their students more firmly toward different sectors of the state-controlled economy. To be sure, these facts do not refute the Marxist analysis of class bias in American public schooling, but they do correct the impression given by Marxists that capitalist schooling alone is guilty of reproduction.

On the positive side, Marxists offer large-scale theories that purport to show how social, economic, and cultural factors to a considerable extent rule our lives. When these theories are wrong, it generally is because Marxists exaggerate the effects of the factors on which they focus. Nonetheless, they often direct our attention to influences that we had not noticed and that we later can assess more accurately. Marcuse, for instance, overestimates the power exercised by the media and corporations.

---

[53]*Ideology and Curriculum*, p. 57.

But he has shown that they guide our choices more than we realized. Habermas judges natural science too harshly (for it is contemplative in intent as well as controlling), and he overestimates the scope of psychoanalysis (which hardly is a model for teaching). Yet he has revealed that supposedly disinterested knowledge is more "interested" than we had thought. Bowles and Gintis exaggerate the hidden influence of the economy on the personal development of American students, but that the economy has *some* influence on their development hardly can be denied. Apple at times attaches too much reality to his Marxist abstractions. Nevertheless, with their aid he points to a web of connections among the individual, the school, the economic base, and the superstructure that we might not otherwise have noticed.

Marxism also is becoming less dogmatic and determinist. The resilience of capitalism has forced Marxists to incorporate other approaches in order to explain the movement of events. The critical theory of Habermas shows how many different ideas Marxism can accommodate from other sources. Apple and his sympathizers combine a Marxist grasp of structural features with a sensitivity to life in the individual school. This eclectic, humanist approach offers more to western education than other forms of Marxism.

Finally, Marxists are genuinely moved by the injustices in our society. This concern gives their work an emotional force absent from much positivist thinking. I myself find some of the emotion misdirected—at "profit-hungry" capitalists, for example, or "greedy" entrepreneurs. But I do believe that this emotion also leads many Marxists to focus on matters of real importance to education.

Romanticism

7

Common Themes

Two hundred years ago the romantic writers extolled the human power to envision and realize ideal states of affairs—ideal love, ideal goodness, ideal societies. Today, when we call someone a "romantic," we mean that he or she is a visionary, an idealist, a utopian. In the philosophy of education, however, the word denotes someone who holds ideas that hark back to the eighteenth-century philosopher and educator Jean-Jacques Rousseau. These ideas may be put as follows: (1) human beings are naturally good; (2) the purpose of education is self-development; (3) children should direct their own learning; (4) there should be no set curriculum; (5) there should be no gap between education and life; (6) grading and competition are harmful. Let me expand a little on each of these ideas.[1]

---

[1]In doing so, I refer back to Rousseau because he not only introduced these ideas but expressed them as eloquently as any subsequent thinker. On Rousseau and his relation to recent romanticist thinking in education, see Robin Barrow, *Radical Education: A Critique of Freeschooling and Deschooling* (New York: Wiley, 1978), chs. 1–3.

1. *In the romanticist view, people by nature are good, honest, and loving.* If they turn out evil, dishonest, and hateful, it is because they have been warped by their upbringing or corrupted by society. As Rousseau puts it, "Everything is good as it comes from the hands of the author of Nature; man meddles with it and it deteriorates."[2] *The central purpose of education is to allow the child to grow naturally under benevolent guidance.*

2. *Only by promoting individual self-development can education help create the good society.* Romanticists value individual happiness and freedom more highly than anything else. Hence they reject any claim that education should prepare people directly for their place in the economy or society, or that it explicitly should further social and political goals extrinsic to personal growth. "Fit a man's education to his real self," says Rousseau, "not to what is no part of him."[3]

3. *If children are to realize their unique potential, they must direct their own learning.* Worthwhile knowledge is the result of personal reflection on experience. Even when this experience includes the study of grammatical rules or scientific facts, the final interpretation and emotional coloring still are the individual's. Children naturally are curious and will seek to make sense of their world with little adult intervention. A teacher should encourage them to inquire, solve problems, and test things for themselves. Thus Rousseau advises, "It is not your business to teach him the various sciences [i.e., branches of knowledge] but to give him a taste for them and methods of learning them when his taste is more mature."[4]

4. *Filling the minds of children with preformed, academic subject matter separates them from the real world to which that subject matter is supposed to refer.*[5] There is, in any case, little formal knowledge that everyone needs to acquire. "Give your scholar no verbal lessons," declares Rousseau, "he should be taught by

---

[2]Jean-Jacques Rousseau, *Emile* (New York: Dutton, 1911), p. 5.

[3]Ibid., pp. 156–157.

[4]Ibid., p. 135.

[5]Rousseau objects to "heraldry, geography, chronology, languages, etc., studies so remote from man, and even more remote from the child, that it is a wonder if he can ever make any use of any part of them" (ibid., p. 73).

experience alone."[6] A teacher may present problems to students, but students should find the solutions themselves. Literacy and computational skills are important, but they should be acquired in the course of other learning experiences rather than formally.

5. *Education should take place in and for the real world.* The child's community and surroundings are educative in themselves, and with adult guidance (though without overt instruction) this environment will lead to his or her full moral and intellectual development. The child's geography, says Rousseau, "will begin with the town he lives in." Again, to find out what life is like, the youngster must move among the poor, so that "the sight of suffering makes him suffer too."[7] Learning by doing and learning from sense experience put the child in touch with real life. "Our first teachers in natural philosophy," declares Rousseau, "are our feet, hands, and eyes."[8]

6. *Grading, competing, and awarding diplomas hinder personal development.* Grading rates children against external standards and so fails to respect their individuality. It also substitutes the teacher's judgment of children's performances for the meaning that those performances have for the children. Competition foments jealousy and hostility. It encourages children to measure themselves against others rather than follow their own desires. Diplomas state that young people have satisfied someone else's standards; they do not say what the youngsters have learned for themselves.

Forerunners

Other writers since Rousseau have expressed these ideas—among them A. S. Neill and Paul Goodman, the immediate forerunners of present-day romanticists.

---

[6]Ibid., p. 56.

[7]Ibid., pp. 134, 213.

[8]Ibid., p. 90. ("Natural philosophy" is what we now call "science.")

Neill

Neill maintains that, since children are born good, they should be surrounded by love and allowed for the most part to do what they want. "My view," he says, "is that a child is innately wise and realistic. If left to himself without adult suggestion of any kind, he will develop as far as he is capable of developing."[9] The prime aim of education, as of life itself, is happiness. If children are given love and freedom, they will grow up happily and will continue to be happy. Next to happiness, the conventional goals of education, such as academic competence or a taste for the arts, are of little account. "My own criterion of success," declares Neill, "is the ability to work joyfully and to live positively."[10]

At Summerhill children pretty much ran their own lives. With few exceptions, everything was settled by majority vote. No one was obliged to learn anything. Classes were held in traditional subjects, but children attended them voluntarily. Teaching as such was not considered important, since (in Neill's view) children learn what interests them and not what doesn't. "The child who wants to learn long division will learn it no matter how it is taught," insists Neill. Moreover, he adds, "Long division is of no importance except to those who want to learn it."[11] To the oft-asked question, "Won't the child turn round and blame the school for not making him learn arithmetic or music?," Neill replies that "young Freddie Beethoven and young Tommy Einstein will refuse to be kept away from their respective spheres."[12]

Critique   Neill has been criticized for pitching his claims too high. Since most of his students already have been "corrupted" by their parents, and some by other schools, how can he be sure that at Summerhill they grow up "naturally"? Again, if people always learn what they really want to and become what they

---

[9]A. S. Neill, *Summerhill: A Radical Approach to Child Rearing* (New York: Hart, 1960), p. 4. Summerhill (in England) was attended largely by children who had difficulty adjusting to regular schools.

[10]Ibid., p. 29.

[11]Ibid., p. 5.

[12]Ibid., p. 12.

are destined to become, what do they gain by attending Summerhill? On the other hand, if children are not all potential Einsteins and Beethovens, a school like Summerhill will fail to give them the disciplined habits from which they will benefit later in life. Neill also puts too much trust in instinct and too little in teaching. He does not see that children's minds and characters are formed as much by others as by the children themselves, and that good teaching can arouse interests that otherwise might remain dormant.[13]

Goodman

Goodman, too, castigates public schools. In his view, they hand out useless knowledge, fail to provide effective vocational training, and, worse, kill the child's natural curiosity. For Goodman, worthwhile learning is self-motivated. "On the whole," he says, "the education must be voluntary rather than compulsory, for no growth to freedom occurs except by intrinsic motivation."[14] Regarding the public schools as beyond rescue, Goodman proposes that the environment itself be made educative and that specific institutions be created to meet the need for specialized training or knowledge. In particular, he advocates mini-schools and apprenticeships.

Goodman's mini-schools are for children under 12 years. They contain about twenty-eight children and four adults (one, a licensed teacher) and they are administered jointly by parents, teachers, and the youngsters themselves. Located in a couple of rooms near the children's homes, the mini-schools concentrate on teaching the children to learn from their communities. There is no prearranged subject matter; the children learn what they want to. In Goodman's words: "It seems stupid to decide *a priori* what the young ought to know and then to try to motivate them, instead of letting the initiative come from them and putting information and relevant equipment at their service."[15]

---

[13]For some assessments of Neill, see Nathan W. Ackerman et al., *Summerhill: For and Against* (New York: Hart, 1970).

[14]Paul Goodman, *Compulsory Mis-education and the Community of Scholars* (New York: Vintage, 1966), p. 61.

[15]Paul Goodman, "Freedom and Learning: The Need for Choice," in *The Curriculum*, ed. R. Hooper (Edinburgh: Oliver & Boyd, 1971), p. 107. cited in Barrow, op. cit., pp. 100–101.

After age 12 there is no more schooling. Instead, youngsters are allowed to try out as many lifestyles and ways of earning a living as they wish. The aim is to "open as many diverse paths as possible, with plenty of opportunity to backtrack and change."[16] Teaching and training now are the responsibility of the appropriate professionals in any sphere. Individuals "apprentice" themselves to whoever can teach them what they want to know, from rock music to philosophy.

Goodman places himself in two traditions: that of Western civilization, from the ancient Greeks to the late nineteenth-century naturalists (e.g., Charles Darwin and Thomas Huxley), and that of Jeffersonian democracy. In the name of the first tradition he denounces the schools for teaching the cultural heritage (science, literature, history) as a means to immediate employment or college entrance rather than for its intrinsic truth and beauty. In the name of the second, he deplores the current practice of teaching people to adjust to authority and the work place rather than to participate as equals in a genuine democracy. Present-day education, he says, is irrelevant to such Jeffersonian aims as "citizenly initiative, the progress of an open society, or personal happiness."[17]

Critique   However lofty Goodman's ideals may be, some of his proposals are shortsighted. For example, youngsters are to learn only what interest them now, regardless of whether it will interest them later and regardless of what else may be of value to them but of no immediate interest. Again, instead of being guided by a carefully thought-out curriculum, youngsters remain exposed to the random conditioning of current society through the media and through the prejudices of their parents and peers. Goodman's apprenticeship system will equip them with some competencies and information but not with the span of related skills and knowledge provided by a standard curriculum. Finally, mini-schools will segregate children by neighborhoods instead of introducing them to a common realm of social concern and public knowledge. In summary, Goodman's proposals are likely to limit the range of knowledge and life choices

---

[16]Ibid., p. 109.

[17]*Compulsory Mis-education*, p. 21.

open to the individual even more than the present system does.[18]

Goodman's criticisms of contemporary education are mostly impressionistic. He makes sharp observations, but advances few deep or systematic explanations. For instance, he often says that the economy and the schools interlock, but he does not propose a mechanism through which they do so. He praises science, but it generally is physics he has in mind, and he fails to draw on the human sciences in his critique of contemporary life. Instead of presenting philosophic arguments, he refers to the two traditions I have mentioned, yet he does not use these traditions to explain his ideas. He keeps repeating that the traditions are missing from present-day education, but he does not show how they are missing (e.g., from the teaching of this short story or that historical event) or how they could be re-introduced. The closest he gets to bringing back the "austere morality" of science, for instance, is to suggest that the average youngster whose chemistry experiment does not "balance out" should "spend the entire semester in explaining the 'failure' and cleaning his test-tubes better."[19]

The Open Classroom: Kohl

Today's romanticists propose three main alternatives to traditional schooling: the "open" classroom, the "free" school, and no school at all. The open classroom may be located inside or outside the conventional school. It is dedicated to individual freedom, self-development, and participatory democracy. In Herbert Kohl's words, it is "an environment where many can discover themselves."[20] Self-discovery depends on personal choice, since the students who simply do what they are told do not know what else they may be capable of. Students in the open classroom choose what they will do, individually or as a

---

[18]Among the many formal criticisms of Goodman, those of Robin Barrow (op. cit., pp. 111–126) are especially incisive.

[19]*Compulsory Mis-education*, p. 98.

[20]Herbert Kohl, *The Open Classroom: A Practical Guide to a New Way of Teaching* (New York: New York Review, 1969), p. 115.

group, and the teacher follows their lead. They may choose to read, paint, talk to friends, or meditate for a while. If they are doing what they really want to, says Kohl, they generally are learning from it.

In such a classroom the teacher is not an authority but another person, older and more experienced than the students. Like them, the teacher expresses feelings. If the teacher is uncertain or angry, he or she says so. The teacher also relinquishes some of the powers conferred by the school. As Kohl puts it, the teacher has to be able to say, "I'm not going to grade, or I'm not going to punish people, or I'm not going to send anybody to the principal—and mean it."[21] Besides, says Kohl,[22]

[The teacher] has to come to realize that the things that work best in class for her are the unplanned ones, the ones that arise spontaneously because of a student's suggestion or a sudden perception. She trusts her intuitions and isn't too upset to abandon plans that had consumed time and energy.

Instead of instructing students, the teacher provides them with "options" to choose from—and add to. Teacher and students bring as many different materials to class as they can (such as second-hand books, rugs, toys, small furniture), so that there always are things they can choose to work with. Says Kohl, "One cannot ask pupils to be free or make choices in a vacuum."[23] As regards subject matter, the teacher introduces students to the possibilities for learning in a particular subject and then lets them decide which of these (or other) possibilities interest them. Mathematics, for instance, offers such activities as measuring, timing, bargaining, and gambling, while history supplies such themes as war, exploitation, love, and power.[24]

Kohl discusses how the teacher might introduce a short story.[25] He or she should present the story not as a masterpiece that students must appreciate but as a work that some may

---

[21]Ibid., p. 79.

[22]Ibid., pp. 41–42.

[23]Ibid., p. 99.

[24]Ibid., pp. 43–44.

[25]Ibid., pp. 54–55.

enjoy and others may not. Both the class as a whole and any individual student are entitled to turn the offer down and do something else. The teacher should try to anticipate what the students may find interesting in the story. If it is about a bank robbery, they may want to talk about prisons, banks, safes, locks, the causes of crime, and the possibilities of reformation. The teacher also should anticipate what the students may want to do in addition to discussing the story. They may want to parody it, write their own stories, act it out, change it, write a sequel, or read other stories by the same author.

How is order maintained in an open classroom? According to Kohl, the class orders itself. Conflict and disagreement, he says, are to be expected in any democratic community and should be resolved in the ordinary course of events. A fight between two boys, for instance, properly is seen as "an affair in the lives of men, not as a breach of discipline." The class must work out its own rules as the need arises, and one cannot tell "which rules or routines will emerge as convenient or necessary."[26] The teacher may arbitrate the application of these rules and, therefore, is "a mediator and not a judge or executioner." The teacher also must give up the idea that noise and movement are necessarily bad. Instead, they are evidence that the class is doing what it wants and so is likely to produce not chaos but "a more complex and freer order than is usually found in classrooms in the United States, or in the society at large for that matter."[27]

Is it easy to create an open classroom? No, replies Kohl, it is "no less difficult than changing one's own personality, and every bit as dangerous and time-consuming. It is also as rewarding." Kohl admits that it took him several years to "function in a freer environment."[28] He advises the teacher to loosen up little by little and to take the students into her confidence, "to tell them where she hopes to be and give them a sense of the difficulty of changing one's styles and habits." The students, too, will find the transition arduous, for they are no more accustomed to choosing for themselves than the teacher is, and

---

[26]Ibid., pp. 78, 29.

[27]Ibid., pp. 12, 43.

[28]Ibid., pp. 69, 70.

they "will even at times insist that the teacher tell them what to do."[29]

What is the philosophy behind the open classroom? At its core is the thesis that human beings naturally are good, and that the aim of education is to enable them to live freely and let this goodness unfold. This philosophy also is individualist, in that it seeks to change society only by changing individuals. On this view, self-expression and self-fulfillment in a particular community are more important than acquiring publicly validated knowledge or internalizing ideals that are good for human beings as such or for a particular society.

Kohl adds three elements of his own to this philosophy. First, he asserts that the chief problem facing educators is the constant presence of authoritarian modes of control and the need to develop open, democratic alternatives. Second, he holds that an open class essentially is a "community" that works together in an open environment, "often spilling out of the school into the streets, the neighborhood, and the city itself." Finally, he distinguishes between an open and a permissive classroom. In the latter the teacher "pretends" that annoying behavior "isn't annoying," and "permits students to behave only in certain ways, thereby retaining the authority over their behavior she pretends to be giving up." In an open classroom, on the other hand, the teacher "tries to express what she feels and to deal with each situation as a communal problem."[30]

Critique The philosophy behind the open classroom is deficient on several counts. First, it makes the false assumption that, if you abolish authority, you also abolish the need for it. In an open classroom the teacher renounces authority so that the youngster may grow up free. But society at large must be governed and organized, and hence depends on authority. If society is to function, its members must accept the authority of employers, judges, policemen, elected officials, bankers, civil servants, physicians, and others. An adult also must exercise authority—as a parent, employee, officer of an organization (PTA, union, camera club), and in crises (deaths, crimes, and

---

[29]Ibid., pp. 80, 98.

[30]Ibid., pp. 14–15.

disasters). An adult must know, too, how to deal with authority (how to apply for jobs and loans, for instance) and also on occasion how to confront it. Now, an open classroom might give the youngster an opportunity to confront authority. For example, the class might decide to support a local strike or boycott. But it provides very little experience in accepting or exercising authority. In these respects it fails in its responsibility to the individual and society alike.

Second, the open classroom undervalues organized knowledge and disciplined thinking. The traditional disciplines—math, science, language, literature, history—contain the knowledge and skills on which the economy, the state, and civil society mainly depend. Since they also are the most effective tools for understanding and operating in these realms, they are equally valuable to the individual. In freeing youngsters from the demands of the academic disciplines, the open classroom denies them the knowledge and habits of thought necessary for exercising their freedom effectively in later life. Thus, the philosophy that states that youngsters cannot be free in a vacuum, itself leads to a knowledge vacuum.

Third, Kohl fails to distinguish satisfactorily between the open and the permissive classroom. Actually, both classrooms are permissive, since in both the teacher permits behavior that is forbidden in a conventional classroom and permits the children's interests to govern what they learn.

Finally, an open classroom requires an unusual teacher—one who is flexible, nondirective, and relatively impervious to noise and disorder. Too few aspiring teachers have the right personality for this role. True, for some students the open classroom may be a desirable alternative to the ordinary public school. It may even be a useful learning experience for every student for a year or two. But for most students it is no overall substitute for conventional schooling, and as a preparation for higher education it is quite inadequate.

The Free School: Kozol

The quintessential free school is small, urban, and dedicated to the needs of the poor and the minorities. It differs from the open classroom in two main ways. (1) It regards its students as members of an oppressed community rather than as unique individuals. (2) It helps them develop abilities that may benefit their community, such as a talent for law or engineering, rather than abilities of no particular social value. One of the most eloquent spokesmen for the free school is Jonathan Kozol.

Kozol is scathing in his denunciation of the public school system. He calls it "an intellectual and custodial Hell" whose "real creative occupation" is "the process of menial-labor manufacture."[31] To keep up its fighting spirit, he advises the free school to locate itself in sight of its enemy, *across the street* from that old, hated, but still-standing and still-murderous construction."[32] Nevertheless, he is not a revolutionary or even a Marxist but an angry American who wants to make society share its benefits with the urban underclass. He tells radical freeschoolers that they must make compromises in order to win the backing of the rich and the foundations, and he suggests ways for the school to earn money, such as operating a franchise or selling college textbooks.

Kozol rejects the extreme individualism of the open classroom. If the children of the oppressed are to survive and succeed, they need the same curriculum and credentials as other children. The free school therefore must teach some of the same content as the public school, but teach it differently. It must condense the academic curriculum for faster coverage. High school French or Spanish, for instance, can be handled in three months rather than three years. The school also must relate subject matter to the lives of its students. Youngsters learn to read more quickly when they see words that excite them, like "sex" and "cops" and "cash" and "speed," instead of words like "postman," "grandmother," and "briefcase." They take to math more readily when it is used to analyze the costs and receipts of the local drug trade (the "Heroin Equation" as Kozol's students called it).[33]

In Kozol's view, the free school needs strong, forceful teachers, men and women who will not conceal the real power they

---

[31]Jonathan Kozol, *Free Schools* (Boston: Houghton Mifflin, 1972), pp. 118, 117. In his *On Being a Teacher* (New York: Continuum, 1981) Kozol is a little more restrained.

[32]*Free Schools*, p. 50.

[33]Ibid., pp. 35, 40, 76.

have as knowledgeable adults. Such teachers have two main tasks: to present the subject matter that is needed, and to be role models of "effective, bold, risk-taking, conscientious and consistent adults." As role models, they show that there is no need to deny one's nature to suit "the oppressor." Hence they express in class "all of the richness, humor, desperation, rage, . . . strength and pathos which they would reveal, as well, to other grown-ups."[34]

Critique   Kozol should be read more for his real-life descriptions and practical suggestions than for any theoretical depth. He cites Freire approvingly, but does not approach him in explaining the psychological effects of oppression. He excoriates society's indifference to the poor, but blames it on individual callousness rather than on any psychological or socioeconomic mechanisms of which people may be unaware. He travesties the public school system, calling it a "concentration camp" and a "prison." He does not analyze its failings in detail and supplies no data to back his charges.

Kozol's notion of liberation is important but limited. He wants to liberate the poor from poverty and their children from an educational system that (in his view) prevents them from improving their lot. He does not consider the need of youngsters to liberate themselves from a narrow outlook on life and from the psychological conditioning of their peers or (irresponsible) parents. It does not occur to him that if all that the oppressed acquire is the knowledge and skills of the oppressor, they may reproduce the same social arrangements over again. In his overwhelming desire to help poor youths to find a career, Kozol forgets to help them find themselves as individuals.

Deschooling: Illich[35]

Some romanticists want to abolish schools altogether. According to Ivan Illich, schools corrupt people by leading them to

---

[34]Ibid., pp. 57, 58.

[35]For other approaches to deschooling, see Everett Reimer, *School is Dead: Alternatives in Education* (Garden City, N.Y.: Doubleday Anchor, 1972); and John Holt, *Freedom and Beyond* (New York: Dutton, 1972).

believe that their needs (e.g., for health, personal mobility, and psychological healing) should be met by institutions providing appropriate services or "treatments." The schools have this effect, says Illich, because they convince people that in order to learn anything, they have to be taught it formally. This conviction gives rise to the belief that other needs too should be satisfied by institutions.

In fact, Illich insists, the schools fail to meet either of the two main needs to which they address themselves: the need for skills and the need for liberal or "humane" education. Schools fail with the first need mainly because they are "curricular." "In most schools," he maintains, "a program which is meant to improve one skill is chained always to another irrelevant task. History is tied to advancement in math, and class attendance to the right to use the playground." Schools fail with the second need because they are compulsory and thus provide "schooling for schooling's sake: an enforced stay in the company of teachers, which pays off in the doubtful privilege of more such company."[36] Since it mainly is the schools that have corrupted society (or so Illich claims), a better society can be created only by abolishing schools altogether and finding new approaches to skill acquisition and humane education.

What are Illich's new approaches? He proposes four educational "networks": (1) reference services to educational objects; (2) skill exchanges; (3) peer-matching; (4) reference services to educators at large.

1.   "Reference services to educational objects," says Illich, "facilitate access to things or processes used for formal learning." Some of these things may be kept in libraries, rental agencies, laboratories, and museums. Others may be in regular use in factories or farms and "made available to students as apprentices or in off-hours."[37] Illich maintains that if the goals of learning were no longer "dominated" by schools, "the market for learners would be much more various and the definition of 'educational artifacts' would be less restrictive." For example, tool shops and gaming rooms would attract learners. "Photo labs and offset presses would allow neighborhood newspapers

---

[36]Ivan Illich, *Deschooling Society* (New York: Harper & Row, 1974), p. 17.

[37]Ibid., p. 78.

to flourish." "Storefront learning centers could contain viewing booths for closed-circuit television." Film clubs would compete with one another and with commercial TV.[38]

2.   The "skill exchange network" would consist of people who possess certain skills and are willing to teach them to others. Teachers of skills, says Illich, could be paid out of public funds in at least two ways. One way would be to create government-supported free skill centers especially in industrial areas. These centers could teach the skills needed for certain apprentice-ships—skills such as typing, accounting, computer program-ming, and handling machinery. Another way would be to create a "'bank' for skill exchange." Each citizen would receive a "basic credit," monetary or the equivalent, with which to acquire cer-tain fundamental skills. Further credits would go to those who earned them by teaching. Those who had taught others for a given amount of time could claim that time from more ad-vanced teachers. Thus, says Illich, "an entirely new elite would be promoted, an elite of those who earned their education by sharing it."[39]

3.   The "peer-matching network" would be used by people who want to share an interest with others. The interest could be a TV series, the work of an author, a game like chess, an activity like bird-watching, and so on. Participants would state their names and addresses and the interests for which they sought peers. A computer then would send them back the names and addresses of those who had given the same description. Bul-letin boards and classified ads could be used if the computer did not produce a match. Illich suggests that space in school build-ings be given over to persons who wish to share their interests with larger groups. "Each could state what he would do in the now abandoned classroom and when, and a bulletin board would bring the available programs to the attention of the in-quirers."[40]

4.   "Reference services to educators-at-large" would meet the need for guidance experienced by participants in the other

---

[38]Ibid., p. 84.
[39]Ibid., p. 90.
[40]Ibid., p. 94.

three networks. Illich distinguishes between three types of "special educational competence . . . [:] one to create and operate the kinds of educational exchanges or networks outlined here; another to guide students and parents in the use of these networks; and a third to act as *primus inter pares* in undertaking difficult intellectual exploratory voyages."[41] Network administrators, possessing the first competence, "would concentrate primarily on the building and maintenance of roads providing access to resources." "Pedagogical counselors," possessing the second competence, "would help the student to find the path which for him could lead fastest to his goal"—for example, by recommending books and places for apprenticeship. Educational "initiators or leaders," possessing the third competence, would act as "masters" with "disciples." Common to all master-disciple relationships, says Illich, is "the awareness both share that their relationship is literally priceless and in very different ways a privilege for both." In the society of the future, he maintains, such "exploratory, inventive, creative teaching would logically be counted among the most desirable forms of leisurely 'unemployment'."[42]

Illich calls for political revolution as well as educational change. If the schools alone are disestablished, he says, other social institutions may be used to condition us more effectively still. The result may be "more subtle and more numbing than is the present society, in which many people at least experience a feeling of release on the last day of school."[43] Illich therefore urges the creation of a democratic, participatory society, in which each person works to fulfill himself, without requiring as a condition "the enforced labor or the enforced learning or the enforced consumption of another."[44] Illich does not predict what new social forms will emerge. If people create their own institutions, he says, rather than receive them from an elite,

---

[41]Ibid., p. 98.

[42]Ibid., pp. 98ff.

[43]Ivan Illich, "After Deschooling, What?" in *After Deschooling, What?* ed. Alan Gartner, Frank Riessman, and Colin Greer (New York: Harper & Row, 1973), p. 16.

[44]Ivan Illich, *Tools for Conviviality* (New York: Harper & Row, 1973), p. 13.

they will discover the forms that suit them in the process of creation itself.

Critque   In my view,[45] Illich makes four crucial, highly dubious assumptions. First, he assumes that children *want* to learn what they need to know for their full development as persons, and hence that they will seek this knowledge from those who offer to teach it. This assumption flies in the face of two obvious facts: (1) children cannot tell what they will need to know; and (2) since this knowledge often is hard to master and of little immediate interest, children rarely are motivated to learn it.

Next, Illich takes for granted that those who possess knowledge and skills will be able and willing to teach them. Here he ignores the fact that people tend to forget how they learned the basic intellectual skills and subject matter on which later academic and much other learning depend. In order to teach reading, elementary math, and introductory science, people must learn both what to teach and how to teach it. They must train themselves, or be trained by others, to be successful teachers— and Illich is opposed to teachers. As for more advanced skills, such as those of the physician or the engineer, how many professionals will want to teach them if they can get more money or greater satisfaction from practicing them? Some, obviously. But how will these professionals meet the potentially high demand for their services unless they teach in institutions offering instruction to large numbers of people—in a word, schools?

Again, Illich assumes that any knowledge or skill can be learned at any age and apparently in any order. But certain skills are learned best when young—writing and computation, for instance, as well as certain work habits and good manners. Indeed, schooling may be regarded as a benevolent form of coercion that creates habits for which adults often are grateful, regardless of what they felt as children. As for knowledge that can be learned later but only in sequence (such as math, science, and languages), who will do the sequencing? Illich expects "something like an invisible hand"[46] to harmonize supply and

---

[45]For other criticisms of Illich, see Gartner et al., and Barrow, *Radical Education*, ch. 6.

[46]Sidney Hook, "Illich's De-Schooled Utopia," in Cornelius J. Troost, *Radical School Reform: Critique and Alternatives* (Boston: Little, Brown, 1973), p. 69.

demand in the educational free market. But if this mechanism works imperfectly in the ordinary market, why expect it to perform better here? For example, the person who taught me elementary algebra may not teach intermediate algebra, and the other teachers of this subject may be occupied. As a result, I may feel obliged to postpone studying physics, which requires intermediate algebra.

Illich's fourth assumption is that people will learn what is intellectually, morally, and aesthetically worthwhile—that they will turn to the novel rather than pulp fiction, to philosophy and not the crossword puzzle. But popular taste in entertainment justifies no such optimism. It is the school that gives many of us our intellectual and aesthetic standards. It is the school that guides us until we are ready to choose intelligently how we will continue to grow. Take the school away, and how will we tell what knowledge is of most worth?

Another serious flaw is the lack of official controls on those who would teach. Expertise would be assessed simply by polling former students and clients. For Illich, anyone has the right to teach anything at all; it is a right as basic as the right of free speech, hence a right that does not have to be earned. If so, the networks might well attract quacks and incompetents eager to thrive off an ill-educated public.

Are there any virtues in Illich's ideas? Certainly. Illich thinks more deeply and systematically than most romanticists, and he is more conscious of history. The very scale of his critique and proposals has led many people to look harder at the purposes and accomplishments of our educational system. Are the schools expected to do too much? Could parents and others be more responsible for the moral and psychological growth of the young? Could the YMCA take over most of the athletics program? Are schools necessary at all? Could students see their teachers in their homes or offices (like physicians)? Illich's work has provoked these and many other questions. It has made the schools more self-critical and more aware of the need to justify their existence.

Moreover, there is much to be said for Illich's networks provided they are not expected to bear the main burden of education. At their best, they would offer a wide range of learning experiences and would respond quickly to new social and cultural developments. They would give many people the joy of teaching and the pleasure of social contact. They would increase participation in cultural and intellectual life. They would stimulate some people to take charge of their own intellectual growth, and they would make education a lifelong process. It is not surprising that some alternative learning centers in our cities partly have been inspired by them.

Illich's networks may prove most useful in underdeveloped nations that cannot afford mass, public education. Where relatively few people can pay for formal schooling, the vast majority need an alternative. For such countries Illich offers a "bootstrap" system that may work. Illich's critique seems designed as much to show the unsuitability of mass schooling for most of the Third World as to find flaws in the educational systems of the industrialized nations.

Appraisal

Most romanticists are inclined to interpret education subjectively. They write less from theory than from direct experience. Their perceptions are apt to be intense rather than exact; their judgments, deeply felt rather than carefully weighed. For the most part they ignore research and, with exceptions such as Goodman and Illich, even organized knowledge. Moreover, except for Illich, they lack a sense of history. They write largely out of the present moment with an eye on the immediate future. As a result they advocate, sans acknowledgment, much that was recommended by certain progressive educators earlier in the century.

Although the romanticists want to transform society, most are individualists by temperament. They rarely state what large-scale social consequences they expect their educational ventures to have. Indeed, they seem uncertain whether these ventures are ideals for the society they want or ways to attain this society. Only Kozol makes detailed proposals for cooperation among radical educators, and he is among the least individualist and most group-minded of the American romanticists.

Romanticist undertakings seem likely to succeed only in

special circumstances. Kohl's open classrooms need unusually dedicated, flexible, nondirective teachers, as well as tolerant principals. Kozol's free schools need to be small and have neighborhood support. Yet how many neighborhoods will back schools that oppose majority values? Illich's deschooling assumes the desirability of a low-growth society. How many societies will make that choice?

Again, many romanticist ventures seem likely to confine young people within their backgrounds. Kohl's open classroom, focusing on children's interests, tends to increase the influence of the environment that originally provided these interests. Kozol's free school tends to bind children to their communities. Illich's networks, it is true, are designed to multiply contacts across regions and social classes. Yet they are unlikely to give individuals firm moral and cultural values and, as a result, may leave them more susceptible to the influences of media, cults, and peers.

The romanticists do not equip young people well enough to deal with today's society. They prepare them to be happy (Neill, Kohl), to be in touch with their communities (Kozol), or to choose their own learning paths (Illich), rather than to cope directly with the larger world they will enter. Since the romanticists do not show how society will change to accommodate the attitudes they foster, they hardly are justified in inculcating them.

The romanticists do not sufficiently appreciate that most adults (parents especially) want the school to train and discipline the young. The romanticists do not see why children must wait before they are called on, why they must tolerate boredom and frustration, take orders, be neat and orderly for no obvious reason, compete with one another, perform uninteresting tasks, defer gratification. But these are precisely the behaviors required of workers everywhere, and that is why the school is expected to inculcate them. Unless there is a major shift in majority values, it is naive to suppose that schools will be allowed to abandon the task of discipline.

The romanticists overlook both the solidarity and the fun of ordinary school life. Granted, the school disciplines and often constrains its students, yet it also gives them experiences of comradeship, sport, and collective enjoyment. In a host of extracurricular activities students can express themselves and meet like-minded partners. These facts largely refute romanticist charges that schools imprison the young (Kozol) and manipulate them (Illich). Moreover, by offering common experiences of learning, playing, and maturing together, schools unite people rather than separate them. Unlike the educational ventures of the romanticists, which would do little if anything to make society less segregated, the public schools play an important part in holding society together.

Nevertheless, the romanticists deserve the last word. Their approach expresses a perennial human desire that the young should grow up free and happy without having to undergo the self-denial of their elders. It articulates the belief that a fresh start can be made and that the young, uncorrupted by the world, should have the chance to express rather than restrain themselves. The romanticists are only the latest to voice this longing. In the years to come we will hear it again and again, and with luck our schools and our society will respond to it.

Conservatism

8

Traditional Conservatism

There are two main strands in conservative thinking, the "traditional" and the "libertarian." The traditional strand descends from Edmund Burke, the eighteenth-century English statesman-philosopher who opposed both Rousseau and the French Revolution. It is represented in education today by such thinkers as Michael Oakeshott, Geoffrey Bantock, and Russell Kirk. What is its essential message?

1. *Traditional conservatives believe in the existence of objective moral and other values.* These values, whether established by God or rooted in human nature, represent an order to which both society and the individual should conform. Although people may differ on details, say traditional conservatives, they nevertheless share, or should share, the same basic values. People may disagree, for example, as to how much democracy is desirable, but they believe, or should believe, that everyone is entitled to some say in how the social order is maintained and strengthened. Again, while people may differ passionately over particular educational issues, they generally agree that school-

219

ing is desirable as a means of passing on the heritage and enabling the individual to fulfill himself.

2.   For traditional conservatives, *society is a finely adjusted organism that has evolved through centuries of trial and reflection.* Over time, say these conservatives, institutions are tested against the needs they are intended to satisfy. Institutions that work, survive; and nothing that long has survived should lightly be discarded. *Since society is finely adjusted, the schools alone neither should nor can engineer fundamental social reforms.* They should not do so because any single institution ought to respect the complex balance of other institutions. They cannot do so because they themselves interlock with such traditional institutions as families, churches, media, and peer groups.

3.   These conservatives maintain that *tradition is wiser than the individual or the group.* If we moderns can see a little further than our ancestors, it is only because we have the benefit of the wisdom for which they had to struggle. Some past achievements cannot be equaled. We are unlikely, says Russell Kirk, "to make any brave or new discoveries in morals or politics or taste."[1] *The prime purpose of education, therefore, is to transmit the wisdom of the past.* Most of this wisdom is contained in the major intellectual disciplines: history, language, literature, mathematics, and science. These represent the tested ways that have been developed to understand and handle the central aspects of human experience. They should form the major part of the curriculum today.

4.   Traditional conservatives *welcome the diversity of social classes, institutions, and ways of life.* Individuals, they hold, largely are formed by the social structures to which they belong, such as families, unions, businesses, professional associations, clubs, churches, and political parties. The more such structures there are in a society, the wider is the range of individuals; and the more such structures people belong to, the more they tend to individualize themselves. Thus, these conservatives *denounce the spread of bureaucracies that take over the work done by other*

---

[1] Russell Kirk, "Conservatism: A Succinct Description," *National Review* (September 3, 1982), 1081. Two recent books in the traditionalist vein are *The Portable Conservative Reader,* ed. Kirk (New York: Viking-Penguin, 1982) and George F. Will, *Statecraft as Soulcraft: What Government Does* (New York: Simon and Schuster, 1983).

social forms necessary for individuality. They deplore the tendency to burden the school with functions that, in their view, are the province of other agencies—such as sex education, which belongs (they say) to the family or the church, and the more specialized forms of vocational training, which belong in the work place. They also advocate a multiplicity of private schools to stimulate the public schools and provide alternatives to them.

Inequality, say these conservatives, is a fact of life and must be accepted. People are equal before God and the law but unequal in other ways. Attempts at leveling lead either to social stagnation, since now one has less incentive to distinguish oneself, or to new forms of inequality no better than the old, as in the case of reverse discrimination. Thus, conservatives generally *oppose attempts to "equalize" education through such measures as forced busing, fixed quotas, and affirmative action over the wishes of the local population.*

5.   Traditional conservatives maintain that *since human beings are fallible, society is bound to be imperfect.* Utopias demand too much of human nature. "All that we can expect," says Kirk, "is a tolerably ordered, just, and free society, in which some evils, maladjustments, and suffering continue to lurk."[2] Public education, too, is limited in what it can achieve. Without parental assistance it cannot make the young morally better than their elders. Nor can it provide an "ideal" learning experience that ignores the economy's need for suitably educated workers and professionals. *In the main, education must reflect the society it serves, while at all times seeking to improve it according to that society's standards.*

Oakeshott: Initiation into a Tradition

For the meaning of "tradition" in conservatism and education we turn first to Michael Oakeshott. For him education is initiation into a tradition or civilization. By "tradition" he means a complex of feelings, thoughts, languages, skills, books, "instruments," and so forth. Tradition is not finished and structured but "miscellaneous and incoherent." It is what human beings

---

[2]Ibid., 1082.

have achieved by exploiting opportunities and exercising their own ingenuity. Tradition "often speaks in riddles . . . . It has no meaning as a whole; it cannot be learnt or taught in principle, only in detail." Tradition also enables people to make the most of themselves, because it contains everything to which value may be attributed ("it is the ground or context of every judgment of better or worse"). Aided by tradition, people see what they can achieve and what they can become.[3]

Oakeshott distinguishes between three types of education: school, vocational, and university. School education passes on the basic skills and "intellectual capital" of a tradition, both of which should be taught rather than discovered by students for themselves. Students also must learn much that does not appeal to them and that they may not fully understand. Oakeshott continues:[4]

School education . . . is not concerned with individual talents and aptitudes, and if these show themselves (as they may), the design in school education is not to allow them to take charge. At school we are, quite properly, not permitted to follow our own inclinations.

Vocational education, says Oakeshott, is not part of schooling but, like university education, follows it. In vocational education a person acquires a body of knowledge in order to practice a trade or profession. He or she studies knowledge in current use but not its history. At a university the student learns to explore one of the basic "modes of thought," such as literature, science, or philosophy. The student does this for its own sake rather than to prepare for a profession or to produce new knowledge. The latter task "properly" belongs to the "professional researcher."

How is the student "initiated into a tradition"? From the teacher's point of view, says Oakeshott, tradition is equivalent to knowledge, and knowledge consists of "information" and "judgment." Information comprises facts, such as names,

---

[3]Michael Oakeshott, "Learning and Teaching," in *The Concept of Education*, ed. R. S. Peters (London: Routledge & Kegan Paul, 1967), pp. 158–162.

[4]Michael Oakeshott, "The Study of Politics in a University," *Rationalism in Politics and Other Essays* (New York: Basic Books, 1962), p. 306.

dates, and meanings of words; and also rules, such as those of grammar and mathematics. What matters about information is "the accuracy with which it is learned" and "the readiness with which it can be recollected and used."[5] Judgment is "being able to think . . . with an appreciation of the considerations that belong to different modes of thought." What does such thinking involve? First, says Oakeshott, the student "learns to interpret and use information." This entails applying a range of rules appropriate to a mode of thought. (Rules that apply in science, for example, do not normally hold in literature, history, or philosophy.) Instead of doing an exercise that involves a particular rule of French grammar, the student writes an essay in French. In this respect, says Oakeshott, judgment is a form of "connoisseurship," of expertise in handling information:[6]

[Judgment] enables him to determine relevance . . . allows him to distinguish between different sorts of questions and the different sorts of answers they call for . . . emancipates him from crude absolutes and suffers him to give his assent and dissent in graduated terms.

But judgment includes more than the interpretation and use of information. It includes the ability to "recognize and enjoy the intellectual virtues," such as unbiased curiosity, exactness, concentration, and skepticism. Above all, judgment involves "the ability to detect the individual intelligence which is at work in every utterance, even in those which convey impersonal information."[7] The manifestation of individuality in every significant act, work, or utterance Oakeshott calls "style." The word "style" conveys that this is not a raw and untutored self-expression but rather one that has been both empowered and tempered by a tradition.

Style, says Oakeshott, is the "self-expression of the culturally formed individual." For the traditional conservative, an act, idea, or utterance is important primarily as the expression of a tradition or civilization. For the romanticist, by contrast, an act, idea, or utterance is noteworthy chiefly as an expression of a

[5]"Learning and Teaching," p. 172.
[6]Ibid., p. 173.
[7]Ibid., p. 174.

unique individual almost regardless of his culture. For a Marxist, it is significant largely as the revelation of the thinking of a social class. For a positivist, it is significant mainly as an effect of some psychological or sociological factor(s), such as intelligence, habit strength, or social role.

Style transcends rules. The rules of a mode of thought only enable us to do or say so much. The rules of French grammar, for instance, do not always tell us which word or tense to use to express a shade of meaning. Where the rules stop, says Oakeshott, we must exercise judgment, a faculty based on rules but not limited by them. Just as judgment recognizes style, so too it is expressed *in* style. For style is "the choice made, not according to rules, but within the area of freedom left by the negative operation of rules," that is, in the realm where rules no longer apply and indeed may not be relevant. Science, philosophy, history, and other disciplines "are not modes of thought *defined* by rules; they exist only in personal explorations of territories only the boundaries of which are subject to definition."[8] Within these territories much is too subtle and complex to be captured in rules and abstractions. We must develop a "feel" for these realms. We must know them intuitively.

How, then, is judgment taught? According to Oakeshott, it cannot be taught separately or according to rules. Instead, it is "imparted" at the same time, but not in the same way, as information:[9]

Judgment is implanted unobtrusively in the manner in which information is conveyed, in a tone of voice, in the gesture which accompanies instruction, in asides and oblique utterances, and by [personal] example.

Thus, the teacher exemplifies the intellectual virtues and "never stoops to the priggishness of mentioning them . . . . Not the cry but the rising of the wild duck impels the flock to follow him in flight."

How is judgment learned? Oakeshott says it is learned chiefly by imitation, conscious or unconscious. Students imitate their teacher until her style or his becomes second nature to

---

[8]Ibid., pp. 174–175.
[9]Ibid.

them. This is not to say that they acquire the teacher's manner-
isms but that they absorb his or her ways of thinking. Once
learned, says Oakeshott, judgment "can never be forgotten. . . .
It is, indeed, often enough, the residue which remains when all
else is forgotten, the shadow of lost knowledge."[10]

Obviously the cultivation of judgment demands a great deal
of teachers. Each must be master of a mode of thought. Each
must have a style that expresses itself throughout his or her
teaching. Each must live up to high standards, knowing that
every turn of phrase, every gesture, every intonation can and
should carry a style that students may imitate. Thus,
Oakeshott's view of teaching is characteristically conservative.
For him, the teacher exemplifies a tradition and, in so doing,
provides a model for the student to emulate.

Critique   Although closely reasoned and elegantly expressed,
Oakeshott's ideas may be criticized on several grounds. First,
Oakeshott underestimates what young people can contribute to
their own schooling. He maintains that, in presenting information, the teacher "quite properly" ignores students' personal
interests, but he does not say why it is "proper" for the teacher
to do so. In my view, since students' interests motivate them to
learn, it is self-evident that at least some of the things that
Oakeshott wants to teach them will be learned more effectively
if they are related to those interests. Moreover, ignoring interests would seem to discriminate unfairly against those whose
education ceases with the high (secondary) school. These students have the most pressing interests, since they will be seeking jobs soonest, yet they alone are educated without reference
to their interests. This is not to say that interests need be merely
job related or that they should determine the course of studies,
but rather that interests other than the purely academic should
be taken into account.

Second, Oakeshott's ideas on judgment and style are by no
means clear. Is style, for example, primarily intellectual, or does
it include morality, aesthetic taste, and some relation to a person's emotions? If style is primarily intellectual, how can it
affect the student as deeply as Oakeshott implies, since adoles-

---

[10]Ibid., p. 175.

cents especially live so much in their emotions? On the other hand, if style is more encompassing, how can it fail to reflect a teacher's ambivalent feelings or inner conflicts? If it does reflect these, it would seem that at least some teachers will impart conflicting attitudes rather than a coherent style.

Third, it is untrue that judgment always is communicated indirectly. Take the cases of literary appreciation and philosophy. A teacher who communicates directly and explicitly, stating that a given poem or argument is good for reasons she explains, surely conveys as much of importance as a teacher who communicates mainly through gestures, tones of voice, and the like. Since the first teacher's reasons form the core of her stated judgment of the poem or argument, they must express the essential content of the mental processes through which she made that judgment. Thus, they must belong to the core of the teacher's "habit of thought" or style. Again, if judgment is imparted in a teacher's style, and if style represents a tradition, how does the student learn to criticize that tradition? Oakeshott should realize that traditions need to be criticized as well as perpetuated.

These flaws, however, are outweighed by Oakeshott's many contributions. For example, he rightly appreciates that a tradition is not a system but the outcome of an infinite number of historical processes, and hence an accumulation that contains many puzzles and inconsistencies. He is correct, too, in his view that judgment consists (among other things) in choosing from a range of rules rather than applying a single one. Again, he is right to say that judgment also comes into play when the rules no longer apply. More importantly, he sets a high value on teaching as the transmission and exemplification of a tradition, and he believes fervently in personal contact between teacher and student in the communication of style. As he himself says, his reflections were stimulated by his own experience as a teacher. His love of teaching shows itself in his concrete, personal manner of writing. All in all, he deserves R. S. Peters' accolade, that here is "an extremely civilized man writing with acuteness, elegance, and conviction about a matter which is of no small account—the passing on of a civilization."[11]

---

[11]R. S. Peters, "Michael Oakeshott's Philosophy of Education," in *Politics and*

Bantock: Culture and Education

Where Oakeshott concentrates on teaching, Geoffrey Bantock focuses mainly on educational studies and the curriculum. He recommends a more historical and a more literary approach to the study of education. He also rejects both "meritocratic" and "egalitarian" curriculums. For the academically less able student he proposes a sensory, action-based curriculum, and for the more able student a curriculum that stresses not only basic knowledge but also an understanding of the uses of political power. I will develop these points in turn.

In his treatment of educational studies Bantock is particularly critical of analytic philosophy, which, he says, like much research in education, is "antihistorical." Instead of drawing on the wisdom of the past, analysis has become "parasitic upon itself," a "private conversation" in which "every effort after analytic precision calls forth rejoinders and counter-rejoinders." The choice of concepts for analysis—such as "indoctrination," "autonomy," and "reason"—rests on unanalyzed assumptions about what is important in education. A historical approach to the philosophy of education would reveal "very different sets of working concepts," some of which, such as "imitation," are relevant still. It would bring to our attention vital needs that are ignored by contemporary curriculums.[12]

Educational research also can be assisted by "the sort of imaginative insight fostered by good literature."[13] Insight enters research, says Bantock, primarily in the choice of hypotheses to investigate. What insights can literature contribute here? Bantock answers this question by pointing out that, like the researcher, the writer starts from the everyday human world. Since the writer "has a tale to tell as well as a social phenomenon to explore,"[14] he or she tends to particularize—to

Experience: Essays Presented to Michael Oakeshott on the Occasion of His Retirement, ed. Preston King and B. C. Parekh, (Cambridge: Cambridge University Press, 1968), p. 63.

[12]Geoffrey Bantock, The Parochialism of the Present: Contemporary Issues in Education (London: Routledge & Kegan Paul, 1981), p. 2.

[13]Ibid., p. 4.

[14]Ibid., p. 48.

show how the social phenomenon (e.g., a public high school) influences the private lives of his or her characters. In doing so, the writer reveals aspects of the phenomenon that often remain closed to less imaginative minds. These are insights on which the researcher can draw.

The researcher also should imitate the writer by trying to enter the inner lives of his or her subjects. For example, the researcher investigating teacher values should not ask teachers merely to rank certain values but should encourage them to express themselves at length. The teachers then may reveal their deepest feelings about their schools and students. To the extent that they do, the researcher, like the writer, will "plumb the deeps within a framework of the familiar."[15]

Turning to the educational process, Bantock analyzes three views of the curriculum that (he says) have emerged from the movement toward social equality set off by the French and Industrial Revolutions. He calls these views the "meritocratic," the "egalitarian," and the "cultural."

The meritocratic view, Bantock holds, arose in response to the demand of industry and government for trained professionals rather than "classically educated gentlemen." For the meritocrat the prime purpose of education is to feed society with "the varieties of expertise it needs for its efficient functioning," that is, with "educated manpower." This means that everyone must have an equal opportunity to be educated in proportion to his or her ability. However, says Bantock, since abilities vary, and since government and industry are hierarchical, "greater educational opportunity" becomes "an opportunity of becoming unequal."[16] The meritocrat also calls for a common curriculum until the early secondary level, in order to identify talent and "hold open the options of selection" for the late developer. Unless children learn something in common, says the meritocrat, it is difficult for them to transfer to different schools or curricular programs.

Bantock acknowledges that education must make some contribution to "the purely functional efficiency of the industrial-bureaucratic society." He also grants that in the meritocratic

---

[15] Ibid., p. 50.
[16] Ibid., pp. 128–129.

school "the able are not neglected or despised." He maintains, however, that a meritocratic system exacts a high price: the intellectually less able children "demonstrably fail to benefit from it." The curriculum fails to respect their more physical and intuitive natures. It develops the intellect rather than the senses and the emotions, and it underemphasizes the arts.[17]

Bantock is even more critical of the egalitarian curriculum, which offers an identical education to all students. In his words, it is "a perverse attempt to homogenize both ends of the spectrum in a mediocre common experience satisfying to neither." It also is "unfair" because it prevents many young people from realizing their full potential.

On the other hand, a cultural curriculum promotes the vitality of the culture. By "culture" Bantock means, not the total pattern of a society's thought and activity, but rather the best that is thought and done in a society. A healthy culture is one to which each level of the population makes a contribution appropriate to "the level of consciousness it can achieve." Each such contribution is "equally appropriate but necessarily different." Contributions vary because people differ in talent, due mainly to genetic potential and family upbringing. Bantock also insists that the family is the chief carrier of culture. The student, therefore, "should not . . . be treated as an atomic unit apart from family culture." His potential for development should be assessed partly in terms of the cultural potential of his family— "partly" because some students obviously will transcend their family backgrounds.[18]

In Bantock's view, education is responsible first to the culture and only then to the individual. A vital culture, he says, enables individuals to "live rewarding lives." A weak culture provides fewer opportunities for creative self-expression. Therefore, he argues, schools should adopt a "differentiated" curriculum, offering content of different kinds to students of different cultural potentials. Such a curriculum will "allow all an equal opportunity to achieve their appropriate level of consciousness and hence to make their own proper contribution to the cultural health of the society." This, he claims, is "the only

---

[17]Ibid., pp. 126, 129–130.

[18]Ibid., pp. 122, 128, 131.

sort of equality which is viable" in education, for it "respects the irreducible diversity of actual minds."[19]

Bantock proposes curriculums for both "low achievers" and "elite" students. Low achievers, he says, should learn through "authentic emotional experience." Their curriculum should be based on "movement" education, which "takes normally random impulses of children and directs them into ordered activities."[20] Disciplined movement will feed into dance, drama, and music, on the one hand, and craft work and art on the other. These children also should learn to benefit from television by, for example, making and editing films and taking photographs. They should learn reading and writing in the course of other activities rather than in themselves. By contrast, elite students should be educated in (among other things) the understanding and exercise of political power. In the Renaissance they would have obtained this education from the literature of the Romans and Greeks, "who had given intensive attention to the business of politics." Today they should acquire it by studying both classical (e.g., eighteenth century) and modern literature, which "open the way to a consideration of the generic problems that all political systems must face."[21] For this purpose, any elite curriculum, Bantock maintains, should include the study of literature.

Critique   While I accept some of Bantock's ideas, I must reject others, mostly on grounds of sheer impracticality. Bantock denies being an elitist, but he maintains that the "upper levels" of society possess a culture that is more "conscious" and "differentiated" than that of the lower. I am not opposed to elitism as such, but I do not believe that consciousness and differentiation necessarily imply greater creativity. Moreover, Bantock does not say how these two concepts are to be used to assess cultural contributions; and if such contributions cannot be assessed, they do not deserve to play such a central role in his theory. The fact that Bantock offers so little evidence for his social and cultural ideas does not inspire confidence in them.

[19] Ibid., pp. 125, 131.

[20] Geoffrey Bantock, *Dilemmas of the Curriculum* (New York: Wiley, 1980), pp. 89–90.

[21] Ibid., pp. 123–124.

Furthermore, Bantock's view presupposes that each social level has a definite nature, giving rise to a determinate cultural potential; that levels are more important contributors than individuals; that levels make contributions as opposed to engaging in activities for their own sake; and that levels *ought* to make their proper contributions regardless of their treatment by other levels. But no modern society is so rigidly differentiated, nor is any society ever likely to be. Again, what precisely is a person's cultural potential and proper contribution? Most of us, looking at our lives, would be hard put to specify some determinate cultural potential that we have. We seem more inclined to do different things at different times in our lives for different personal as well as cultural reasons.

Some of Bantock's proposals derive from dubious assumptions or false information. Philosophic analysis has much to say to practicing educators and it is more attuned to history than Bantock supposes. The concepts he mentions have been analyzed not just in themselves but frequently enough in their historical contexts. Certainly the concept of "indoctrination" is every bit as practical and relevant as Bantock's concept of "imitation." And contrary to his belief, much educational research today uses in-depth, face-to-face interviews. Qualitative (as opposed to quantitative) studies are on the rise, and new methods of doing them constantly are being proposed.

Finally, I am troubled by Bantock's view of the "proper" education for the "less able." Although he believes that education should provide an understanding of history and political power, he excludes these subjects from his curriculum for this group. In effect, he relegates a quarter of the population to the position of a permanent underclass with less preparation for political participation than the rest. In a democracy the least that education can do, in my view, is to give all youngsters some insight into political decision making, even if too few of them will be making these decisions later themselves. Put another way, the less able should receive ample preparation for political participation, for at the ballot box the vote is expected to represent the best judgment of *all* voters. Is there a better place than the school for *all* people to develop the capacity for good political judgment?

Nevertheless, it is by virtue of his literary and historical approach that Bantock makes his important contributions. He rightly points out, for example, that an analysis of past educational concepts will reveal forgotten possibilities for present-day education. He reminds the educationist and the researcher of the insights that await them in literature. He draws our attention to the importance of educating people to understand and exercise political power. He also is right in his view that the study of literature is a better preparation for this than many of today's classes in ephemeral current affairs. His proposals for the education of the emotions especially should be taken seriously. They also might be applied to the elite students. In summary, by pursuing the implications of Bancroft's unusual approach, we are challenged to look more critically at the usual. This contribution alone makes a study of his ideas well worthwhile.

Kirk: Ethics and Intellect

Bantock, as I have shown, wants education to invigorate culture. By contrast, Russell Kirk wants education to civilize individuals. However, just as Bantock believes that a healthy culture will offer more to individuals, so Kirk maintains that civilized individuals will contribute more to society. For Kirk, a civilized person is one who possesses "moral imagination," nurtured through intellectual study. Thus, education's central aim is ethical and its method is intellectual. More broadly, its purpose is "to enable man to order his own soul and thereby come to a condition of moral worth," while its method is "to impart an apprehension of reality through disciplines which concern the nature of man and the condition in which we find ourselves in this world." People who have been educated in this way, says Kirk, will permeate society, "leavening the lump" through both professional and public work.[22]

If education is to succeed, Kirk asserts, it must impart "dogmas," especially in the elementary school. A dogma is "a theory or doctrine received on authority—as opposed to one based on

---

[22]Russell Kirk, *Decadence and Renewal in the Higher Learning* (Southbend, Ind.: Gateway, 1978), pp. xviii, 296, 302.

personal (or general short-run) experience or demonstration." Because dogmas are "sound and firm," they "liberate us from enticement by fad or foible, from intellectual servility." Society depends on dogmas; without "a core of common belief" it will fall apart. The central dogmas are ethical and at bottom common to all peoples. They include the law of general beneficence; duties to parents, elders, ancestors; duties to children and posterity; the law of mercy; the law of magnanimity. There also are political dogmas, such as "adherence to the benefits of representative government . . . and the assertion that a humane and free economy is better than a servile economy." The school, says Kirk, should teach these dogmas instead of "asking 'What do you think?' about grave matters concerning which a child has no basis for comparison."[23]

To nurture the moral imagination, says Kirk, we should turn primarily to literature. Great literature presents the abiding realities of the human condition. It "confers upon the rising generation a sense of what it is to be fully human." Literature "wakes us to truth through the imagination rather than through discursive reason." Four types of literature especially foster the moral imagination: fantasy; narrative history and biography; creations in verse or prose; and philosophic writing.[24] Works of fantasy, such as Shakespeare's *A Midsummer Night's Dream*, arouse that sense of awe and wonder which is the beginning of philosophy. Works of narrative history and biography, such as Benjamin Franklin's *Autobiography*, "do something to form decent lives." Creations such as George Orwell's *Animal Farm* "require serious interpretation and discussion." Philosophic writing, such as George Santayana's *The Last Puritan*, present "poetic and moral truths" more directly. If all schools were to teach the same books, declares Kirk, they would "give us all a common culture, ethical and intellectual, so that a people may share a general heritage and be united through the works of the mind."

The development of moral imagination also depends on the "social-studies disciplines." Whereas literature for the most part teaches private morality ("the order of the soul"), the social

---

[23]Ibid., pp. 249, 254–256.
[24]Ibid., pp. 273ff.

studies, says Kirk, teach public morality ("the order of the commonwealth"). There should be a hierarchy of social studies running from the first grade to the college level. These courses should combine the study of ethics and politics, for politics is "the application of ethics to the concerns of the commonwealth" and "a political structure without discernible ethical foundations will attract little interest or loyalty from young people."[25]

How should political theory and precept be taught? Kirk recommends the "biographical examination of great men" rather than "abstract or chronological analysis." Like other conservatives, he believes that young people need models or "exemplars." Therefore, he says, crucial historical events should be studied through the lives of men and women who shaped them. Kirk also recommends a course in the history of ideas and institutions, beginning with the Old Testament and the Greeks and proceeding to the twentieth century. This course would be "a study of moral philosophy . . . as related to social institutions." It would analyze the "standards" we inherit from the past and would emphasize "authority and freedom, the inner order of the soul, and the outer order of the commonwealth, the complementary character of permanence and change."[26]

Turning to higher education, Kirk urges the college of arts and sciences to follow fundamental conservative principles. The college, he says, should dedicate itself to "wisdom and virtue" or the attainment of "an ethical purpose through intellectual means." These means are the "disciplines of the mind," notably religion, history, moral philosophy, humane letters, languages, and the theoretical sciences. The college should eschew "amorphous 'survey' courses, vocationalism, and professional studies." Instead of encouraging "socialization" and "person-

---

[25]Ibid., pp. 280, 288–291. By "social studies" Kirk does not mean a collection of interdisciplinary topics or an amalgam of subject matter from such disciplines as economics, sociology, psychology, political science, and history, but rather these disciplines studied individually.

[26]Ibid., p. 289. Kirk does not specify the level at which this course would be taught. I infer, however, that the subject matter would be graded according to the level at which it was taught, beginning perhaps in the late elementary or early secondary school. In my view, such a course should be an essential part of the secondary school curriculum.

ality building," it should aim at "the improvement of the human reason, for the reason's own sake. . . . The development of sound character will follow from that." In order truly to respect individuality, the college should set high entrance standards and should remain small. In order to preserve structure and hierarchy in learning, it should offer few electives, for the undergraduate "ordinarily is not yet capable of judging with discretion what his course of studies ought to be." Finally, the college should inculcate "a sentiment of gratitude" toward past generations and a sense of obligation toward those to come:[27]

It should remind the rising generation that we are part of a long continuity and essence, a community of souls transcending time; and that we moderns are only dwarfs standing upon the shoulders of giants. This consciousness lies at the heart of a liberal education.

Critique   It is possible to regard Kirk as both authoritarian and exclusivist. As an authoritarian thinker, he wants the young to accept certain dogmas from their elders, not because these dogmas *necessarily* are appealing or even persuasive, but because they have been accepted for a long time and older people believe in them. He wants imagination, creativity, and independence, but only within the framework of these dogmas, certainly not in defiance of them. He wants people to fulfill themselves, provided they submit to "right" reason, because he apparently regards reason as inadequate without dogma.

I would reply that it is as important to question dogmas as it is to live by them. I believe that instead of freeing one from "intellectual servility," belief in dogmas actually can constitute servility. And I am inclined to doubt the wisdom of older people who have learned so little from life that they still accept uncritically the dogmas imposed on them in their youth.

Kirk may be considered exclusivist in two respects. First, he regards those who are educated on his lines as morally superior to the rest of the population. They will "leaven the lump" of society, he claims. His only ground for this claim is the prior claim that they will believe in certain moral absolutes. Moral beliefs, however, do not guarantee moral behavior, while belief

---

[27]Ibid., pp. 300ff.

in moral absolutes may tend to produce intolerance of other beliefs. A pragmatic, pluralist society, dependent on flexibility, consensus, and compromise, seems unlikely to be leavened by people educated according to Kirk's prescriptions. Second, Kirk wants to limit higher education to a minority of the most intelligent. However, if we are to respect both the individual and society (as Kirk claims we should), it seems more reasonable to allow *any* person to have a (more broadly conceived) higher education, provided that he or she is intellectually and emotionally prepared for it and that society too will benefit.

Nevertheless, I am impressed with much that Kirk proposes. I share his conviction that education primarily is a moral enterprise—one whose purpose is to develop moral worth through the study of basic disciplines. Like him, I believe in recognizing our debt to the past and our obligation to the future. Nothing is more likely to create a sense of obligation than the knowledge that a great deal of what we hold dear (our moral code, our sense of beauty, our love of country) has been given us and deserves to be passed on by us in finer form than we received it. I also agree with Kirk on at least two other matters. I believe that young people need models to emulate. Hence I endorse his proposal that they study the lives of historical figures. I also favor combining the study of morality and politics. Although democratic politics depends on compromise, it is important that politicians work for morally defensible goals. A citizenry educated to be aware of the moral dimensions of public life is the best guarantor of an enlightened politics.

Libertarian Conservatism

The libertarian strand in conservative thinking reaches back to Adam Smith, moral philosopher and founder (in 1776!) of laissez-faire (free-market) economics. Libertarians generally agree with traditionalists on the importance of transmitting the cultural heritage. (By "libertarians" here I mean nontraditional conservatives, who emphasize individual and market freedom, rather than the small group of conservatives who call themselves "Libertarians.") For example, most libertarians favor a return to basic disciplines and the teaching of traditional values. However, they are not committed to a belief in universal (or supracultural) values. They maintain that some values are objectively good in a certain society (e.g., the United States) but not necessarily good in all societies. We therefore should not try to export them, and we should not import alien values.

Libertarians also take a more practical view of tradition. They regard it as a collection of ideas and practices, many of which have proved useful to a society, rather than as a venerable and organic growth some of whose elements cannot be improved on. They are less strongly attached than traditionalists to the classical and Renaissance disciplines of literature and history. Instead, they place more weight on science and current affairs.

The libertarian departs from the traditionalist's rather cautious view of individual human nature. For the libertarian, human beings naturally are rational, competitive, and self-interested. In a free society with a free market, self-interest in the long run is "enlightened," in that society as a whole benefits when its members are allowed to pursue their own interests with minimum regulation. Because libertarians have more faith in individual human nature, they are ready to undertake more radical experiments in education—such as providing all parents with vouchers, which they can exchange for educational credit at any school they choose, public or private. Libertarians also differ from traditionalists in their view of society. For libertarians, society is an association of individuals rather than an organism superior to them. Social institutions work well, they say, only to the extent that they promote personal freedom. Like traditionalists, libertarians oppose the use of schools to reform society—but for another reason. They believe that this denies children the right to be educated for the society in which they will have to make their way.

More than traditionalists, libertarians maintain that schools should foster competition and the quest for excellence through examinations, sports, school spirit, and teacher example. Schools should reward intellectual attainment rather than serve as socializing agencies. Instead of quotas, affirmative action, and compulsory busing, there should be scholarships and other aids for individuals who deserve them regardless of ethnic or social background. Schools should make every effort to seek out and cultivate talent wherever it can be found, because the nation needs all the expertise it can produce.

Friedman: Parental Control of Schooling

The work of economist Milton Friedman exemplifies the libertarian approach to education. Friedman contends that the public school is wasteful and inefficient because it has fallen under the control of government and professional educators. He proposes several ways to restore parental control, improve the quality of education, and spread its costs more fairly.

In principle, says Friedman, parents can control their children's schooling in two ways. They can choose and pay for the schools they want their children to attend, and they can elect representatives to school boards. In fact, they have lost both forms of control. There are three reasons, he maintains, for this sad state of affairs. (1) The practice of taxing everybody to fund the public schools has made it too costly for most parents to send their children to private schools. (2) Power has shifted from the local community to the state and federal government. (3) Professional educators (mostly in university faculties of education) have come to exercise increasing control over every phase of schooling.

Under government and educationist control, schooling, contrary to an earlier tradition of local control, has become more and more centralized. As the number of school districts has declined, the size of those that remain has increased dramatically. Centralization, however, has not brought economies of scale. According to Friedman, size and efficiency go together only if the consumer is free to choose. A firm, for instance, can expand to meet demand and then produce more cheaply because it is producing (and selling) more goods. But when the consumer is less free to choose, as in political arrangements, size generally leads to inefficiency and even less freedom. In small communities, for instance, the individual can have some say in what happens, and if he does not like a particular community he lives in, he can move to another. But when power belongs to a central government, the individual has little control over the authorities and little opportunity to move elsewhere.

In education, too, size works against the consumer. As Friedman puts it,[28]

In schooling, the parent and child are the consumers, the teacher and school administrator the producers. Centralization in schooling has meant larger size units, a reduction in the ability of consumers to choose, and an increase in the power of producers. . . . The same phenomenon is present whenever government bureaucracy takes over at the expense of consumer choice.

To assure parents greater freedom of choice, Friedman proposes a voucher plan. All parents, he says, should receive from the government a piece of paper redeemable for a sum of money, provided it is used to pay for the education of their child at an "approved" school, public or private. Friedman justifies this plan on several grounds. It would "end the inequity of using tax funds to school some children [those attending public schools] but not others." It would compel public schools to compete with one another and with private schools in order to attract students. It would reduce violence, because parents would choose schools that could keep order. It would militate against class differences, since "schools defined by common interests— one stressing, say, the arts; another, the sciences; another, foreign languages—would attract students from a wide variety of residential areas." It would improve the quality of schooling available to all classes, especially the poor. Finally, it would produce many more alternative types of schools, "unless it was sabotaged by excessively rigid standards for approval.[29]

For higher education Friedman proposes a "contingent-loan" program. Students, he says, could receive the funds needed to finance their education on condition that they agree to pay the government a specified portion of their future earnings. The government then "could recoup more than [its] initial investment from relatively successful individuals, which could compensate for the failure to do so from the unsuccessful." This program, he argues, not only would make higher education

---

[28]Milton and Rose Friedman, *Free to Choose: A Personal Statement* (New York: Harcourt Brace Jovanovich, 1980), p. 157.

[29]Ibid., pp. 163ff.

available to all interested and qualified persons, it also would end taxpayer subsidization, and hence the injustice of compelling the poor to pay for a service that their children use less than the children of other classes.[30]

Unlike the other authors I have discussed, Friedman has written his most recent book partly to refute objections brought against his ideas. Take, for example, the objection that under the voucher plan schools no longer would bring together members of different races and classes. Friedman makes two points in reply. First, he maintains that, since people no longer would need to live in the same district as the school they choose, neighborhoods would tend to become more varied and, therefore, "the local schools serving any community might well be less homogeneous than they are now." He then asserts that "secondary schools would almost surely be less stratified," since each would tend to specialize in certain subjects and thus would attract interested students from a range of neighborhoods. Or take the objection that the voucher plan might stimulate the creation of private schools, leaving the bulk of the poor to inferior public schools. Friedman replies that money saved on taxes would "open a vast market that could attract many entrants, both from public schools and other occupations." He admits that "there is no way of predicting the ultimate composition of the school industry." Nevertheless, he emphasizes, "Only those schools that satisfy their customers will survive— just as only those restaurants and bars that satisfy their customers survive. Competition will see to that.[31]

Now take a more serious charge. Friedman's voucher plan, it has been said, would destroy the public school system that has taught the democratic way of life to each generation and, more than any other institution, has embodied the ideas for which this country was founded. What is Friedman's reply? He contends that in small, close-knit communities with reasonably satisfactory public schools, the latter "would remain dominant, perhaps somewhat improved by the threat of potential competition." Elsewhere, he says, and especially in the urban

---

[30]Ibid., pp. 814ff. As a second-best alternative for higher education, Friedman proposes a voucher plan.

[31]Ibid., pp. 167ff.

slums, there would be some transitional difficulties during and after the time in which parents transferred their children. This undoubtedly would leave some public schools "even poorer in quality than they are now." However, he argues, "As the private market took over, the quality of all schooling would rise so much that even the worst, while it might be *relatively* lower on the scale, would be better in *absolute* quality."[32]

Critique   However, Friedman does not meet all objections. First, under his contingent-loan program private universities with large endowments would have an initial advantage over public universities that no longer would be funded by tax monies. Private universities would use their generally larger endowments to hire better teachers and provide better facilities. Second, Friedman ignores government's positive contribution in funding certain special programs, such as education for the handicapped, bilingual education, and expanded programs in math and science—programs in which private suppliers might not be sufficiently interested. Third, under the Friedman plan the estimated return on investment in schools in slum areas might be too low to attract the capital needed to raise the quality of schooling above its pre-voucher level. Instead, potential investors might prefer educational ventures in better-off areas. Fourth, the voucher plan might make suppliers of education more powerful than parents. Like suppliers of other goods and services, they might spend heavily on deceptive advertising, and parents might not find out until they had paid their fees, if then. Finally, vouchers and loans would not end government control of education but would redefine and redirect it. Funding is the ultimate means of control, and national and state loan and voucher operations would be subject to constant government review.

Nevertheless, although Friedman's proposals have their faults, I believe that the underlying principles are sound. I agree with Friedman that government should intervene in school affairs as little as possible, and that a free market with minimal government regulation not only would expand freedom of choice but, through a voucher system, would promote class

---

[32] Ibid., p. 170.

harmony and racial integration. In my view, too, most parents are better qualified than government to make decisions about their children's education. If parents choose their children's schools, both they and their children will gain in autonomy. Teachers, too, will become more independent, more like other professionals (such as lawyers and doctors), as they consult with parents and are less subject to school bureaucracies. I also believe that a diversity of schools, and a more equal balance between public and private schools, fits our pluralist society better than a monolithic public school system, however wide its offerings. Finally, I commend the voucher plan as a stimulus to the public schools. Competition among themselves and with private schools could propel these schools into much-needed reforms. Far from killing the public school system, as many opponents claim, a voucher plan could very well reinvigorate it.

Central Libertarian Issues

Liberty and Equality

Let us take some other issues important to libertarians. As their name implies, libertarians value liberty more highly than any other quality. Harvard philosopher Robert Nozick defends this valuation in his theory of the "minimal state."[33] Each of us, holds Nozick, is endowed with three basic rights—not to be physically injured, not to have our liberty limited, and not to have our property taken without our consent. How are these rights best guaranteed? In any territory, says Nozick, "protective associations"—groups of people pursuing compatible goals—arise naturally, and the dominant association takes over the responsibilities of the minimal state. These responsibilities are twofold: to exercise a monopoly over the use of force and to defend the basic rights of everyone in the territory. The minimal state may tax people, for example, but only in order to protect them.

---

[33]Robert Nozick, *Anarchy, State, and Utopia* (New York: Basic Books, 1974), p. 27: "The sole legitimate function of the state" is "to protect rights against violation," and "all other functions are illegitimate because they themselves involve the violation of rights."

According to Nozick, the individual, and only the individual, is entitled to the products of his own labor. The individual has full right to use and dispose of these products as he wishes. Without his or her permission, the government has no right to redistribute any of these products to other individuals, even less fortunate ones.[34] On this view, inequality is natural, and equality is an artifically imposed condition. This principle, he says, is self-evident; it stands to reason. It is only departures from this principle that need to be justified. What does the principle imply for education?

Taken literally, it implies that there should be no system of public education at all. In Nozick's view, each family is entitled to use whatever portion it chooses of its full, untaxed resources for the education of its children. Hence all education should be private, paid for by each family out of its own resources, and controlled by educators rather than by government. However, few libertarians actually take this position. In their view, it is unfair to tie a child's education totally to the resources and wishes of his or her parents. If the parents are negligent or improvident, the child's education and life chances will suffer.

Nevertheless, while most libertarians accept the need for a public school system, they seek to maximize freedom within it. Take the issue of compulsory busing. Libertarians concede that because of their differing backgrounds different children can be regarded as resources for the learning of other children. Even so, they say, no authority has the right to redistribute these resources in order to provide a supposedly more equal education for all children, since this results in an inferior education for many. At the very least, each family is entitled to choice of school by choice of residence. This view affirms parental freedom and accepts the inequalities that may result. Libertarians also insist that local communities be left free to decide how much they will tax themselves to fund their own schools. In

---

[34]Ibid., p. 238: "No one has a right to something whose realization requires certain uses of things and activities that other people have rights and entitlements over. Other people's rights and entitlements to *particular things* (*that* pencil, *their* body, and so on) and how they choose to exercise these rights and entitlements fix the external environment of any given individual and the means that will be available to him. If his goal requires the use of means which others have rights to, he must enlist their voluntary cooperation."

order to make education within a state more equal, the state government may supplement the resources of communities with a low tax base, but it may not limit the educational expenditures of other communities. Here libertarians uphold local freedom over statewide equality.

Authority and Discipline

Libertarians maintain that in a free society each individual must respect the freedom of others and therefore must exercise rationality and self-discipline. Now rationality and self-discipline have to be learned both at home and in school. Youngsters, then, should not be treated as adults who are presumed to have acquired these qualities. On the contrary, they are both more vulnerable and more volatile than adults. Hence they need "more intense protection, scrutiny, and constraint."[35] At school they need both adult (teacher) authority and a sense of community—two factors that, in the libertarian view, go together. Adult authority provides the external discipline from which self-discipline is learned, and also the community structure needed by the young who have less experience than adults in community living. The existence of a school community in turn makes the young more responsive to adult authority.

Libertarians criticize the legalistic concept of educator authority, which treats children as possessors of legal "rights" and educators as "custodians" who can be taken to court for infringing those rights. In the libertarian view, if teachers and administrators are to exercise legitimate authority, apply necessary discipline, and create a sense of community, they must act *in loco parentis*. When teachers and administrators fear litigation, they no longer promulgate and enforce clear, firm rules of conduct. As a result, students prey on one another more, threaten and even assault their teachers, and defy authority whenever it interferes. Teachers, feeling relatively powerless, hesitate to exercise control. How can authority and discipline be restored? Libertarians propose two steps. First, they say, we must "constrain and reverse" court decisions that limit the educator's traditional authority. Second, we must give parents freedom to

---

[35]Edward A. Wynne, "What Are the Schools Doing to Our Children?" *Public Interest*, **63** (Summer 1981), 18.

choose their children's schools and thus express disapproval of schools that abandon their responsibilities.[36]

Moral Education

Libertarians advocate free choice in most things, but not in basic morality. Every society, they say, depends for its existence on its members' awareness that they share a core of deeply felt moral values. Americans, for instance, believe in such values as honesty, fairness, readiness to work, repudiation of violence, and respect for the democratic process. Without some such core, society must collapse, and with it freedom, for all persons then are at one another's mercy. The transmission of a moral code to the young is therefore no less essential to society's survival than the maintenance of a police force and the levying of taxes.

Habitual moral behavior does not come naturally, says the libertarian. The young have to be *told* to do what is right, and punished (as well as reasoned with) if they do not heed. *Basic moral education must be directive.* It also must lead the young to feel deeply about morality. Simply to know that lying and stealing are wrong is not enough. If youngsters are to avoid wrongdoing, they must find it repugnant, and teachers must express repugnance when faced with it. Teachers must care passionately about right and wrong and make sure that their students know they do. If teachers are detached, they will give students the impression that morality is no concern of the school.

Reasoning about moral controversies (such as abortion, school prayer, and racial quotas) comes later. Students can benefit from such reasoning only if they already have internalized the relevant principles. As one libertarian puts it,[37]

If students are taught dilemmas before or in place of principles, they will think that morality is nothing but dilemmas; and if they discuss exceptions to principles without first having internalized the princi-

---

[36]Edward A. Wynne, "Courts, Schools, and Family Choice," *Public Interest*, **67** (Spring 1982), 139.

[37]Andrew Oldenquist, "'Indoctrination' and Societal Suicide," *Public Interest*, **63** (Spring 1981), 85.

ples themselves, the exceptions, meeting no resistance, will come all too easily.

Does this mean that basic morality has to be taught by indoctrination? Yes, replies the libertarian. And, he adds, there is no need to feel uneasy about it. Honesty, fairness, and aversion to violence must be inculcated openly, and their opposites condemned. If anyone objects, let him show that failure to teach these values is socially beneficial.

Basic Subjects

For libertarians, the central purpose of schooling is to enable people to develop their intelligence and talents to the full. One's intelligence includes the powers of thinking, imagining, appreciating, observing, questioning, and judging. These powers enable one to read critically, weigh evidence, appraise arguments, and form and express one's own opinions. They enable all of us to understand the world and make our way in it. In order to train intelligence, the schools first should teach children the basic skills they need to continue learning—the skills of reading, writing, computing, speaking, and listening. Once they command these skills, children should proceed to the subjects that enlarge their intellectual powers and acquaint them with nature, human nature, society, other cultures, and the past. These subjects are science, mathematics, language, literature, social studies, history, and the arts. Youngsters need to acquire these skills and disciplines in school because, except for those rare individuals who can teach themselves, they are unlikely to get another chance to learn them.[38]

To encourage excellence, schools should require specific levels of performance. At each level, exit criteria should be set higher than entrance criteria. Ideally, all fifth-graders should understand the multiplication tables; all eighth-graders should comprehend punctuation and fractions; and all high school diplomas should stand for genuine literacy. There should be no automatic promotions. More than this, schools should reward outstanding academic achievement. Once again libertarians say

---

[38]See, for example, Dianne Ravitch, "Forgetting the Questions: The Problem of Educational Reform," *American Scholar,* **50**:3 (Summer 1981), 329–340.

that intelligence is not equally distributed and that basic education is not fundamentally egalitarian. Equal educational *opportunity* should be provided, but its purpose is to enable all to realize their differing abilities to the full rather than to reach the same intellectual level.

Critique   How persuasive is the libertarian position on the issues I have considered? Take the issues of liberty and equality. Here the libertarian belief in individual freedom is apt to conflict with the concomitant belief in equal educational opportunity. If libertarians accept the goal of equal educational opportunity, they surely should accept compulsory busing as one means to this goal. True, some suburban children may receive an inferior education as a result, but educational opportunity will be more equal among races and classes. Again, to ensure that all children enjoy equal educational opportunity, all communities surely should spend the same or a similar amount per child on education. If certain people or groups in a community wish to spend more on their children's education, they should found their own schools rather than impose their wish on public schools. The libertarian cannot achieve equal opportunity by allowing some communities to spend more money per student than others—money which tends to attract better teachers and pay for better facilities.

Now consider authority and discipline. Recent court decisions have strengthened *legitimate* student rights. Students are citizens and, as such, are protected by the Constitution. Exercising their rights in school prepares them for adult citizenship. True, placing restraints on teachers and administrators may make some of them anxious, but this is a price that must be paid if student rights are to be respected. Naturally, this does not deny that students must be taught duties as well as rights, the value of authority as well as its limits.

On the issue of moral education, it should be pointed out that, although uncritically held moral values lead to a measure of moral behavior, they also can promote hypocrisy and self-deception. The right course for schools is not to neglect moral education but to pursue it through discussion rather than precept alone. Granted, it makes little sense to debate moral dilemmas before the principles at stake have taken hold. On the other hand, it does make sense to discuss the principles themselves. If people know why their principles are justified, they are more likely to pay them genuine respect.

On basic subjects, one may object that the libertarian conception of schooling is too narrow and selective. Especially in today's world, schools must do more than cultivate the intellect at the expense of the whole person. Other important objectives of education are to foster emotional and physical growth, develop the capacity for a rich and productive personal life, reduce prejudice by promoting contact between diverse groups, and improve the quality of cultural and political life generally.

Libertarians reject these arguments, however. In defense of liberty some libertarians maintain that freedom of choice is more important than equality of educational opportunity. Parents, they say, are entitled to choice in the public as well as in the private school sphere, and they may choose to keep their children in local schools rather than have them bused elsewhere. Other libertarians are more moderate. They propose giving more weight to equality by, for example, allowing children to transfer to the school of their choice, provided the latter school has a smaller proportion of their race or class than the school they leave. This proposal preserves the right to choose a school by residence, but adds the right to choose a school in an area from which the parents are excluded for ethnic, social, or economic reasons. Thus, on the side of liberty, children are not required to be bused, but on the side of equality, schools are required to accept children from outside their residential areas. James S. Coleman observes:[39]

> By this alternative full equality is not realized, nor is the full liberty of the economically advantaged to maintain homogeneous schools realized. But neither is equality fully sacrificed for that liberty, nor is liberty fully sacrificed for equality.

In defense of traditional discipline, libertarians contend that the courts are a blunt and awkward tool for altering human relations within the school. The attempts of the courts to rem-

---

[39]James S. Coleman, "Rawls, Nozick, and Educational Opportunity," *Public Interest*, **43** (Spring 1976), 126, 128.

edy the real or imagined abuses suffered by some individuals and groups have helped undermine the morale and community life of schools generally. A better remedy, they say, is to give parents, and hence students, more choice between schools and between programs within schools.[40] In defense of moral indoctrination, libertarians argue that hypocrisy and self-deception are the price to be paid for having effective moral values at all. Only a strong inhibition enables us to resist temptation when no one is around to see us fall. The alternative to inhibition is either relative indifference (the attitude that moral values are matters of taste) or the absence of moral values altogether. Finally, on basic subjects, libertarians insist that intellectual and moral education together are prerequisite for most other objectives proposed for the schools. Without intellect and character, how can one expect to live abundantly, participate fully in cultural and political life, overcome prejudice, and contribute to human progress? If the schools succeed in their two central tasks, the other objectives will be attained as a consequence.

Appraisal

In discussing libertarian conservatism, I have paid most attention to the ideas that distinguish this form from traditional conservatism. Hence I now appraise the two forms separately. Nevertheless, since both share some common beliefs—for example, in the importance of teaching basic intellectual disciplines and traditional values—some points that I make about traditionalists will also apply to libertarians.

Traditional Conservatism

One weakness of the first form is its relatively uncritical attitude to tradition. These conservatives are apt to regard tradition as altogether beneficial and even sacrosanct. Oakeshott is a wholehearted champion of tradition and believes that it is passed on most effectively in a teacher's style, which is manifest mainly in gestures and intonations. Yet if (as here) tradition is not made explicit, how can students properly evaluate it? In-

---

[40]Wynne, "Courts, Schools, and Family Choice," 137.

stead of appropriating tradition critically, students are appropriated by it. Again, Bantock believes that education is responsible first to culture (which for him is mainly, though not entirely, tradition) and only secondly to the individual. For him, students are potential contributors to culture rather than unique persons. Thus, he proposes a sensorimotor curriculum that will make it easier for the less intellectually able to act on their feelings, which Bantock believes is the mode of expression "proper" to low achievers. This curriculum, however, will make it harder for them to rise in a meritocratic society. Finally, Kirk is so devoted to tradition that he advocates a curriculum built mainly around the great books with little room for science or standard social studies. This may suit the literary student, but it is not likely to be of much help to many who come from unbookish homes.

Partly because of their attachment to the past (when social inequities were accepted more readily), traditional conservatives tend to be anti-egalitarian and elitist. For example, Oakeshott's principle that in primary and secondary schools the student's personal interests ought to be ignored discriminates against all those who do not receive a further education. These students are educated regardless of their interests, yet they are the first to enter the job market. Even more elitist is Bantock's provision that the intellectually able alone should be educated to exercise political power. When we consider that an intellectually demanding education in itself tends to confer a political advantage, it surely is excessive to add to it an explicit training in political leadership. Kirk denies that he is an elitist, and certainly he is less of one than Oakeshott or Bantock. Nevertheless, he believes that those who are educated as he recommends will be morally better than other people and will enlighten the rest of society. In fact, however, an indoctrination in moral absolutes seems as likely to result in self-righteousness as in enlightenment. Kirk also would limit higher education to the most intelligent—a proposal that clearly conflicts with the more general view that such education should be available to all persons who can improve themselves and benefit society as a result.

Traditional conservatives tend to be authoritarian. Oakeshott maintains that primary and secondary school students must learn much that they neither like nor see the point of. Unlike most writers on education, he suggests no way to make this process more palatable to the student. Kirk insists that the young must be taught certain dogmas, on the grounds that wisdom and virtue in the individual, and order and freedom in society, depend on adherence to certainties. It may be replied that much wisdom and virtue can be learned only from experience, and that the inculcation of dogmas makes one less inclined to learn from this source. Bantock is more paternalist than authoritarian. He does not recommend instilling absolute truths, but he does advocate differentiating subject matter for the young according to the school's judgment of their cultural potential. Granted, the school often may be a better judge of student potential than the students themselves. Nevertheless, Bantock's differentiated curriculum is likely to make it harder for youngsters to rise above the consequences of a school's misjudgment of their potential than a curriculum that divides students and subject matter less strictly.

Traditional conservatives also seem out of touch with some important aspects of present-day culture. Oakeshott holds that students should imitate the cultural style of their teacher. Yet many students today have a culture of their own, received largely from media and peers, and some of the most intelligent are likely to question a teacher's style rather than absorb it. Bantock admires a complex culture, but he believes in a hierarchy of cultural levels distinguished by degree of consciousness and differentiation. Thus, he does not seem to envision a pluralist society like the United States, in which each social and ethnic group is considered capable of making potentially equal contributions in all areas of culture. Moreover, in its tendency to limit social mobility, Bantock's curriculum for the intellectually less able runs counter to the American ethos with its vital element of social mobility. Kirk advocates a curriculum, centered on history and literature, which (to my mind) is oriented toward an earlier, European, preindustrial era. This heritage, however valuable in itself, can have only limited influence in the urban, media-influenced, rapidly changing milieus in which American youngsters grow up. Kirk also neglects the need to equip the young with the technical expertise so important in today's economy. Again, Kirk recommends the teaching of the Judeo-Christian religion. It is doubtful, however, whether a core of moral or religious beliefs can be presented at all effectively without alienating many parents and students. Finally, the moral absolutism that Kirk favors seems unlikely to produce the ability for compromise and consensus so much needed in our pluralist society.

Traditional conservatives tend to undervalue educational research. Bantock urges researchers to seek personal, in-depth answers to their questions. Yet many researchers already do so and, contrary to Bantock, they need no rationale from literature for this practice. More tellingly, when Bantock presents his view of the low achiever, he cites no research whatever. Similarly, Oakeshott insists that student interests are irrelevant to schooling, even though there is abundant evidence that interest motivates learning more strongly than any other factor. Finally, Kirk mentions research infrequently and cites no empirical studies to support his claims for the efficacy of indoctrinating students in absolute moral principles.

Far more important, however, are the achievements of traditional conservatism. Proponents of this movement remind us that education above all is a moral enterprise. Kirk rightly proclaims that the ends of education are virtue and wisdom. This is to insist, not that every unit and lesson must make a moral point, but rather that the purpose of studying any subject is to live better, with more respect for ourselves and others, more in harmony with the universe, and closer to God (if we believe in Him). Kirk points out that politics, too, is or should be a moral endeavor, and that schools should teach the history of the political institutions of Western civilization in the light of the moral goals for which they were designed. Bantock, for his part, maintains that those who later will exercise political power should study its nature first in works of literature, which movingly present the personal responsibilities and moral dilemmas that power entails. Oakeshott, too, in his ideal of the culturally formed individual, makes us aware that education should form the character as well as the intellect.

In line with this emphasis on the moral purpose of education, traditional conservatives tell us that the young must have models to emulate. For Oakeshott, the essence of education lies in the informal, often unconscious, imitation by the student of the teacher's personal style. Oakeshott loves teaching, and throughout his writing he conveys that the teacher is a guide and mentor to the student. Like Oakeshott, Kirk insists on personal contact between teacher and student. Hence he calls for small colleges with an emphasis on teaching rather than research. Kirk also maintains that students should find models of good character and right action in literature and history. Since the media today tend to highlight the influence of power-hunger and self-interest in politics, it is salutary for the young to study the ways in which great historical figures strove against odds to realize the ideals for which we revere them still. Bantock wishes to adapt to modern times the Renaissance ideal of education as largely the imitation of patterns of conduct depicted in literary works (such as epic poems, tragedies, and histories).

Libertarian Conservatism

I find the libertarians vulnerable in several respects. First, they seem unaware of some of the limits to individual freedom and rationality. They are inclined to think that, if parents are free to choose their children's schools, they will do so wisely and rationally, and that over time the interests of different families will harmonize. Yet parents also think and act as members of social groups and classes, and they may prefer schools with cachet to those with sound programs. If class interests play a large part in choices, then a voucher plan or a totally private system of education (which Friedman, among others, supports) might increase the power of the elite schools and exacerbate class conflict. Libertarians sometimes overlook human frailty; they believe, but do not show, that maximum freedom in the long run promotes social harmony. Granted, most parents will act in the best interests of their children, but some will not, and their children therefore should be protected by an outside agency. Libertarians also do not allow for the possibility that entrepreneurs will make false claims and operate schools for profit at the expense of education.

This same, rather simplified, view of human nature lies behind the libertarians' advocacy of moral indoctrination and their opposition to values-clarification approaches to moral education. Libertarians are inclined to regard moral values as objective, moral issues as clear-cut, and moral conduct largely as a matter of personal discipline and willpower. To this it may be replied that moral issues are tangled and controversial, and therefore reflection is as important to morality as exercise of will. There certainly is a case for moral indoctrination, especially to form good habits, but it is no less vital to introduce young people both to the difficulties of moral choice and to the fundamental relativism of many (though not all) values.

Although libertarians support private charity for those unable to help themselves, they seem otherwise to lack compassion. Freedom, they say, matters more than equality. If people are to be free to succeed and enjoy the results of their skill and enterprise, then some people are going to suffer and fail. Governments seek to help these people by increasing educational and employment opportunities and by redistributing income, but in the libertarian view they have had only limited success. Despite the existence of monopolies and oligopolies, libertarians think that somehow the "invisible hand" of the free market is going to eliminate over time the suffering and disharmony caused by unfettered competition.

Thus, libertarians at heart are meritocrats. They believe that the prime aim of the school is to allow the talented and energetic to prepare themselves to move up the ladder of success. Other aims, such as socialization and racial harmony, are secondary. The school is not obliged to promote good fellowship, if this involves restricting the energies of a dynamic and productive minority. Similarly, as meritocrats, libertarians fail to appreciate the hardships that must accompany the introduction of a voucher system. They assume that competition will ensure that most genuine educational needs are satisfied and that the quality of education will rise accordingly. In fact, the opposite might happen. It seems just as likely that some forms of education, especially those made possible by government subsidy, and some economically depressed areas may fail to attract the capital they need. If so, public schooling, which is bad enough now, could well get worse.

However, no social or educational system is perfect, and the faults I have mentioned in the libertarian approach seem to me inevitable in a society dedicated to individual freedom. The less that government intervenes in education, the more it will be possible for individuals and groups to work out solutions that meet local and individual needs. It hardly can be denied that most parents know their children better than anyone else does, and that they can judge best whether their children are getting the right kind of education. If parents are free to choose their children's schools, then some, it is true, may choose carelessly. Nevertheless, other agencies, including government, can be careless; and in an enlightened democracy I prefer parental choice to government mandate.

Allowing parents basic control over their children's education is an important step in restoring the freedom that individuals, in my view, increasingly have ceded to government in the course of this century. People who take charge in this area of their lives are likely to take charge in others. Hence free choice in education would take us closer to the ideal of a society of self-fulfilling individuals. It also would enhance the self-respect of teachers, who now would be responsible mainly to individual clients rather than remote officeholders. Finally, it would serve notice on the public schools that many of their current faults no longer will be tolerated.

For Further Reading*

Adler, Mortimer, *The Paideia Proposal: An Educational Manifesto* (New York: Macmillan, 1982). Adler is an Aristotelian leaning toward traditional conservatism. He argues that a truly responsible public school system will offer the same academic education to all students, allowing no elective or vocational courses. Electives, he claims, are undemocratic because they separate future toilers from future leaders.

Bowers, C. A., *Cultural Literacy for Freedom: An Existential Perspective on Teaching, Curriculum, and School Policy* (Eugene, Ore.: Elan, 1974). A phenomenological examination of the process by which the student, who already has his or her view of the world, absorbs through formal education the world view of adult society. Similar in spirit to the New Sociology, but more literary and philosophic in manner.

Eisner, Elliot W., *The Educational Imagination: On the Design and Evaluation of School Programs* (New York: Macmillan, 1979). Eisner proposes an aesthetic, as opposed to scientific, approach to the educational process. In his view, the student, the teacher, and the researcher all resemble the artist in that

---

*Publications cited in footnotes to the chapters are not repeated here.

they try to create patterned wholes, or "organic entities that 'work'" (e.g., personal projects, lesson plans, case studies). Eisner's approach is strongly anti-positivist and has affinities with phenomenology and romanticism.

Giroux, Henry A., *Ideology, Culture, and the Process of Schooling* (Philadelphia: Temple University Press, 1981). Giroux is a humanist neo-Marxist with a deep interest in Critical Theory and phenomenology. Opposed alike to positivism and doctrinaire Marxism, he emphasizes the power of students and teachers to resist the dominant culture.

Green, Thomas F., *The Activities of Teaching* (New York: McGraw-Hill, 1971). In this inquiry into the nature of teaching, Green states what philosophic analysis is and also practices it. Among other topics, he discusses the analytic view of meaning, the analytic method, and the nature of concepts.

Hamlyn, D. W., *Experience and the Growth of Understanding* (London and Boston: Routledge & Kegan Paul, 1978). A philosophic analysis of the development of language and understanding in children. Hamlyn examines the theories of Skinner, Chomsky, and Piaget, and presents his own. He shows that philosophic reflection is vital to the human sciences.

Harris, Kevin, *Education and Knowledge: The Structured Misrepresentation of Reality* (London and Boston: Routledge & Kegan Paul, 1979). An informal presentation of the Marxist view that schools systematically lead people to perceive the world in a way that favors the ruling class, while at the same time getting them to believe that they see the world objectively.

Holt, John, *Teach Your Own* (New York: Delacorte/Seymour Laurence, 1981). Romanticist John Holt has given up on schools altogether and argues that most children are educated better by their parents, whether permissive or authoritarian.

Matthews, Gareth, *Philosophy and the Young Child* (Cambridge, Mass.: Harvard University Press, 1982). With the aid of some fascinating examples analyst Matthews argues that many young children think philosophically and are only later socialized to abandon the activity. Matthews highlights what Piaget overlooked, that children not only acquire highly general concepts (such as those of space, time, and the self) but also puzzle over them.

Petrie, Hugh G., *The Dilemma of Enquiry and Learning* (Chicago: University of Chicago Press, 1981). Like Piaget, Petrie proposes a testable theory of learning that unites philosophy with psychology. Drawing on evolution theory, systems theory, and contemporary philosophy of science, Petrie maintains that learning aims at a "reflective equilibrium" more dynamic than Piagetian equilibration.

Postman, Neil, *Teaching as a Conserving Activity* (New York: Delacorte, 1979). A former romanticist, Postman now argues that the task of education is to strike a balance between the conserving and innovating tendencies in society, stressing conservation in times of change and innovation in times of retrenchment.

Shor, Ira, *Critical Teaching and Everyday Life* (Boston: South End Press, 1981). Shor applies some of Freire's ideas to U. S. education, though not Freire's vision of revolutionary political action. He describes ways to teach literacy and communication skills and develop critical consciousness among open admissions students in universities and community colleges.

Vandenberg, Donald, *Being and Education: An Essay in Existential Phenomenology* (Englewood Cliffs, N.J.: Prentice-Hall, 1975). A Heideggerian reflection that draws on the work of other European educationists in the tradition of existential phenomenology. Vandenberg inquires into what it is in the being of youth and children that makes education possible.

Index

Accommodation, 101, 109,
Accountability, 35, 152, 153, 188
Achievement, academic, 58, 59,
    153, 161, 164, 165, 237, 246
Action, 21, 31, 43, 58, 61, 78, 82,
    83, 109, 114, 128, 156,
    175n, 194, 195, 223, 253
  affinity with texts, 66, 85
  intentional, 14-16, 150, 163n
  mental, 27
  understanding of, 66, 68
Administrator, educational, 25,
    31, 35, 40, 133, 179, 188,
    195, 289, 244, 247
Adolescence, 36, 123, 226
Aesthetic education, 74
Affirmative action 26, 221, 237
Alienation, 57, 167, 169, 182
Alternative school, 183, 207, 239
Althusser, Louis, 180

Analysis, 1, 23, 25
  of concepts, 1-9, 10-16, 139,
    140, 227, 231
Analysis, philosophic, 1, 3, 13,
    16-17, 27, 60, 66n, 175, 327
  appraisal of, 23-26
  and common sense, 10
  contrasted with phenomenology,
    27, 62, 63
  and educational practice, 20, 25,
    231
  and educational research, 13,
    15, 231
  forms of, 4-5
  method of, 10-13
  on nature of action, 13-16, 66n
  and philosophy of education, 5,
    10, 23-26, 140
  see also Language; Ordinary
    language philosophy

Analyst, philosophic, 4-5, 14,
24-26
Anxiety, 33-34, 35-36, 63
Apple, Michael W., 184-193, 196
advice to Marxist educators,
190-191
on class conflict and school,
184-185
critique of, 190-195
on education and the
production of knowledge,
187, 191
on logic of capital, 188-189
on school and reproduction,
186-188, 194
on student response to
reproduction, 187-188,
192, 194
on use of prepackaged
materials, 186
Apprenticeship, 92, 201-202,
210-212
Arguments, 81, 113, 177, 226,
246
construction and appraisal of, 3-4
philosophic, 4, 17, 115, 203
Aristotle, 22, 88
Arts, fine, 18, 20-21, 42, 45-46,
75, 172, 189
Assimilation, 101, 104
Austin, John L., 6, 8, 10, 17
Authenticity, 34-36, 45, 67
limitations of, 37
Authority, 13, 24, 110, 144, 177,
179-180, 206-207, 232, 234,
247
epistemic, 7, 9
Peters on, 6-9
social/political, 7, 8-9
and speech acts, 6, 8-9
of teacher, 6-9, 29, 50-51, 78,
130, 178, 206, 244, 247
Aversive control, 147

Bacon, Francis, 178
Bantock, Geoffrey, 217, 227-232,
253
critique of, 230-232, 250-252
on curriculum, 227-230,
250-252
Barrow, John, 2n, 197n
Behavioral objectives, 151-153,
163, 165
critique of, 153-154, 163
Behaviorism, 15, 45, 93, 144-146,
165
contrasted with cognitive
science, 155-157
critique of, 15-16, 23, 30-31,
163, 165
Behaviorist, 144-145, 154, 162
Behavior modification, 189
Being, 68-71, 73-76
and education, 69-71, 97
see also Heidegger
Bernstein, Basil, 129-131,
133-134
critique of, 130-131, 134-135
Bourdieu, Pierre, 127-129,
130-131, 133
critique of, 129, 131, 133-135
Bourgeoisie, 169
Bourgeoisie, petty, 186, 188
Bowles, Herbert, 179-184
critique of, 183-184, 193, 195
on schools and division of labor,
180-182, 194-196
Buber, Martin, 46-51, 61
critique of, 50-51, 63
Burke, Edmund, 219
Busing, compulsory, 221, 237,
243, 247-248

Calculative thinking, 72, 74
Capital (Marx), 170
Capitalism, 169, 170-171, 180n,
182, 190n, 192-195

education under, 169-170,
179-185, 195
Causation, 14, 18, 20, 79, 117,
125, 138, 145, 154
role in explanation, 14-16, 66n
scientific concept of, 14-16
Character, personal, 49-50, 150,
201, 235, 249, 252-253
Child, 45, 128, 157, 201, 242
and concept-formation, 31-32
102-103, 106
intellectual development of, 42,
56, 104-109, 156, 201
linguistic development of,
120-123, 126-127, 201
moral development of, 110,
112-113
rights of, 26, 141, 237, 244
Chomsky, Carol, 121-127, 135
Chomsky, Noam, 116-121
contrasted with Piaget, 116, 125
critique of, 123-127, 133-134
research program of, 127
Class, social, 40, 56, 59, 167-168,
171, 174, 177, 179, 193-194,
224, 248
conflict between, 131, 134,
167-168, 182, 184, 253
structure of, 127-129, 132, 170,
179, 195
Cognitive science,   109, 144,
155-162
contrasted with behaviorism,
155-157
critique of, 158-160, 163
on mind as information-
processing system,
155-156
and positivism, 155
on problem solving, 157-158
Common sense, 45-59
and ordinary language, 10
and phenomenology, 28, 61

and philosophic analysis, 10
Communication system,
education as, 128-129
Communism, 170
Community, local, 51, 162, 165,
199, 201, 206, 208, 221, 238,
240, 254,
and spending on schools,
243-244, 247
Competition, 197, 199, 216,
237, 239, 242, 254
Computer program, 155-156, 160
as representation of mind,
158-159, 165
Comte, Auguste, 137n
Concepts, 4, 6-32, 44-45, 53,
57, 62, 71, 140
child's formation of, 31-32
prereflective, 43-44
role of in arguments, 3-4
role of in structuring experience,
18, 28, 30-31, 54, 62, 64,
101, 117
and words, 2, 4-5, 18, 54
Conceptual truth, 3
Conditioning, 150, 202, 209, 212
operant, 146, 148, 151
Conformism, 34-35, 52, 87, 95,
134, 182
Consciousness, 18, 81, 229, 251
false, 84
working-class, 183
Consciousness-raising, 54, 56,
173, 179
Consensus, 175, 177-178, 185,
235, 251-252
Conservatism:
libertarian, 219, 236, 249,
253-255
on basic subjects, 246
critique of, 247-249
on educator authority, 244
on equality of educational

Conservatism (Cont'd)
  opportunity, 243-244, 247, 254
  on human nature, 237
  on liberty, 242-245, 254
  on moral education, 245-246, 253-254
  on parental choice of schools, 243-245
  on purpose of schooling, 246
  on role of government in education, 243-244
  on society, 237
  traditional:
    on education as moral enterprise, 252
    on inequality, 221
    on limits of public education, 221
    and objective values, 98, 219-221
    on society as organism, 220-221, 237
Consumerism, 171, 173-174, 193
Contradiction, 104
  logical, 6-7, 14, 190n, 191
  social and cultural, 167n, 189-192
Control, 145-146, 151, 175n
  aversive, 147
  in school, 7, 141, 147, 165, 189, 206
  technical, 188-189, 191, 193
Corporation, 180-181, 195
Correspondence thesis, 179-182
Crafts, 73-75, 97, 230
Creativity, 48, 73, 75, 96-97, 109, 174, 182, 229, 235
  encouragement of, 123, 126
  linguistic, 116-117, 119-120, 122-123, 126-127
Critical Theorists, 170-171
Critical thinking, 83-84, 87, 176-177, 226, 253-254

Cultural capital, 128-130
Culture, 20, 31, 40, 42, 55, 63, 88, 95, 99, 131, 149-150, 175, 185, 190-195, 229-233, 246, 250
  dominant, 129, 179n
  middle-class, 193-194
  of school, 129, 187, 192
  of students, 251
  working-class, 179n
Curriculum, 16, 26, 62, 73, 98, 129n, 130, 140, 180, 186, 197
  cultural, 229-230, 251
  design of, 23, 107, 160n, 176-177
  egalitarian, 227, 229
  for the elite, 227, 230
  Hirst on, 17-23
  knowledge and, 17, 57, 176
  for the low achiever, 227, 230-231, 250-251
  meritocratic, 227-229

Darwin, Charles, 90, 93, 202
Death, 34, 63
Deduction, logical, 18, 21, 62, 143
Democracy, 195, 217, 240, 255
  Jeffersonian, 202
  participatory, 202-203, 212
  in school, 113, 205-206
Descartes, Rene, 117
Deschooling, 203, 209-216
Determinism, 145, 149-150, 163
  economic, 171, 175, 184
Development:
  accelerated, 104, 109
  biological, 101
  emotional, 159
  intellectual, 17, 23, 101-109, 125, 159, 200, 215
  linguistic, 120-125
  moral, 23, 110-113, 134, 199, 214

stages of, 110-115
Dewey, John, 17
Dialectic, 190, 191n
Dialectical materialism, 167n
Dialogue, education as, 46-50, 53, 68, 78-82, 96
Dilthey, Wilhelm, 65-67, 89, 91, 96
Disciplinary matrix, 90-91
Discipline, 46, 51, 907, 205, 216, 247-248
  concept of, 10-13
  contrasted with punishment, 10-11, 24
  self-, 12, 201, 244, 254
Discipline(s), academic, 9, 13n, 31-32, 44, 75, 198, 207, 220, 224, 232-236, 249
Discovery learning, 109
Discrimination, 26, 154, 221
Dogmas, 232-235, 251
Drama, 21, 126, 230
Drill, 148
Duckworth, Eleanor, 105n
Duty, 110, 112, 114, 247

Economics, 75, 168, 170, 175, 179, 180n, 183, 193, 196
Economy, 20, 72, 161, 168, 184-189, 194-195, 198, 207, 251
Education, 6, 10, 26, 52, 82, 93, 99, 129, 142, 164, 211, 214
  aesthetic, 74
  as "banking," 52, 55, 57
  under capitalism, 169-170, 179-184
  of character, 18
  as communication system, 128-129
  concept of, 4, 23, 28
  as conditioning, 150-151, 163
  control of, 153-154, 174
    by community, 238

    by government, 174, 238-239, 243
  in a democracy, 231
  discipline of, 4
  and the economy, 179-185, 221
  as game, 68, 81, 96
  higher, 207, 234, 236, 239-240, 250
  as indoctrination, see Indoctrination
  intellectual, 248-249
  liberal, 16-23, 25, 182, 210, 235
  moral, 97, 245-246, 249
  as moral endeavor, 236, 252
  objectives of, 16-19, 22, 48, 52, 132, 152, 182, 198, 206, 228, 232, 248, 254
  physical, 18
  for political participation, 231
  private, 243, 253
  process of, 4, 57, 59, 64, 81, 88, 128, 131, 139, 143, 153-154, 162-165, 215, 228
  public, 194, 215, 243
  and reproduction, 128-129, 180-182, 185-188, 194-195
  and society, 128, 163, 169, 198, 221, 228, 237
  under socialism, 169-170
  student's experience of, 134, 179
  study of, 10, 66, 88, 127, 143, 227
  theories in, 24-25, 29, 133, 135, 139-143, 171
  and understanding of texts, 77, 80-85, 96-97
  vocational, 180, 201, 221, 222, 234
  see also School; Schooling
Educational opportunity, equality of, 228-230, 247-248

Educational reform, 26, 60, 113, 129, 182-183, 193, 212
Educational research, 85-88, 93-94, 130, 135, 139, 160, 227, 231, 252
and literature, 227-228, 232
and New Sociology, 56, 59
objectivity in, 59, 143-144, 164-165
and philosophic analysis, 13, 15
schools of thought in, 93
Educational system, 31, 128, 131, 181, 184, 209, 215, 256
and the economy, 181
and production of knowledge, 185, 187, 191-192
Educationist, 99, 127, 138, 142, 195, 232
Educator, 162
as custodian, 244
Marxist, 183, 189-190, 192-193
professional, 238
Efficiency, 35, 153, 161, 163, 238
Einstein, Albert, 178
Elitism, 156, 230, 250
Emotion, 18, 22, 45, 108, 172, 198, 225-226, 248
and curriculum, 74, 230-232
Empathetic understanding, 66-67, 89, 91, 93, 96
Empiricism, 145. See also Logical empiricism
Enculturation, 128
Equality, 16, 23, 182, 243, 254
in education, 26, 183-184, 192, 243-244
see also Educational opportunity, equality of
Equilibration, 101-102, 104-105, 108-109, 134
Ethnicity, 171, 192, 237, 251
Evaluation, of students, 9, 186
Evolution, 32, 93, 102, 165

Examination(s), 128, 135, 148, 150, 237
Experience, 16-17, 20-22, 25, 29, 31, 53, 64, 82, 101, 117, 127, 141, 158, 162
immediate, 30, 215
personal, 37, 57, 62, 141
role of in learning, 45, 62, 149
role of in teaching, 62-63
structured by concepts, language, 18, 28, 30-31, 54, 62, 64, 101, 117
Experimentation, 18, 90, 102, 105, 107, 133, 142-145, 237

Family, 108, 220-221, 243, 253
and enculturation, 128, 229
Fine arts, 18, 20-21, 42, 45-46, 75, 172, 186
Forms of knowledge, 17-23
Frankfurt School, 170. See also Critical Theorists
Freedom, 24, 48, 50, 62, 141, 171-175, 224, 234, 238, 240
Free market, 186, 236-237
educational, 214, 240-241
Free school, 171, 183, 203, 207-209, 216
contrasted with open classroom, 207-208
see also Kozol, Jonathan
Freire, Paolo, 51-57
critique of, 55-56, 63
Freud, Sigmund, 82-83, 98
Friedman, Milton, 238-242, 253
critique of, 240-243
Froekel, Friedrich, 141

Gadamer, Hans-Georg, 75-82, 87
contrasted with Heidegger, 76-78
contrasted with Ricoeur, 83, 98
critique of, 80-82, 98
Galileo, Galilei, 30, 89-90

Game, as model of understanding, 80-81, 96
General theory of relativity, 90, 117, 178
Genetic programming, 102, 116, 118, 124, 132, 134, 163
Gintis, Samuel, *see* Bowles, Herbert
God, 18, 46, 51, 198, 219, 252
Goodman, Paul, 199-204
  critique of, 203-204
Government, 172, 194, 228, 243, 250
  role of in education, 174, 184, 211, 238-241, 244, 255
Grading, 9, 39, 59, 62, 147, 197, 199, 204
Grammar, 120, 126
  rules of, 125-126, 223-224
  universal, 119
Gramsci, Antonio, 179n, 185n
Greeks, 65, 69, 70, 202, 230, 234
Greene, Maxine, 45n, 61n
Growth, personal, 37, 39, 46, 48, 50, 53, 154, 182, 198, 214, 248

Habermas, Jürgen, 170, 175-179
  critique of, 177-179
Happiness, 172, 198, 200
Hardie, Charles D., 139-141
Haroutunian, Sophie, 109n
Hawthorne, Nathaniel, 172
Hegemony, 185, 187-188, 190
Heidegger, Martin:
  as existential phenomenologist, 32-37, 45-46, 67-68
    critique of, 37
    and national socialism, 37
  as hermeneuticist, 67-75, 82, 87-88
    contrasted with Gadamer, 76-77
    critique of, 74-75, 98
    on meditative *vs.* calculative thinking, 71-72, 74, 97
    on role of interpretation in understanding, 67
    on science, 70, 72, 74
    on technology, 70, 74-75
    on truth, 71n, 72-74
Hermeneutics, 26, 64, 66n, 88, 171
  appraisal of, 68n, 95-98
  contrasted with philosophic analysis, 66n
  contrasted with structuralism, 85-87, 99
  and educational research, 143
  and industrial civilization, 97-98
  and nihilism, 98
  relativism of, 98
  themes of, 68
Hermes, 65
Higher education, 234, 236, 239-240
Hirst, Paul H., 2n, 16-25
  critique of, 20-23
Historical materialism, 167-168
History, teaching of, 176, 178, 189, 202, 220, 234, 246, 252
Human beings, 22, 30, 70, 117, 141, 150, 163, 169, 174, 237
  as naturally good, 172, 197-198, 200, 206
  as passive, 150, 163
  as purposive, 67
Human condition, 34, 62, 67, 232
Humanities, 66n, 82, 99, 129, 176, 234, 239
Human sciences, 14, 45, 66n, 82, 98-99, 127, 131, 135, 139-142, 176, 203
  contribution to education, 142
  method of, 66, 87
  purpose of, 118, 145, 175

Husserl, Edmund, 27-33, 41, 56
Hypotheses:
    creation of, 122, 137-138, 143,
        152
    testing of, 103, 152, 164

Idealism, 24, 117
Ideology, 180, 185-186, 187-192
Illich, Ivan, 209-217
    critique of, 213-215
Imitation, 224-225, 231
Individual, 77, 88, 108, 128, 131,
        144, 161, 170-173, 193-196,
        206-209, 219-220, 231-232,
        237-244
Individualized learning, 186, 188,
        189
Indoctrination, 4, 24, 171, 174,
        227, 231
    moral, 112, 115-116, 246, 249,
        250, 252
Industry, 70, 153, 161, 170-171,
        186, 228
Inequality, 128, 182, 221, 228, 243
Infancy, 42, 100, 149
**Information-processing
    approach,** 93, 155
Inhelder, Barbel, 103n, 106n
Innate ideas, 101, 117, 132
Inner life, 66, 144-145, 228
Instinct, 48, 134, 172-174, 201
Instruction, 16, 151-154, 157,
        161, 163-164, 199, 204
    method of, 153, 162, 164, 176
    programmed, 163
Instructional design, 160, 163
Instructional materials, 105-107,
        121, 132
Integration, 111, 134
Intellect, 103, 229, 248-249
Intelligence, 142, 223-224, 246
    concept of, 2, 23, 56
    traits of, 101
Intention, 21, 24, 145

and action, 14-16, 66
    author's, 66, 69, 73
    nature of, 14-15
    in speech, 124
Interaction, student-teacher,
        58-59, 85-86, 129, 134, 144,
        183, 194
Interdisciplinary approach, 109,
        135, 179
Interest, 186, 211, 253
    immediate, 148
    knowledge-constitutive,
        175-178
    self-, 194, 237, 253
    of student, 96, 145-148, 160,
        200-202, 207, 216, 222, 225,
        250, 252
Internalization, 11, 13, 52,
        102-103, 106, 120, 125,
        181, 206, 245
Interpretation, 44-45, 57, 72,
        77-78, 84-86, 91, 96, 107,
        149, 156, 176
    as defined by hermeneutics, 65
    individual, 68, 144, 198, 215
    of literature, 69
    role of in understanding, 65-67
    of texts, 65-66, 68, 77, 81-84,
        97-98
    varieties, 66, 77-81, 86-87

James, Henry, 29
Judgment, 8, 215, 223-226
    by teacher, 9, 13, 59, 199
    moral, 141
    value, 141
Justice, 16, 110, 130-131

Kant, Immanuel, 17, 117, 156
Keats, John, 73
Kirk, Russell, 217, 232-253
    critique of, 235-236, 250-253
Knowledge, 16-17, 23, 50, 53, 62,
        72, 91, 117-118, 124, 137,

145, 155, 169-170, 175-176,
186, 196-198, 201-202,
206-209, 213, 222
academic, 7, 62, 106-107, 227
acquisition of, 17-18, 101, 108
forms of, 17-23
and preunderstanding, 72, 90
and teacher, 7, 9
technical-administrative,
185-187
theoretical, 59, 178
transmission of, 53, 57, 59,
128, 164
Kohl, Herbert, 203-216
critique of, 206-207, 215
Kohlberg, Laurence, 110-133, 175
critique of, 113-116, 133
Kozol, Jonathan, 208-217
critique of, 209, 216-217
Kuhn, Thomas, S., 88-97
critique of, 93-95

Labeling, 58-59
Labor, division of, 169-170,
180-182, 187, 190, 192
Laissez-faire, 236
Lakatos, Imre, 94
Language, 5, 17, 22, 24, 27, 63,
85, 100, 108, 127, 140, 213
as acquired, 176
capacity for use of, 116-117, 126
development of, 120-123
as innate, 117, 176
ordinary, 4-5, 10, 25
and poet, 70-73
rules of, 100, 118-126, 132, 134
child's construction of,
120-122
as structuring experience, 54
use of for communication, 133
written, 121
see also Chomsky, Noam
Language game, 5, 10, 17
Laws, 90, 99-100

contrasted with rules, 125, 134
judicial, 16, 60, 65, 168
of learning, 164
Newtonian, 71, 90
scientific, 7, 72, 101, 125,
138-139, 164
Learning, 11, 14, 17, 23, 31-32,
85, 96, 141-142, 151-156,
161, 164, 199, 214, 217
active, 105, 132
by discovery, 109, 135
by doing, 199
from experience, 199, 210-211
as exploratory, 157-159, 212
as imitation, 224-225
to learn, 105-106
as observable behavior, 152,
154, 163
as operant behavior, 146, 148
self-directed, 122, 126, 163,
197-198, 200-201
self-paced, 148, 186
and teaching, 3, 24, 85, 152
theories of, 108, 142, 162
Leibnitz, Gottfried, 117
Lenin, Nikolai, 169-170
Liberal education, 235
Hirst on, 16-23, 25
Life, 20, 25-26, 164, 200
meaning of, 44, 110
way of, 23, 171-173, 220
Lifestyle, 173, 202
Lifeworld, 30, 42, 52, 56
Linguistic analysis, 4-5, 62
Literacy, 52, 199, 246
training in, 54, 56
Literary criticism, 66n, 226
Literature, 18, 20-21, 34, 45, 75,
84, 121, 180, 220-223, 230,
232, 337, 252-253
classic, 81
and human nature, 74, 85, 172,
176, 233
interpretation of, 69

Literature (Cont'd)
  as model for educational
      research, 227-228, 232
  as revelatory of Being, 70, 73-74
  teaching of, 73-74
Locke, John, 17
Logic, 21, 71, 100, 137-138, 159,
      163
  of capital, 188-190
  definition of, 4n
  symbolic, 4, 10
Logical connectedness, 6-7, 14-15,
      18
  of action and intention, 15, 163n
  of mind and knowledge, 17
Logical empiricism, 138-139
Logical positivism, 140-141
  critique of, 138
  theory of knowledge, 137
  theory of meaning, 138, 140
  theory of science, 137-138
Love, 200

Male-domination, 175
Marcuse, Herbert, 170-175
  critique of, 173-175, 193
Market, 187, 192, 210, 214
  educational, 214, 241-242
  free, 186, 236-237
Marx, Karl, 83, 98, 167-170, 191n
Marxism, 175, 179
  on alienation and liberation,
      167, 169, 193
  appraisal of, 193-196
  on class struggle, 167-168
  and determinism, 171, 175, 196
  on education, 93, 167, 169, 193
  and historical materialism,
      167-168, 193
  humanist, 170, 179, 193-196
  and New Sociology, 60
  reductive, 192
  and revolution, 169

on state, 167, 193
structural, 170, 179, 193-194
Marxist educators, 183, 189, 193
Marxists, 170, 179, 190-196,
      208, 224
Materials:
  instructional, 105-107, 121, 132
  prepackaged, 185, 188, 191-192
Mathematics, 20-21, 28, 100,
      132, 137, 145, 163, 204,
      208, 213
  as school subject, 18, 31, 106,
      109, 130, 180, 186, 207, 223
  in science, 30, 90
Meaning, 21-22, 67-68, 75, 104,
      123-124, 138, 140, 141n,
      199, 224
  author's, 73, 80, 95
  concealed, 83-86
  interpreted, 77, 80-81, 95
  of life, 44, 110
  recreation of, 66, 77, 80-81, 87
  of situations, 30, 111
  of texts, 65-66, 77, 80-81, 87,
      89, 95
  as use, 5-6, 124
  of words, 3, 70, 74
Measurement, 153, 154, 204
Mechanism, 145
  mind as, 155, 158-159, 163
Media, mass, 52, 171, 177, 180n,
      195, 202, 216, 220, 251,
      253
Mediation, 185, 188, 190
Meditative thinking, 71-75, 97
Memory, 28, 144-145, 156-157
Mental operation, 33, 102-103,
      107, 132, 156
Mental process, 27, 60, 67, 138,
      144-145, 155, 157, 163, 226
Meritocracy, 181, 250
Merleau-Ponty, Maurice, 41-46,
      56

critique of, 45-46
Metalearning, 157
Metaphysics, 137, 141
Mind, 16, 18, 20, 27, 57, 76, 79,
    96, 100, 117, 132, 135, 140,
    159, 228, 230
  as active, 101, 156, 159
  acts of, 27
  of child, 42, 56, 156, 198
  conscious, 27, 33
  contrasted with computer
    program, 158-159
  development of, 17, 100, 159
  as information-processing
    system, 155-156
  as mechanism, 155, 158-159,
    163
  open, 77, 79, 98, 174
  "organs" of, 117
  as structure of substructures,
    116-117, 133
  as structuring experience, 28,
    71, 116, 118, 131, 156
  theories of, 101
Minorities, 207
Modes of thought, 222-224
Model, scientific, 142-143, 144n
Montessori, Maria, 141
Moral dilemmas, 50, 245-247, 258
Moral education, 26, 97, 112, 221,
    233-234, 236, 245, 247
  directive, 116, 135, 245
  via discussion, 112-113, 115,
    247-248
  via values clarification, 116,
    135
  see also Kohlberg, Laurence
Morality, 45-46, 110, 114-115,
    168, 185n, 220, 225, 245
  private, 233
  public, 41, 234
Moral principle, 141, 233
Moral thinking, 110-113, 234

Moral value, 50, 98, 110, 216,
    235-236, 245, 247, 249, 252,
    254
Motivation, 142, 144-145, 164,
    252
Movement education, 230
Movement of thought, 68, 85, 97,
    99, 133, 144, 178
Music, 117, 172, 200, 230

National socialism, 37
Natural selection, 20, 146
Nature, 37, 46, 73-74, 167,
    169, 176, 198, 246
  child's response to, 72
  despoliation of, 70, 74
  science on, 72
  and technology, 70, 74
Nature study, 72-73
Neighborhood, 206, 216-217,
    239-240, 248
  segregation by, 202
Neill, A. S., 199-200
  critique of, 200-201
Neisser, Ulric, 155
New Sociology of Education,
    56-60
  critique of, 59-60
Newton, Isaac, 71, 84, 90, 92, 94
Nihilism, 76, 98
Novel, 22, 72, 83-84, 126, 214
Nozick, Robert, 242

Oakeshott, Michael, 219-227
  critique of, 225-226, 249-252
Objectivity, 59, 91, 99, 111, 115,
    127, 132, 139, 144, 175
Observation, 72-73, 92-95, 107,
    127, 137-138
O'Connor, D. J., 139, 141-143
Open classroom, 171, 203-207,
    216
  critique of, 206-207
  order in, 205

Open Classroom (Cont'd)
  philosophy of, 206
  role of teacher in, 204-206
  student choice in, 203-205
Operant conditioning, 146, 148, 151
Opportunity, educational, equality of, 184, 243-244, 247, 254
Oppression, 52-56, 208-209
Ordinary language philosophy, 4-6
  mature phase of, 16-17
  suitability to education, 5, 10
  see also Analysis, philosophic
Organism, 109
  human, 101, 144-145
  interaction with environment, 101-102, 109, 111

Paradigm, 89, 90-91, 93, 95-97
Parental choice of schools, 238-245, 248-249, 255
Parents, 29, 34-35, 40, 44-45, 76, 147, 172, 188, 206, 209, 237-239
Pavlov, Ivan, 144
Peers, 44-45, 145, 148, 202, 209, 216, 220, 251
Perception, 27, 32, 41-42, 45, 52-57, 60, 128, 142, 156, 164, 215
Pestalozzi, Johann Heinrich, 141
Peters, Richard S., 2n, 14
  on teacher authority, 6-9
Phenomena, 27-28, 31, 66, 114, 135
  mental, 138, 145
  natural, 30, 75, 92
  social, 60, 86-87, 131, 138, 144, 164, 227-228
Phenomenologist, 27, 32-33, 45, 51, 58, 60, 62, 82, 130, 143, 194

Phenomenology:
  appraisal of, 61-64
  on bracketing, 28-29
  and concepts, 27-31
  contrasted with philosophic analysis, 27, 62-63
  on curriculum design, 32
  on education, 33, 64
  in educational research, 31-32, 93, 162, 187, 192
  existential, 26, 33, 61, 68
  on freedom, 61
  Husserlian, 28, 61, 63
    critique of, 61
    on education, 31
  and knowledge, 31-32
  method of, 27-30
    applied to education, 31
  on role of experience in learning, 62
  on role of experience in teaching, 62-63
  and stream of experience, 27
  and systematic variation, 29-30
Philosophic analysis, see Analysis, philosophic
Philosophy, 4, 18-19, 21, 24, 26, 98, 202, 214
  of education, 24, 140, 197
  problems of, 69, 98
  purpose of, 1, 25, 118
Physicalism, 138-139
Piaget, Jean, 43, 99n, 100-110, 116, 125, 133, 135, 175
  critique of, 107-109, 133-134
Planning, 19, 151, 162, 164-165
Plato, 17, 70, 78
Play, 31, 217. See also Game, as model of understanding
Poet, 69, 70-71, 84, 97
Poetry, 69-74, 97, 105, 126
Politics, 31, 42, 220, 230, 253
  as moral endeavor, 234, 252

study of, 75, 227, 230, 234, 236, 250-253
Positive reinforcement, 147-151, 163-165
Positivism, 56, 141, 155, 161, 196
appraisal of, 162-165
approach to educational research, 139, 143-144
approach to human sciences, 101, 131, 163, 175n
and Comte, 137n
and determinism, 163
doctrines of, 137-138, 162, 175n
in education, 139-143
see also Logical empiricism; Logical positivism
Positivist, 60, 143n, 144, 224
Poulantzas, Nicos, 180n
Power, 84, 179, 204, 238
and authority, 6-8
economic, 168
political, 168, 227, 230-231
will to, 70
Preconception, 76-77
role of in learning, 79-81, 84, 87
Prediction, 88, 125, 139-142, 145, 164
Prejudice, 84, 174, 202, 249
Prepackaged materials, 185, 188, 191-192
Pre-Socratics, 70, 87
Presupposition, 27, 33, 61
Preunderstanding, 68, 86, 90, 96-97
of child, 92
in science, 90, 93
in science education, 72, 92
Private school, 221, 237, 239-242, 248
Problem solving, 92-93, 132, 157, 160, 164, 198-199
method of, 91, 109, 157-158
Production, 175, 187-188

forces of, 60, 168-169, 172
means of, 109
process of, 161, 187
relations of, 168
Program, instructional, 16n, 148, 161-163, 165
Programmed materials, 149, 151
student response to, 149-150
Psychoanalysis, 175-178
Psychology, 30, 66n, 93, 101, 109, 127, 142, 145, 155
Public school, 175, 195, 201, 207-208, 217, 221, 239-243, 247-248, 254
criticism of, 208-209, 238
Punishment, 15, 31, 63, 108, 110, 204, 245
contrasted with discipline, 10-11, 24

Qualitative research, 231
Quantitative research, 101, 143, 165
Quotas, 221, 237, 245

Race, 40, 59, 192, 194, 242, 247-248, 254
Rationality, 44, 235, 244, 253
Readiness, 96, 164
Reading, 54, 80, 83-84, 96-97, 109, 121-123, 135, 208, 213, 230, 246
Realism, philosophic, 24
Reality, construction of, 30, 52-58, 62-64, 134, 144, 161, 164, 183
Reasoning, 23
moral, 110-115, 245
Reasons, 11, 34, 40, 61
role in argument, 4
role in explanation, 66n
Reform:
educational, 26, 60, 113, 129, 182-183, 193

Reform (Cont'd)
  social, 51, 60, 129, 174, 206, 220
Reinforcement, positive, 147-151,
    163, 165
Relativism, 57, 91-94, 98
  critique of, 60, 98
  moral, 112
Religion, 18, 40, 234
Reproduction:
  cultural and economic, 170,
    180-181, 185-190, 194
  social, 128, 170-171, 190, 195
  student response to, 185,
    187-188
Research:
  qualitative, 231
  quantitative, 243
Research, educational, 85-88,
    93-94, 130, 135, 139, 227,
    231, 252
  and literature, 227-228
  and New Sociology, 56, 59
  objectivity in, 59
  and philosophic analysis, 13, 15
  schools of thought in, 93
Research program, 94-95, 127,
    135
Research tradition, 89-94, 97
  Darwinian, 90, 93
  Kuhn on, 89-92, 97
  Lakatos on, 94
  Newtonian, 90, 92, 94
Responsibility, 14, 29, 34-42, 47
Ricoeur, Paul, 82-88
  contrasted with Gadamer, 83,
    98
  critique of, 87-88, 98
Rights, 16, 24, 112, 114
  basic, 214, 242
  of children, 16, 141
  of students, 247
Role model, 173
Romanticism, 197-199

appraisal of, 215-217
Romanticists, 214-217, 224
Rousseau, Jean-Jacques, 17,
    197-199, 217
Ryle, Gilbert, 17

Sartre, Jean-Paul, 37-41, 46
  critique of, 40-41
Scheffler, Israel, 141
School, 28, 30, 68, 132,
    154-155, 213, 242, 250
  alternative, 183, 207, 239
  as arm of state, 185, 188
  as black box, 183
  and class conflict, 134-135
  concept of, 1-2
  control in, 147
  culture of, 129, 187, 192
  and division of labor, 180, 182
  and the economy, 179-185, 203
  elementary, 92, 121
  and enculturation, 128
  experimental, 162
  free, 147, 171, 183, 203, 216
  high, 40, 84 92, 98, 181, 25
  and inculcation of democracy,
    113
  and inequality, 128, 182
  and legitimation, 129, 180
  parochial, 51
  and personal development,
    182
  primary, 178, 180, 191, 250
  private, 221, 237, 239-242, 248
  and production of knowledge,
    192
  public, 97, 171, 195, 201,
    207-209, 217, 221, 237-242,
    247-248, 256
  and reproduction, 129, 180-181,
    185-186, 190, 195
  secondary, 75, 178, 180, 191,
    225, 240, 250

and social reform, 220, 237
and stratification of student
   body, 181, 184, 191
systems-designed, 162
and transmission of knowledge,
   130
Schooling, 23-24, 74, 126, 164,
   176, 220, 222, 238-241,
   252
School system, 85-86, 99, 131
Science, 133-137, 140, 145, 176,
   180, 186, 199, 250
history of, 70, 88, 91, 92
method of, 137-138
philosophy of, 88
preunderstanding in, 45
skills of, 90
Science education, 72, 74, 189. *See
   also* Kuhn, Thomas S.
Searle, John R., 6n, 159
Segregation, 202
Self-development, 197-198, 203
Self-expression, 80, 122, 206, 217,
   223, 229
Self-fulfillment, 34-37, 161, 169,
   198, 206, 212, 220, 223,
   229, 255
Self-interest, 237, 253
Semantics, 123, 133
Sex education, 221
Shakespeare, William, 77, 84,
   172, 233
Simulation, 156, 162-163
Skills, 49, 90, 130, 209-211
intellectual, 154-157, 165, 186,
   199, 202, 207, 213, 246
pedagogical, 189
scientific, 90
Skinner, Burrhus F., 145-152
critique of, 149-151
Smith, Adam, 136
Social change, 52, 55, 134, 167,
   173-174

Social class(es), 127-128,
   131-134, 167-170, 179, 184,
   179, 184, 188, 190, 192-195,
   216, 239-240, 247, 253
Socialism, 169-170
Socialization, 108, 130, 177, 234,
   237, 254
Social reconstruction, 169-170,
   215
Social reform, 51, 60, 129,
   169-170, 174, 206, 215, 220
Social studies, 233-234, 246, 250
Society, 20, 22, 99, 151, 161,
   167-171, 174-175, 179,
   185-186, 202, 205, 220,
   229-235
consumerist, 171
forms the individual, 179
as imperfect, 221
industrial, 74-75, 228
as organism, 220, 237
pluralist, 220, 236, 242, 251-252
repressive, 172-174, 184
as warping, 198
Sociology, 30, 66n, 75, 93, 137n,
   170
Soltis, Jonas F., 10n, 13n, 16n
Speech acts, 5-6, 123-124, 175
and authority, 8-9
and communication, 124
intentions and, 124
Spelling, 122-123, 135
State, the, 167, 189, 191, 195, 207
and education, 185, 188, 192
Stratification:
of student body, 181, 184, 187,
   191
of work force, 182, 184
Streaming, 59
Strike, 168, 207
by teachers, 174
Structuralism, 26, 98
appraisal of, 131-135

Structuralism (Cont'd)
approach of, 82, 85, 93, 99-100
contrasted with hermeneutics,
85-87, 99
Structuralist, 127, 131, 133,143
Structure, 77-80, 99, 109, 127,
131-133, 143, 156-157
cognitive, 101-111, 117-119,
132-134, 155
logical, 18-21
natural *vs.* cultural, 132-133
nature of, 99-100
social, 127-129
as system of moral rules,
110-111
Student, 9, 11-13, 17, 31-32, 35,
57-60, 75, 105-106,
112-113, 161, 195-196, 239
as active, 105-106
and authenticity, 34
and choice, 34, 36, 39, 61, 155,
205-206
as citizen, 247
and discussion, 78-82, 96
and employment, 128, 169
enculturation of, 128, 130
and existential anxiety, 36
and freedom, 50, 61-63, 206
and game of understanding, 80
interests of, 96, 145-148, 160,
200-202, 207
and interpretation of texts,
78-84, 96-98
makes sense of own experience,
154, 164, 183
as passive, 53, 129, 131, 145,
147, 150, 164, 183
resistance of, 49-51, 59, 63,
129-130, 154, 180, 185,
187-188, 192-194
response of to reproductive
process, 185
rights of, 247

self-assertion of, 40, 60
and self-expression, 80, 161, 217
and self-government, 113
and self-realization, 161, 164,
229
and social criticism, 172, 174
upper and middle class, 128
and use of own experience in
learning, 62, 208
violence of, 51, 244
working-class, 128-129
Student-teacher interaction,
58-59, 129, 134, 144, 183,
194
Summerhill, 200-201
Swift, Jonathan, 87
Syntax, 123, 125
System, 85
definition of, 85, 160
school as, 161-162
Systems engineering, 93, 144, 163
critique of, 161-164
definition of, 160
and positivism, 161
and problem solving, 160
school and, 160-161, 164-165
teacher and, 160

Taxation, 239-245
Teacher, 15, 24-44, 48-50, 57-60,
64, 69-72, 75
attitude of toward students,
34-35, 40, 49, 59, 147, 174
as authentic, 34-37
authority of, 50-51, 78, 130,
204-206
as "an" authority, 7-9, 178
as "in" authority, 7-9, 178
and Being, 69-73
and class discussion, 78-82,
112-114, 135, 142-147, 154,
178, 1865, 201, 205-206,
239-247, 252-255

and discipline, 11-13, 29, 39, 51,
     63, 130, 178, 205
as example to student, 35, 39,
     174, 209, 224-225, 237
and existential anxiety, 35-36
and freedom, 38-39, 61, 150,
     242
and grading, 9, 29, 59
and moral commitment, 245
as passive, 164-183
and presentation of subject
     matter, 29, 95-96, 106-107,
     132, 163, 177, 199, 209, 225
as professional, 242
and self-expression, 35, 161,
     204, 209, 228
as social critic, 172, 180
as systems engineer, 160
and transmission of knowledge,
     49, 59, 175, 194
and unionization, 189-191
Teachers, 57, 62
moderate views of, 174, 183,
     194
as political force, 174
and social change, 174
women as, 173
Teaching, 29, 62, 66-67, 96,
     153-154, 202-203, 211-214
art of, 45, 95, 165, 224
authentic, 34
concept of, 2-5, 23-24, 28-31, 62
craft of, 189
and learning, 3, 24, 85, 152
as operant conditioning, 146-47,
     163
ordinary vs. successful, 3n
profession of, 26
role of experience in, 44
styles of, 34, 144n
Teaching machine, 148
Technology, 70-74, 92, 95, 107,
     168, 178, 194

Testing, empirical, 88, 108, 133,
     137-139, 143, 151, 178
Tests, educational, 35, 62, 72, 129,
     152, 180
Text, 65, 75-76, 85, 88
affinity with action, 66
and analogues, 68, 95-96
as answer to question, 68, 78,
     80, 96
appropriation of, 82-83
and author, 77, 89, 95-96
canonical, 66
and game of interpretation,
     80
interpretation of, 65-68, 76-78,
     80-84, 87, 89, 95-98
literary, 66, 97
as model of action, 85, 88
as model of social institution,
     86-88
and plurality of interpretations,
     77-81, 86-87
world of, 82-84, 87
Theory, 21, 25, 32, 72, 91, 114,
     215, 242
construction of, 143
in education, 24-25, 29,
     133-135, 139-143, 171, 230
structure and content of,
     139-140
of language, 116-117, 119,
     123-127
scientific, 130, 133, 135, 138,
     142, 151, 164
Thinking, 109, 128, 145, 160,
     163, 168, 207, 246
calculative, 72, 74
critical, 83-84, 87
meditative, 71-75, 97
rational, 132, 159
scientific, 117, 141, 152
Thorndike, Edward L.,
     152

Thought:
  modes of, 141, 222-223
  movement of, 68, 85, 97, 99,
    133, 144
Thrownness, 34, 63
Tradition, 34, 68, 76, 81, 91-92,
    97-98, 202-203, 221-222,
    225, 237, 249-250
  and the individual, 64, 220, 223
  need to criticize, 81, 226
  teaching and, 76-77, 225
Truth, 18, 21, 25, 45, 97, 105, 178,
    202, 233, 251
  and art, 21-22
  conceptual, 3
  as disclosure, 71n, 72, 75, 78,
    96-97
  in science, 91-94, 176
  search for, 177, 179
  in virtue of meanings of
    terms, 135, 140

Understanding, 13, 17, 20, 57-60,
    68, 74-76, 95-97
  as conversations, 68, 78
  empathetic, 66-67, 89, 91, 93, 96
  as game, 68, 80-81, 96
  as like interpreting a text, 68,
    77, 81, 95
  as mode of being, 67, 74
  priomordial *vs.* everyday, 67
  role of interpretation in,
    65-67, 78-81
Unions, 189, 191, 207, 220
University, 129, 133, 187, 191,
    222, 241

Values, 13, 165, 190, 194-195
  absolute, 50, 250-252
  intellectual, 98
  moral, 50, 98, 110, 216, 219,
    235-236, 245-252
  objective, 41, 219, 234

  presentation by teachers, 49,
    50
  of teachers, 228
  traditional, 222, 236, 249
  universal, 237
Values clarification, 116, 135
Verification, empirical,
    138-140
Verification, theory of meaning,
    138-141
Verstehen, 66-67. *See also*
    Emphathetic
    understanding
Virtues, 34, 114, 146, 234,
    251-252
  intellectual, 223-224
Vocational education, 180, 201,
    221-222, 234
Vouchers, 237-242, 254
  criticisms of, 240-241, 253-254
  see also Friedman, Milton

Wittgenstein, Ludwig, 5, 6, 17
Women, 173, 189-190
Words, 21, 70, 80, 100, 103,
    118-122
  and concepts, 2, 4-5, 18, 54
  generative, 54-55
  meaning of, 3, 5-6, 74, 190-191
  use of, 5-6, 10
Work, 52, 167, 169, 171-173, 176,
    185, 195, 200, 223, 232
  manual, 187-188, 191
  mental, 187, 191
  social organization of, 168,
    179-180
Workforce, 180
Working class, 173, 183
Workplace, 177, 182, 202, 221
World, 27, 33-34, 72, 91, 167, 199
  categorized by concepts, 2, 58,
    117, 131
  everyday, 30, 87, 92, 227

independent existence of, 28-31,
53, 60, 62, 70
as object of knowledge and
control, 70

World view, 128, 132, 135, 185n,
186

Writing, 54, 109, 122-123, 126,
132, 135, 153-154, 230, 246